The Explorer's Garden

A view of the remote Gola Pokari, a sacred lake in eastern Nepal thought to be inhabited by a goddess. I botanized the area, with four associates, three Sherpas, and twenty-four porters, in 1995. The fantastically rich valley below is home to numerous species of *Disporum*, *Mandragora*, *Meconopsis*, *Polygonatum*, *Primula*, *Rheum*, *Smilacina*, and *Streptopus*. (Photo by Daniel J. Hinkley)

The Explorer's Garden

Rare and Unusual Perennials

DANIEL J. HINKLEY

Timber Press
Portland, Oregon

Fifth printing 2002

Timber Press, Inc.
The Haseltine Building
133 S.W. Second Avenue, Suite 450
Portland, Oregon 97204, U.S.A.

Printed in Hong Kong
Part title page photo: *Disporum uniflorum*
Title page photo: *Glaucidium palmatum*
Designed by Susan Applegate

Library of Congress Cataloging-in-Publication Data

Hinkley, Daniel J.
   The explorer's garden : rare and unusual perennials / Daniel J. Hinkley.
      p.   cm.
   Includes bibliographical references (p.   ) and index.
   ISBN 0-88192-426-1
   1. Perennials. 2. Rare garden plants. I. Title.
SB434.H56 1999
635.9'32—dc21   98-48722
                                                                      CIP

To J. C. and Gerald,

whose spirits are eternally bound to every plant I will ever know.

CONTENTS

FOREWORD

It is more years ago than I care to remember that, as a schoolboy, I was asked by a man I knew simply as Vicar Shaw if I would like to join him in search of the wild spignel or baldmoney. Vicar Shaw, or to give him his full name, the Reverend C. E. Shaw, was my first plant guru, and it is to him that I owe a good deal of my own enthusiasm and admiration for the natural world, especially its vegetation. His winter lectures at the local Field Naturalists Society had captured my imagination with their stories of adventure, triumph, and disappointment on the trail of unusual wild plants, and his invitation to help him find them was in every way a godsend, releasing me from aimless if harmless activities on the cobbled streets of my hometown.

Shaw was one in a long tradition of vicar-naturalists stretching back at least to Gilbert White, whose *Natural History and Antiquities of Selborne*, first published in 1789, is still regarded as a classic, and whose interests covered a galaxy of objects, from flowers and animals to fossils, minerals, and opera. He would often sing out loud on finding a new plant, and I have found myself doing likewise in places as far removed as the mountains of China and the woodlands of Washington. Shaw and I eventually did find the spignel, otherwise known as *Meum athamanticum*, a fuzzy clump of emerald-green, finely dissected foliage, in the mountains of the English Lake District, and the circumstances of its discovery has occupied a special corner of my memory until now, when I find it mentioned here in Dan Hinkley's book.

Dan describes it well: "fretted white flowers, opening from pinkish-blushed buds" above "low mounds of soft, filigreed, fennel-like foliage in spring," and with these words he rekindles my childhood memory. A small, unassuming member of the carrot family, *Meum* cannot hold a candle in the ornamental stakes to the likes of *Arisaema candidissimum* and *Myosotidium hortensia*, but in common with many other perennials, it has its own special charm, and in recognizing this, Dan shows an unusual and laudable even-handed approach to his garden plants.

Dan believes, as I do, that ideally a gardener needs to see both sides of the coin in order to better understand a plant and its likely requirements in the garden. That is, the gardener should try to visit plants in their natural environment, where they *choose* to grow, if he or she wants the plants to succeed in cultivation. Of course, such opportunities are not available to every gardener, which is why Dan's experiences are so valuable. Having myself traveled in many of the wild places visited by Dan, I can sense in his words the keen edge of his quest, the passion of his discovery, and beyond this, the simple satisfaction of a plant growing well.

His descriptions come as naturally as those of a Reginald Farrer, but without the sneaky bite or petulance, which is not to say that he isn't critical where he deems it necessary. Where Dan's writing succeeds most is in its successful union of artist's eye and poet's pen together with the hands-on approach of one who has grown these plants and propagated them too. Having on several occasions visited his garden and nursery at Heronswood in Kingston, Washington, I have seen for myself how successful and sympathetic a grower he is, and I can recommend to anyone intent on plant exploration in the cool temperate regions a visit to this remarkable collection as a primer.

Dan's decision to focus on herbaceous perennials for this volume is hardly surprising given their current popularity with gardeners in North America as well as in Britain and Europe. As he explains in his introduction, there is something quite special, magical even, in plants that disappear underground for a good chunk of the year, only to reappear with the first swallows each spring. Dan is right: our anticipation and hopes increase with the rising sap, whilst the first sign of emerging growth is in itself almost enough to justify their cultivation.

But these are not, by any stretch of the imagination, your typical border perennials. For his selection, Dan takes us to a weathered volcanic crater off the coast of Korea, a cool dappled woodland in Japan, the wind-blasted shore of a Chilean island, and a yak pasture on the roof of the world, the Himalayas. These are just a handful of native locations in which his plants are found.

Like Dan, I have rejoiced at finding *Glaucidium palmatum* in the deep, leafy loam of a wood in the Japan Alps, a far cry from my first memory of this lovely poppy relative in the woodland garden of Peter Chappell not far from my home in Hampshire. I have seen the outsized rough-and-ready leaves of *Gunnera tinctoria* in many different situations in Chile, always, however, in spring when the big, red, chunky inflorescences are emerging. I can also share Dan's amazement in finding outsized specimens of solomon's seal in Chinese scrub and thickets, the stem of one example of *Polygonatum cirrhifolium* being no less than 13 ft. (3.9 m) long!

A sense of wonder and a willingness to give credit where credit is due are two other attributes of Dan's approach to plants. Despite his familiarity with most of these plants in cultivation, Dan has not lost what I can only describe as the child's sense of surprise and excitement at finding them in the wild, and if it makes him dance and sing, so much the better, for gardening and the plant world are as much about entertainment and joyous outbursts as they are about serious study and the pursuit of knowledge.

His accounts are almost as much about people as they are about plants, which aside from helping the narrative, place on record the opinions and endeavors of those whose names or deeds may otherwise receive no mention in the history of horticulture. Dan has benefited from his own versions of my Vicar Shaw, and it is only right that those who inspired him be acknowledged in the text. Indeed, his book is an example of descriptive writing that others might well try to follow, whether they are professional botanists, horticulturists, amateur enthusiasts, students, or dirt-under-the-nails weekend gardeners.

Finally, this is an account of some of the most exciting, challenging, and satisfying perennials currently available to Western gardeners. Whether you try to grow them or simply read about them, the outcome will be the same—pure pleasure.

Roy Lancaster

PREFACE

With each plant-exploration adventure, whether in my backyard of the Olympic and Cascade Mountains of the Pacific Northwest or in more exotic locales like the Chilean Andes or the island of Cheju-do in the East China Sea, I anticipate the unveiling of yet another remarkable inventory of plants. A sort of emotional overload confronts me as I set out to explore the botanical riches offered by a particular slice of the globe—marveling in its landscapes, hearing the songs of its birds, witnessing the night sky, and embracing the human interaction with the whole.

For nearly as long as I can remember, I have gathered plants, one by one, like so many pebbles picked along a rocky shore. These have been sorted and assembled, forming an aggregate of a somewhat discernible shape and an understandable, pleasurable substance. Through this process we have come to Heronswood, for the past decade my home and garden in Kingston, on the Kitsap Peninsula of Washington, about 30 miles northwest of Seattle. Yet it is not only the plants that have been collected and stored along the way. My garden is also a collection of moments and people—of stiff winds in the Himalayas, dining with good friends in an English manor, the gentle smile and gift of fruit from a Korean hiker. Associated with each species in my garden is a gallery of memories, garnered in the process of collecting, growing, and propagating. In what country, in what year, with what friends, on what day, did this plant become my acquaintance? The richness of these memories is as important as the plant itself, which in turn hides within its biology its own remarkable heritage. What flower, what fragrance, what pollinator? To what is it related, where does it grow in nature, who originally found it and introduced it to the gardener's palette?

Heronswood, marking neither the beginning nor the end of my odyssey, represents a merging of the paths upon which I first set out as a child in northern Michigan. Seeds of oranges and avocados were gathered from the kitchen and planted, and I impatiently waited—in fact, I would repeatedly exhume the seeds, wondering why they had not germinated. When they finally did emerge, I would watch, in awe of the miracle as it unfolded: the lifting of soil, the emergence of the cotyledon, the appearance of the first leaves. Nothing could quite compare with this mystery, and I am happy to say that the emotions summoned in these early interactions with plants have remained unscathed through the trying realities of adulthood.

Pivotal moments can be identified in any passionate pursuit, and mine came when I was a 19-year-old sophomore at Michigan State University. One beautiful August day, I left with a friend and my dog to find the last virgin stand of the eastern white cedar (*Thuja occidentalis*), which was reported to exist on a small island in northern Lake Michigan known as South Manitou. After three days of searching, we finally found this small old-growth stand, and it was an electrifying experience. The trees were not particularly huge; in fact, compared to the mammoth trees that inhabit the Pacific Northwest where I now garden, they would hardly turn a head. But to me, these old-growth cedars remain quite immense, both physically and in what they represent. I had searched for the plants and had discovered my quarry. My perceptions of what my life could and would be were dramatically altered. The excitement of finding, observing, describing, and ultimately cultivating such plants is what has guided me in my life's pursuit.

This smoldering passion burst into full flame only after I came to own land. The five acres on which Heronswood stands in the benevolent climate of the Pacific Northwest envelops a variety of exposures and soils. I at last had the opportunity to explore our kingdom of plants unchecked. My interests branched like hoarfrost on glass: at once seemingly random while assuming a discernible, beautiful pattern over time. Each new plant is never thought of as a bauble or a prize, but rather as another piece of the puzzle. One by one, plant by plant, my understanding of the larger picture has grown, bringing into focus an astounding, mind-boggling portrait of life on Earth.

At Heronswood I am able to experiment with a variety of species, whether growing them in full-sun perennial borders or in our dank, moist woodland. Traveling near and far, I have introduced new plants to the property myself, and friends and colleagues the world over have sent seed or divisions of their own collections. The result has been an exciting array of material: conifers, trees and shrubs, vines and grasses, and perennials. The database at Heronswood currently lists more than 9000 plants in the garden inventory. This number is not given in order to impress, intimidate, or aggravate; it is simply a quantitative statement of the assemblage of plants that we currently tend and that I have come to know during my life, thus far, as a gardener, as well as plants with which I am in the process of acquainting myself. Certainly, many intriguing new additions that come to my garden on a yearly basis are only momentarily savored, and countless acquisitions conjure little more than curiosity. Still, I remain hard pressed to name a favorite genus or species.

The collection of the herbaceous perennials, including my observations of many of them in their native haunts as well as my understanding of their cultural needs and propagational demands, will occupy us here. Unusual and uncommon

Pemba Sherpa, one of the guides during our expedition to eastern Nepal, is pictured with the immense, and immensely bizarre, bracts of *Rheum nobile*, which protect the flowers from climatic extremes at such high altitudes. (Photo by Daniel J. Hinkley)

My friend and fellow explorer Bleddyn Wynn-Jones, with *Meconopsis paniculata* on the Milke Danda in eastern Nepal in 1995. (Photo by Daniel J. Hinkley)

perennials native to Asia, Europe, South America, or right here in North America have been brought together at Heronswood, and subsequently into this book, with the hope of a successful introduction to cultivation and exposure to an ever-growing population of plant enthusiasts.

It is an astounding time for horticulture across the planet. A growing awareness of and reverence for our world's natural heritage, coupled with the wave of baby boomers approaching retirement age, has infused new blood, a fever-pitch excitement, and an increasingly sophisticated following of the herbal craft. I have witnessed this remarkable transformation firsthand during the last decade, in the role of nurseryman, lecturer, author, and consumed gardener. Tastes in style and popularity of certain plants may come and go, but the passion for gardening will only continue to expand.

This surging interest in horticulture has not been overlooked by marketing agents and publishers. Great heaps of books about plants and gardening are found on the shelves of gardeners and horticulturists in every city and town. So, why write yet another?

I have been blessed during the four-and-a-half decades of my life to be able to earn my keep by complete submersion in a subject that I love. Over the past ten years, my interest in traveling to areas of the globe to observe plants in their native habitats has brought alive a new element of horticulture for me, each new experience broadening my perceptions and my approach to the field. But most paramount, these travels have made me a better gardener and a better teacher. They have humbled me in regard to the knowledge I possess, inspired me to learn more, and allowed me to appreciate the common, generous heart of gardeners around the world. This is perhaps why I decided to write.

Of course, I continue to find valuable advice within the faded pages of books by Elizabeth Lawrence, Gertrude Jekyll, Reginald Farrer, Lincoln Foster, and a host of other ghosts of gardening. Though many of the plants they espoused may now be considered old hat or have fallen out of favor, many that they nurtured in their gardens have come full circle, to once again inspire waves of enthusiasm from us, a fickle gardening community. Any book on plants tells us what is or was being grown, sought, or recommended during one point in time. As we approach the end of a millennium, this provides further motivation for adding yet another.

I have chosen to concentrate on relatively few plants, and these for a variety of reasons: obscurity in literature, poorly understood culture, or previous assessment as a poor garden plant. Mostly, these are plants that I simply admire and wish to know and cultivate better. To be sure, my treatment of many genera or families is vastly incomplete. I have avoided genera to which I would be incapable of doing justice, as well as genera that have been intelligently covered in recent monographs—*Hellebore*, *Lilium*, and *Trillium*, to name a few—even if I have large collections of these in my garden.

For the most part, I am including plants that I have grown in my own garden, observed in the wild, and/or propagated in our nursery. I am uncertain how one can possibly know enough about a plant to discuss it in writing if one does not first tend it. Marveling at their colors and textures, respecting their propagational intricacies, noting their petulance, and witnessing how they have adapted to survival in nature are what has made me a better gardener. It has also allowed me to better report my findings in this book.

A book that places its emphasis on the rare, elusive, and undercultivated runs the risk of having its pages filled to the brim with plants precariously balanced on the line between minimally ornamental and decidedly, solely, botanically interesting. Although as my own gardening life continues I find more and more satisfaction in simple subtlety, most gardeners require more compensation to urge them along the path to additional exposure to the wondrous world of ornamental horticulture. My intention is not to serve up a lofty inventory of unavailable plants. I have included plants that can be found in the trade (though perhaps not always readily), supplementing their descriptions with my personal observations and with cultural and propagation information that will make for more satisfying gardens.

Although herbaceous plants should never be considered a garden's only need, or even the most important element of the garden—I am a vehement opponent of blind dedication to the plants that migrate south for winter, while ignoring the structural importance of trees, shrubs, and vines—there is something quite magical in the discovery of the hardy perennials, those plants that entertain passionately for short bursts and then depart predictably, only to return again more exuberantly in later years. I equate the excitement of the herbaceous border to that of unpacking each year the trunk in which we store our collection of antique Christmas ornaments, accumulated from friends and family over many years. The unwrapping of each is in essence its rebirth, of its heritage and intrinsic beauty. The yearly resurrection of these moments may be all too brief, but their anticipated departure is made more palatable by the knowledge and comfort that they will reappear the following year with equal portent and (hopefully) greater ebullience.

When all is said and done, it will forever be the garden that sustains me and provides my purpose. But what is all this commotion that I feel, that we all feel in our hearts and minds? It is not just plants; it can't be. If we garden for the right reasons, we garden in reverence for this sphere that we inhabit as it hurls through space. We as gardeners gather like druids to celebrate the mind-boggling complexities that our gardens embody. Our gardens become an aggregate of history and moment blended with equal parts of tantalizing reality, polished by perfect light.

The island of Ullung-do in the Sea of Japan is an isolated land mass where numerous endemic species of plants and birds can be found. Here I have collected seed of *Hepatica maxima*, *Arisaema angustatum* var. *peninsulae* f. *variegata*, *Campanula takesimana*, *Sedum takesimense*, *Acer pseudosieboldianum* subsp. *takesimense*, and *Acer mono* subsp. *okamotoanum*—taxa found here and nowhere else. (Photo by Daniel J. Hinkley)

ACKNOWLEDGMENTS

I wish to thank the following people and organizations, who have assisted me in a variety of ways in the course of researching and writing: Lynne Harrison, for her dedication in artfully capturing on film the plants presented in this book; Bleddyn and Sue Wynn-Jones, for inspiring me to be more adventurous in the field; Roy Lancaster, for inspiring me through his writings to experience all of life's remarkable creations while in the field, and not simply plants; Elizabeth Strangman, Marina Christopher, and John Coke, for demonstrating how nurseries can indeed transcend gardens; Darrell Probst, for his friendship, generosity of plants, and knowledge of *Epimedium*; Tony Avent, for his help during a busy season in dissecting my observations of the genus *Asarum*; Dr. Jim McClements, for assistance in providing materials on *Podophyllum* and *Paris*, two genera for which we share a common enthusiasm; Kihun Song, Im Unchae, Chong Mun Yong, and Ferris Miller from Chollipo Arboretum in South Korea, for their assistance and great friendship; our guides and porters in Nepal, in particular Sonam Sherpa, Chappal Sherpa, and Pemba Sherpa, for helping in the experience of a lifetime; the staff of the Yunnan Institute of Botany, Kunming, for their kindness in sharing with me their remarkable country; Dr. Clem Hamilton, of the Center for Urban Horticulture, for his assistance in preparation for my first trip to Chile; Kevin Carrabine and Jennifer Macuiba, for their support and friendship during trips to Nepal and Chile; Dr. John Wott, director of the Washington Park Arboretum in Seattle, for his wise direction and guidance during my travels abroad; the staff of Briggs Nursery, Olympia, Washington, for their generous financial support of my plant-collection efforts; Dr. Bruce Macdonald, David Tarrant, Peter Wharton, and the staff of the Botanical Garden of the University of British Columbia, for sharing so freely their knowledge and access to their remarkable garden; Val Easton and Martha Ferguson of the Elisabeth C. Miller Library, for their kind and consistent help in research for this book; Myrna Ougland, for reading through the text and offering many helpful suggestions; Glen Withey, Charles Price, Marco Polo Stufano, Pamela Harper, and Nori and Sandra Pope, for inspiring me to be a better gardener; Dr. James Compton, for prompting me to be a more observant botanist; Jamaica Kincaid, Allen Lacy, Ketzel Levine, Margaret Roach, and Kim Tripp, for inspiring me to be a better writer; Tom Cooper, Tom Fischer, and the staff of *Horticulture* magazine, for providing me the opportunity to write about the plants I love; Mom and Dad, for taking the time; Duane West and the entire staff of Heronswood, for respectfully shouldering the responsibilities of the garden and nursery during my long absences; and above all, to my partner, Robert L. Jones, for selflessly letting me shine in my craft, keeping steady at the helm from the shadows.

INTRODUCTION

A Word About Nomenclature

I have grown weary of reference books that have an overriding assumption that one need not attempt to paint a complete picture, or books that cannot admit that taxonomy and nomenclature remain considerably muddled. I feel confident that the horticultural communities of North America and Europe are emotionally able to accept that science has not yet mastered the complete dissection of the plant kingdom. If there are gray areas, so be it. Let us relish that a step-by-step botanical tour has not yet been developed for every mountain on this planet. The plant kingdom is a multifaceted celebration of adaptation and interaction. The more I study and observe, the more I realize how little I know. And this is a scrumptious, delicious realization, not a troubling one. All that might be interpreted as shortcomings in our understanding of the electrifying webwork of life on Earth should rather be valued as suggesting the richness of things yet to be learned.

Despite the infancy of our understanding of the variation that exists in our natural world, seeking proper nomenclature is paramount. Paramount, yes, but also exceedingly challenging. The genus *Paris* becomes *Daiswa* one day, then changes back to *Paris* the next. Even before the ink on the nursery labels of recently transplanted *Dysosma* has dried, the accepted nomenclature returns to *Podophyllum*. Those who try to capture in print the current state of knowledge find themselves surrounded by moving targets and vehement arguments. Finally, one must simply act. I have aspired to be current in the plant names that I offer, but I remain steadfast in my commitment to not lose sleep over the fact that some of the nomenclature on these pages will, in all likelihood, not withstand the test of time.

Plant Exploration and Ethics

Plant exploration: these two words at once conjure scenes of exotic locations while provoking questions about ethics and ecology. A consciousness concerning the need to care for our planet is now greater than ever before, a fact in which I secure a vast amount of satisfaction. We all must garden and collect plants with an understanding of the complexities of the global ecosystem. For the purposes of this book, however, my hope is that "plant exploration" is understood in the broader, gentler sense. As keen gardeners seeking out the best for our gardens, we are all in a sense plant hunters. Receiving a cutting or division from a fellow keeper of the earth, visiting nurseries in our own country or abroad, or raising some treasure from seed obtained in a society seed exchange is indeed exploring for new plants. It is within this framework that I have written this book. Included are many plants that I have acquired or observed in localities around the globe. Whether from eastern Nepal or a local garden center, good plants do not discriminate about how or where they make themselves available to the gardener.

On Exotics and Natives

The debate on planting exotics versus natives has recently joined the parboil subjects of politics and religion that should be avoided during cocktail parties of mixed company. For several years now I have traveled abroad and brought back numerous plants to trial in my garden, while at the same time developing a greater appreciation for the native flora of the mountains, forests, and high deserts of the Pacific Northwest. From both endeavors, I have witnessed the focusing of a discernible picture by the placement of one small piece of the puzzle at a time.

During this period, some of the introduced plants proved overly vigorous and steps had to be taken to eradicate them. Most, as expected, settled in contentedly and modestly. None has been allowed to invade the areas of the garden that remain in native vegetation. As a responsible horticulturist, I believe that our vegetable and ornamental gardens can harbor a cache of plants that speak different languages yet still communicate in a respectful tone to our surrounding environments.

All life, since inception on this planet, is mobile and adaptive. On that classical model of evolution itself, the Galápagos Islands, life in its intricate beauty has unfurled and embraced the circumstances of the environment, each new species coloring the blank canvases that rest a thousand miles from the coast of Ecuador. For us, as reborn ecologists, to call for a moratorium on movement of non-native species into our cultivated spaces has ramifications for conscience and morality as well as impracticality. Before we heed the call to shut the barn door now that the horses are out, we must first ask if that closure is more unnatural than allowing the interface of the natural world with our human condition to continue. Life, diversity, and the forces of change that mold our natural world are stronger than anything we as humans can imagine, or that we can force upon the planet.

Zones Schmones: The Question of Plant Hardiness

The hardiness zones of the U.S. Department of Agriculture and those of *Sunset* garden books are at once meaningless yet also useful as appropriate points of departure for efforts to discern any species's potential suitability for a particular climate. I have always felt that minimum temperature ranges are more relevant to helping cross-country skiers select the wax they should carry in any part of the country than to determining a plant's chances for survival. As a gardener in the maritime Pacific Northwest, I share the same hardiness zone as my friends in North Carolina. Yet compare our gardens and the inventories within; examine the number of genera that I lose to excessive winter moisture but which thrive in their drier winter climate; observe the plants that thrive in our cool maritime summers but dissolve in the Southeast like popsicles on a sultry Piedmont afternoon. All zone 8 gardens are not created equal.

As horticulturists, we often do an injustice by assigning zone numbers to plants without firsthand knowledge of their appropriateness, or lack thereof, in each climate. Certainly, many a plant has been killed in the process, but at the same time gardeners have bypassed countless plants long thought unsuitable for their climate but which would in fact thrive. The adventuresome gardener who tries plants that supposedly "will never live," who carries that proverbial snowball through the depths of hell, enriches our lives and expands the pleasures that we all can share. While there is no question that every plant has its hardiness limits—I will never successfully grow mangoes in the Pacific Northwest, for example (considering my aversion to them, that's a reasonable sacrifice)—the potential flexibility of hardiness within each taxa is far greater than most people realize.

Countless factors come into play on the question of plant hardiness. I will discuss those that deserve greater consideration by the diverse and ever-more-sophisticated gardening community.

Provenance

Because many species have a broad natural range, assigning hardiness zones often provides little help in determining an individual plant's optimal natural conditions. A plant's provenance refers to the more specific location within that natural range, and so it plays heavily in considering a plant's adaptability and potential hardiness. Though this was clearly understood by the classical plant explorers of the nineteenth century, limited access to higher elevations where hardier forms of a species may have existed meant that collections were made of only those specimens that were more easily encountered and thus represented the least hardy individuals of the species.

Improved accessibility to more remote locations and elevations is perhaps the most exciting aspect of contemporary plant exploration. To be sure, the majority of the plant kingdom has been mapped and remapped. Yet we are now rediscovering the intricacies of the earth's ecosystems, while witnessing the interplay of individuals and their environments.

Siting and Microclimates

Within every garden there exists a world of climates. This is truly one of the pleasures of making a garden: reveling in the kindly sites and being keenly suspicious of the less-forgiving areas. Planting perennials under trees will push the hardiness envelope significantly, as will siting plants of questionable hardiness on slopes or high spots. In my own five-acre garden, I have found that the areas in the bright woodland, "up slope" from the garden and with overstory protection, push the hardiness at least two zones warmer. In this area, I successfully cultivate numerous species not designated as hardy for the climate. By contrast, on the south side of the house, in an area that receives little direct sun during the winter, there is a frustrating frost pocket. Here, year after year, I lose plants that are considered extremely hardy. Walk through your garden on frigid winter mornings to observe the patterns of frost that develop, and this will help you to determine your "safe zones" and allow you to site accordingly.

Drainage

Water is very much like a high-fat diet: too much of a good thing often proves fatal. Keeping excessive moisture away from the crown and root system of a plant aids in its survivability in two ways. First, the soil will not become waterlogged during the rainy season, thus preventing root rots and other fungal disorders. Second, and more important, without a rich diet from the soil, a plant often will shut down earlier in the growing season, thus better preparing itself for the coming frost. Such a shut-down effect can also be brought about by summer heat.

Hardening Off for Winter

On any plant, robust new growth will ultimately "ripen" or harden off, putting in place a set of physiological changes that work to protect a plant from the cold temperatures of winter. The environmental conditions in late summer and early autumn are key elements in this transformation. In the Pacific Northwest, for example, we experience relatively mild winter temperatures (especially compared to the heartland regions of North America), but the first frosts of late autumn follow a moist, warm autumn that begs for a vigorous flush of new growth in many plants. Ignoring our warnings and protests, the plants busy themselves with ignorant, blissful growth, as the shortening days of autumn mimic the lengthening days of spring. From what would be considered light frosts in many other areas, in the "mild" Northwest we lose much of the flowering wood of our trees, shrubs, vines, and perennials when early frosts are experienced. So much for a carefree gardening climate! Holding back supplemental water in late summer will help encourage a complete shutdown before frost. Once a plant realizes that it has reached the end of the road of the growing season, it will be difficult to resurrect growth in even the most delicious of autumns.

Cultural Considerations

Approaches to pruning, fertilization, and watering have a decided effect on plant hardiness. Pruning late in the season will not allow subsequent new growth enough time to sufficiently harden before the first frosts of late autumn. The same applies to late-season fertilization and watering; either practice will revitalize growth and bring about a chain of events that will assuredly influence hardiness. In the Pacific Northwest, it is recommended that one not fertilize or prune after the first of August. When to wean a plant of supplemental watering offers less dogmatic solutions, since plants that are under a great deal of drought stress may also be prone to winter damage. A day-by-day, year-by-year assessment must be given due consideration; late-summer heat waves must also be accommodated.

Common Sense

Practicality is the gardener's worst enemy. "This plant is from Florida—of course I can't grow it in my Michigan garden"; "I saw it growing in standing water—it will never tolerate my well-drained, sandy loam." Not so fast! Common sense all too often results in a stiff, boring inventory of plants and a garden that looks mass produced. Throw all preconceived notions out the window, plant wildly, laugh at the failures, and smugly savor the successes.

The steep valley walls in the Wenchuan Wolong Nature Reserve in Sichuan Province harbor an overwhelming diversity of plant species, and in the surrounding mountains is one of the last remaining populations of the giant panda. Along the limestone cliffs, I have seen *Epimedium davidii* and *Corydalis flexuosa*, along with many other treasures. (Photo by Daniel J. Hinkley)

CHAPTER 1

Woodland Ranunculids:
Anemone, Anemonella, Anemonopsis, Ranunculus, Trollius, and *Glaucidium*

The family Ranunculaceae contains a multitude of members with decidedly distinguished qualities, and considering the legions of cultivated species and hybrids in its ranks, from alpines to vines, the merits are recognized by vast numbers of gardeners worldwide. The family is believed to be quite ancient by taxonomists, with the floral parts arranged in a perfect spiral along the receptacle, sequenced from sepals to petals (or just tepals) to stamens and finally pistils. Simple observation of any seed head, either immediately after petal drop or later after the seed is dispersed, makes very apparent this exquisite symmetry, which embodies the great mysteries of "order from chaos" that surround us. (As someone who has studied taxonomy, however, I will admit to exasperating similarities between the flowers of the Ranunculaceae and those of the Rosaceae.) Another great tool in identifying members of the Ranunculaceae is the often (but, alas, not always) deeply cleft foliage. That this family has come to be commonly called the "bird's foot" family attests to the numbers of taxa within it that embrace such a folial format. The tripartite foliage of many *Clematis* and the rounded leaf blades of *Caltha* should make it quite clear, however, why the science of plant taxonomy is no longer based on foliage characteristics.

Anemone

When I lived in Wenatchee, Washington, in the late 1970s, I would ride my bicycle across town to my job at the USDA Research Laboratory. One autumn day, I passed a garden that I had come to know from my daily commute, and blossoming there was a magnificent plant with willowy, erect stems carrying large, porcelain-pink flowers that rose from clumps of bold maplelike foliage. With no time to spare that morning, I decided I would return that evening to ask the gardener its identity. Nine hours later, I arrived to find that my plant had vanished without a trace. I was about to leave in a state of bewilderment, when the gardener emerged from the house, so I inquired as to whether I had imagined the entire scene. "Oh, the Japanese anemone," she said. "I've been trying to rid the garden of the beast for years. It's in the trash bin if you'd like to take it home." So, having had my first introduction to *Anemone ×hybrida*, off I pedaled with an enormous plant under my arm, looking like an overdone float in the Rose Bowl Parade and pleased as punch. If there is one constant among gardeners worldwide, it is their refusal to take another gardener's word when it comes to invasive plants—especially when smitten by that momentary excitement of a new introduction. Years later, I continue to harvest vast clumps of this anemone (and numerous others) from my own garden, never succeeding in ridding the garden of it, never quite sure if I actually want to rid the garden of it, while finding a paucity of patronizing peddlers to deliver me from this excess compost.

To be sure, a number of *Anemone* species and hybrids must be carefully introduced into the garden, if they are to be used at all. I would rethink my earlier decisions to include *Anemone canadensis* and *A. sylvestris* in my woodland, as the rampant marching stands of low foliage refuse to share the space with other woodland companions. Of course, this degree of vigor might be warranted in certain situations, and the masses of pure white flowers atop 10-in. (25-cm) stems offered by these species compose a tempting scene in early spring.

The anemones that I will discuss here possess varying degrees of invasiveness, but after several years in the garden, I have yet to reconsider my decision to include them.

Anemone trifolia hails from the high mountains of central Europe, where it forms low, spreading colonies of deep green, thrice tripartite foliage. The star-shaped, upturned, white to blue ½-in. (1.25-cm) flowers are produced in early spring. This endearing species superficially resembles a more robust, later-blossoming form of *A. nemorosa*, though Reginald Farrer thought the latter species "rather wizen and douty by comparison." I first saw *A. trifolia* 'Flore Pleno', which is considered an antique hand-me-down cultivar, offered for sale in a tiny nursery on northern Honshu in Japan in 1995. It thrives in my woodland, already having formed substantial colonies, while presenting fully double, white flowers atop 8-in. (20-cm) stems for a long period from spring into early summer. How I would love to hear the sojourn of this plant, chapter by chapter, from its day of discovery to its eventual travel across the planet, one garden at a time.

While botanizing in the parched volcanic soils of Chile's Conquillo National

Anemone trifolia (Photo by Lynne Harrison)

Park in 1998, I observed drifts of *Anemone magellanica* growing under magnificent stands of the monkey-puzzle tree (*Araucaria araucana*) and interspersed among low mats of the evergreen *Baccharis magellanica*. The flowering stems of the anemone rose to 8 in. (20 cm), each carrying a cottony mass of seed, above low mounds of deeply cut, gray-green foliage. I was excited to find and collect seed of this plant, not only because the resultant seedlings would perpetually bring to life the memories of that day in Chile, but also because I had lost this species from my garden years earlier when I was reconfiguring a border. The handsome seed heads follow an early spring showing of ivory-colored flowers to 1 in. (2.5 cm) across.

A vast contingent of cultivars of the wood anemone (*Anemone nemorosa*) have become decidedly more popular, or at least rediscovered, among an ever-increasing number of gardeners across the United States. For several years, on plant-buying forays to Europe, I have collected numerous named forms that bring an assured and early elegance to the woodland garden, as many have done for centuries in European gardens. For reasons that probably stem from handling difficulties (the rhizomes of the wood anemone are quite small and present marketing challenges for large, wholesale operations), very few nurseries offer any form of *A. nemorosa* in North America. I have observed the species as it exists in the wild—no great shakes, I'm sure, for those living within its native range of northern Europe and England, yet still an exciting discovery for me. Alongside *Primula vulgaris* in the deciduous woodlots of Surrey and Kent, the single white flowers emerge on 6-in. (15-cm) stems in late March and early April slightly above low, spreading colonies of deeply cut foliage. *Anemone nemorosa* is adapted to moist, humus-rich soils in partial shade, and as it slips into early dormancy, it can tolerate drier conditions during the summer months.

Undoubtedly, there are many cultivars of *Anemone nemorosa* that will never become widely known, but some of the more commonly grown and most worthy cultivars that I currently have in my own garden include: 'Alba Plena', which possesses fully double flowers of pure white petaloid stamens centered among white petals; 'Allenii', large lavender flowers of luminous quality; 'Amy Doncaster', large flowers opening white and fading to rich rose; 'Blue Bonnet', the latest to flower at Heronswood, with translucent lavender-blue flowers; 'Blue Eyes', a startling double white centered with blue; 'Bowles' Variety', also sold as 'Bowles' Purple', with large flowers of medium lavender; 'Bracteata Pleniflora', a lovely form with green and white jagged bracts surrounding semidouble flowers of white; 'Buckland', an extremely vigorous clone and one of the earliest, with lilac-lavender flowers; 'Dee Day', a good blue collected by an English soldier in France during World War I; 'Green Fingers', with a central boss of green petals held within pure white flowers; 'Leeds Variety', exceptionally large, white flowers; 'Lismore Blue', a tender form offering large, sky-blue flowers with lavender markings; 'Lychette', with large, pure white flowers in late winter; 'Parlez Vous', with soft blue flowers, collected in France during World War I; 'Robinsoniana', similar to 'Allenii', though deeper blue-mauve; 'Vestal', one of the best double white forms; 'Virescens', vigorous mounds with curious heads of double, deeply cut green bracts on vigorous spreading mounds; and 'Wyatt's Pink', nodding flowers opening in shades of rosy red but quickly fading to a soft pastel-pink and then to near white.

During my trip to Yunnan Province in 1996, while botanizing the hills around Zhongdian, I climbed the high hills behind my hotel one afternoon to a magical and quiet wooded site that I had seen far in the distance. There, amidst a most remarkable birch forest dripping with long chains of moss and lichen, I

Anemone nemorosa 'Blue Bonnet' (Photo by Lynne Harrison)

Anemone nemorosa 'Leeds Variety' (Photo by Lynne Harrison)

Anemone nemorosa 'Lismore Blue' (Photo by Lynne Harrison)

Anemone nemorosa 'Lychette' (Photo by Lynne Harrison)

Anemone nemorosa 'Wyatt's Pink' (Photo by Lynne Harrison)

found a most curious seed head arising from a rosette of three-lobed, deeply incised, gray, felted leaves. The dry, flattened seed was presented on umbels composed of 4-in. (10-cm) pedicels, atop a scape to 8 in. (20 cm). The species was identified much later as *Anemone demissa*, and the resultant seedlings of my collection on that remarkable day blossomed for the first time in the late summer of 1998 in the woodland at Heronswood. Numerous elegant and large white flowers are centered by a bright golden boss of stamens. Literature cites this species as being quite variable in flower color, with pink- and blue-flowered forms reported from the wild. I am eager to return to this part of China to continue a search for additional clones of this species, which has found a permanent place in my heart and garden.

While traveling in eastern Nepal and again in western China, I collected seed of a widespread species known as *Anemone rivularis*. The starry heads of dry, brown seed rising on 15-in. (38-cm) stems make for easy identification in the field, as do the simple but elegant sprays of white flowers that feature a purple boss of stamens and purple staining on the back of each petal. The trait of purple staining is variable among different populations, and of my two distinct wild collections of this species, neither has been as good as the small colony that I established in my garden from seed received through the Hardy Plant Society seed exchange in 1987.

I find the bright buttercup-golden flowers of *Anemone ranunculoides* indispensable to the early spring woodland, especially cheery on the gray, overcast days that the Pacific Northwest excels in producing. The flowers blossom atop 15-in. (38-cm) stems, and the low mats of finely cut foliage create sizable colonies quite quickly in moist, humus-rich soils in partial shade. I grow a vigorous form that I received from Elizabeth Strangman of Washfield Nursery in England, who collected it in Bosnia in 1971. I also have an older cultivar known as *A. ranunculoides* 'Flore Pleno', which has semidouble flowers of gold. The species is closely allied to *A. nemorosa*, with which it has crossed to form the hybrid known as *A. ×lipsiensis* (also seen as *A. ×seemannii*). The butter-yellow flowers of *A. ×lipsiensis* are produced on low stems above spreading colonies of dark green foliage, adding an endearing presence to the spring woodland. It is especially good when used as a low-running foil to the darker hued hellebores.

Reginald Farrer, in his book *The English Rock Garden*, told us that *Anemone apennina* needed no introduction or description. That he was so hopelessly smitten I might understand, yet it is unlikely that many American gardeners are on such intimate terms with this species that we can forgo a bit of polite conversation. It is native to southern Europe, in close proximity to the Mediterranean, where it grows under deciduous woods, producing low mounds of finely dissected foliage. On the type form, sky-blue flowers nestle within the foliage in early spring. Numerous cultivars are available, offering flowers ranging from pure white to red-violet, but of these I grow only a rare form known as 'Flore Pleno'. It bears fully double heads of lilac-lavender to $1\frac{1}{2}$ in. (3.8 cm) across that are present for a long period in April and May. Though perhaps less dogmatically than Mr. Farrer, I have come to greatly admire this species and will continue to seek additional forms for the garden. *Anemone apennina* and its variations must be grown in a rich diet in wooded sites. It can be divided in late summer or very early spring before growth resumes.

Hardiness: The majority of *Anemone* species are hardy in zones 5–9, though the European species, such as *Anemone nemorosa* and *A. ranunculoides* will tolerate even colder temperatures and are considered hardy to zone 4, perhaps even lower with protection. *Anemone magellanica*, hailing from higher elevations in its native Chile, is hardy to zones 5–8 and will resent summer heat and humidity, such as is found in the deep South.

Cultivation: Across the board, these *Anemone* species respond best if provided a rich edaphic environment and plenty of spring moisture. Siting should

Anemone ranunculoides (Photo by Lynne Harrison)

Anemone ranunculoides 'Flore Pleno' (Photo by Lynne Harrison)

be carefully considered, as anemones will spread throughout the garden at a respectable clip and may overwhelm more diminutive companions nearby.

Propagation: Division in early spring is the best method of propagation, certainly for the named forms and hybrids. Propagating by seed is convenient for the species, and the seed will germinate the following spring if sown fresh. Self sowing in the garden is generally not a problem.

Anemonella

Anemonella thalictroides is a clever woodland herb that charms the deciduous woodlots of the eastern half of North America, from New England to Florida and west to Kansas, though it remains largely unsung in its native land. It has made its way about the planet under one name or another, including *Anemone thalictroides* and *Thalictrum anemonoides* in addition to its current moniker, though the story may not end there. Work is threatening its present standing in favor of *Thalictrum*, and in line with the rules of priority, its name will change to *Thalictrum thalictroides*, which literally means a thalictrum that looks exceedingly similar to a thalictrum. Comforting.

The wiry, 6-in. (15-cm) stems, cloaked with tiny, bluish green foliage, carry delicate, solitary flowers of white or pink in mid- to late spring, creating sizable clumps over time. After seed is dispersed in early summer, this tuberous perennial generally goes dormant. *Anemonella thalictroides* has offered up a considerable number of highly collectible cultivars, which are more readily found in specialty nurseries in England and Japan than in its home territory. 'Rubra' has a deeper saturation of petals than the species form, though more of a rich rose than a deep, low-throated red. An exceptionally vigorous seed strain currently known as *A. thalictroides* "Semidouble White" has, not surprisingly, semidouble flowers of pure white. *Anemonella thalictroides* 'Green Hurricane' produces endearing, tiny, fully double buttons of lime-green. Fully double white flowers are found on *A. thalictroides* 'Alba Plena', while 'Oscar Schoaff' and 'Cameo' each have astounding fully double flowers of smoky pink. These cultivars may be listed under a plethora of synonymous names, but the names are generally close enough to allow deciphering.

Hardiness: Hardy in zones 4–10, tolerating the heat and humidity of the American Southeast.

Cultivation: Best in bright, shaded sites in humus-rich soils with adequate spring moisture. Plants will falter if allowed to dry out too early in spring. A good companion plant is *Cyclamen hederifolium*, at least in climates that can ac-

Anemonella thalictroides (Photo by Daniel J. Hinkley)

Anemonella thalictroides 'Rubra' (Photo by Lynne Harrison)

Anemonella thalictroides 'Oscar Schoaff' (Photo by Lynne Harrison)

commodate it, since the *Cyclamen* fills in the blanks just as *Anemonella* departs for the season.

Propagation: Seed is produced on single and semidouble forms and should be collected and sown fresh. The semidouble forms will generally come true to type. The fully double-flowered cultivars must be divided, which is best accomplished in early spring or after they have gone completely dormant in late summer. You will understand the paucity of named forms of the species that are available on the market once you have divided your first plant, as very few divisions are offered up from even a sizable specimen.

Anemonopsis

Anemonopsis macrophylla is one of those plants that takes you away when you first see it. And unlike so many plants that so soon become old hat in the garden, this species continues to excite the eyes each and every year as it comes into blossom in my woodland. The plant has a precious and beguiling demeanor about it, as the nodding, waxen flowers of light lavender, appearing quite like those of a somewhat modified columbine (*Aquilegia*), begin to blossom in the late days of June and continue through most of July. These are held on striking ebony stems,

Anemonopsis macrophylla (Photo by Lynne Harrison)

Anemonopsis macrophylla flowers (Photo by Lynne Harrison)

which ascend to 2 ft. (0.6 m) or slightly higher from a ferny clump of pinnate foliage. A monotypic genus, the single species of *Anemonopsis* is native to mountainous woods in central Honshu, where it is extremely rare. I have not yet observed it in the wild.

Hardiness: Zones 5–9, in climates with moderately warm to cool summers only.

Cultivation: This species does not politely ask for a sheltered and cool location—it demands it. The flowers and foliage will scald if exposed to full sun and wind, even if provided supplemental water and a rich edaphic environment. It is slow to establish in the garden, a trait that I always find admirable in a herbaceous species, because it means that it will be long-lived and rather nuisance-free.

Propagation: Division is reasonable for small quantities over time, but seed seems to be the best approach for commercial purposes. The plants in my garden generally set healthy amounts of seed, and if sown fresh, the seed will germinate readily the following spring. It takes three to four years before the first blossoms are formed, and more than one clone grown together will ensure better seed set.

Ranunculus

A vast number of *Ranunculus* species and selections are available for enjoyment in the garden, as well as some fairly dastardly species that are to be avoided. *Ranunculus repens*, a common and aggressive species, quickly spreads to command impressive chunks of earth, especially in perpetually moist soils. Double-flowered forms offered under the names *R. repens* 'Flore Pleno' and *R. repens* 'Timothy Clark' may tempt the weak at heart, but I implore you to stand fast. A good biomass subject this may be; a good garden plant it is not. With that said, I collected a form that I believe to be of this species in the mountains above Monterrey, Mexico, in 1994. Though numerous individuals of *R. repens* may possess some silver marbling on the center of each leaf, the plant I collected in Mexico had a sensational pewtered leaf that would quickly dissipate any frustrations associated with the species. Furthermore, this version has not proven to be overly vigorous in my garden; in fact, it is a little on the shy side, which may be due to a lack of summer heat. *Ranunculus repens* 'Buttered Popcorn' (offered as 'Joe's Golden' in the United Kingdom) is a somewhat yellow-variegated form introduced by Plant Delights Nursery in 1997. Unlike my Mexican collection, 'Buttered Popcorn' showed no objection to the chilly wash of Pacific air that descends upon the garden after nightfall. It whooped and hollered its way to a 6-ft. (1.8-m) colony within less than six weeks, at which point it was containerized—a plastic container with a lid. The foliage of this cultivar is quite striking and could be useful as a vigorous groundcover in extremely moist soils. The species and its various cultivars are hardy in zones 4–9.

The double yellow, green-eyed buttons of *Ranunculus repens* 'Timothy Clark' are virtually identical to those found on a much more sophisticated and refined plant known as *R. constantinopolitanus* 'Plenus'. (Even though I consider botanical Latin a second language, I cannot bring myself to attempt this name in public.) The species itself hails from the moist meadows of southeastern Europe and would be an impressive specimen for the poorly drained border, if it could only be located. The double-flowered form far exceeds the general availability of the species, which isn't saying much, as it is extremely difficult at present to locate 'Plenus' outside of the specialty nurseries of Europe. Cultivated in gardens for more than 200 years, 'Plenus' makes a very handsome perennial, with flowers on stems to 15 in. (38 cm) held above dark green, deeply incised foliage. Its clumping nature adds to the exquisite floral effect to make *R. constantinopolitanus* 'Plenus' a sensational addition to the border. Though I grow this in fairly deep shade, it will tolerate full-sun exposure if provided adequate moisture. It is hardy in zones 4–9.

Many species of *Ranunculus* have been selected for their doubleness in flowers, and the vast majority make distinctive and good garden-worthy plants. I have found *Ranunculus aconitifolius*, a species from the mountains of central Europe, to be a refreshing addition to a lightly shaded border in moist soils. It forms tight clumps of ferny foliage and sprays of $^3/_4$-in. (1.9-cm) white flowers produced in early summer on stems rising to 18 in. (45 cm). The species type is, sadly enough, rarely encountered in American gardens. Instead, keen gardeners have sought out *R. aconitifolius* 'Flore Pleno', its antique, double-flowered form that possesses the vernacular names fair maids of France or fair maids of Kent. It is indeed a charming selection, with fully double white buttons held atop airy 2-ft. (0.6-m) stems for an immensely long time in early summer. It remains a difficult clone to acquire for the garden, which is somewhat odd considering the fact that this plant has been in cultivation since the 1500s. (Five centuries, in my mind, provides more than sufficient lead time to build up numbers of any plant for sale.) I have grown this cultivar, as well as the typical species, in the light shade of my woodland for a number of years, and it has been a shy increaser and allows division only every four to five years. *Ranunculus aconitifolius* and its more common cultivated variety are hardy in zones 4–9.

When I looked at the transplants of *Ranunculus gramineus* in my nursery several years ago, I was certain that we had mislabeled the flats or had received misnamed seed (not that THAT ever happens). With a name like "*gramineus*" (which means grassy or grasslike), however, I should have considered the plant's resemblance to a broad-bladed grass before jumping to conclusions. Since then, I have come to rely on this species for superb effects in the late-spring and early summer border. The distinctive foliage rises to 8 in. (20 cm) in height and forms a dense rosette. Wiry, 8-in. (20-cm) stems emerge from the foliage and carry 1-in. (2.5-cm), quarter-sized, rich yellow flowers. I have included *R. gramineus* in a relatively well-drained site on the east side of our home, where it combines nicely with *Corydalis flexuosa* 'AGM Form' and *Iris setosa* 'Nana'. All three blossom concurrently in April and May to make an entertaining assemblage. A double-flowered selection of *R. gramineus* is known to exist, although I have been unable to locate it. The species, which is native to the Mediterranean region, is hardy in zones 7–10.

Ranunculus gramineus crossed with *R. amplexicaulis*, a white-flowered, spring ephemeral species from northern Spain, has given rise to a series of lovely hybrids known collectively as *R. ×arendsii*. An outstanding selection of this cross, named 'Moonlight', was made by Elizabeth Strangman, using *R. gramineus* 'Pardal' as one parent. The hybrid grows in a bright location in my woodland garden, presenting its soft yellow flowers and strappy, bluish green foliage in midspring,

Ranunculus constantinopolitanus 'Plenus' (Photo by Lynne Harrison)

Ranunculus aconitifolius 'Flore Pleno' (Photo by Lynne Harrison)

though it is ideally suited to full sun and well-drained positions. Hardy in zones 7–10, 'Moonlight' offers greater durability than its white-flowered parent, which I have lost on numerous occasions, and it is easily propagated in early spring by simple division.

The same soft butter-yellow flower color that is provided by *Ranunculus* ×*arendsii* 'Moonlight' is also brought forth by *R. bulbosus* 'F. M. Burton'. The species type, which has bright orange-yellow flowers, is native to grassy meadows of south-central Europe and northern Africa. I have not grown this species in its raw state, but the cultivar has been a superb addition to the woodland. In mid-spring to early June, low mounds of deeply cut, grayish green foliage emerge, growing to 6 in. (15 cm) in height, followed by a long succession of flowers rising to 8 in. (20 cm). As soon as the temperatures rise in early summer, the plants fade to dormancy, though we generally are granted a regrowth and reblossoming by late August. 'F. M. Burton' forms a fleshy root system (as is suggested by the specific epithet "*bulbosus*") that can be divided in spring to increase the plants. It is hardy in zones 5–9.

The lesser celandine, *Ranunculus ficaria*, is a common perennial in moist meadows and road ditches throughout much of north-central Europe. Mounds

Ranunculus bulbosus 'F. M. Burton' (Photo by Lynne Harrison)

of green, ovate-rounded foliage emerge from a tuberous root, while masses of bright, glistening yellow flowers, to $^3/_4$ in. (1.9 cm) across, are produced in very early spring. *Ranunculus ficaria* subsp. *chrysocephalus* is more robust in every regard, rising to 1 ft. (0.3 m) in height and bearing quarter-sized flowers to 1 in. (2.5 cm). Countless cultivars of the standard species offer an outrageously huge assortment of flower and foliage types. *Ranunculus ficaria* 'Brambling' is one of the best in foliage, with muting of silvers, purples, and greens, along with its single flowers of golden-yellow. *Ranunculus ficaria* 'Brazen Hussy', found and named by Christopher Lloyd at Great Dixter, produces mounds of black-purple foliage that provide remarkable contrast to the bright yellow flowers. 'Collarette' creates a pompom effect, with the center of the flower transformed to a golden boss of petaloid stamens. *Ranunculus ficaria* 'Coppernob' presents a glazed tangerine-orange flower against somber, bruised foliage. The foliage of 'Crawshay Cream' is similar to that of 'Brazen Hussy', but this cultivar produces flowers of a lovely ivory color, rather than glaring yellow. *Ranunculus ficaria* 'Double Mud' offers fully double, creamy yellow flowers with a bronze reverse to the petals. *Ranunculus ficaria* 'Green Petal' is a curiosity but lovely, with fully double "roses" of glossy green. Pure white and creamy white flowers are borne on 'Randall's White' and 'Salmon's White', respectively, above dark mottled foliage. Invoking the appearance of a hardy cyclamen, *R. ficaria* 'Tortoiseshell' produces foliage with handsome muted marblings of green, purple, and pewter, in addition to its soft ivory-colored flowers. The lesser celandine and its cultivars survive best in hardiness zones 5–9.

I find the plethora of named cultivars of *Ranunculus ficaria* to be supremely good choices for the early spring garden, but I am aware of the species's potential to self sow too exuberantly throughout moist borders in full sun, especially on the East Coast of North America. Double-flowered forms set little if any seed and can be planted without fear of this overexuberant self sowing. In this species, the small tuberous roots will dislodge from the parent plant to form new plants, so care must be taken to not disturb the site where they grow. (Rototilling a garden that contains a small colony of any cultivar will ensure enough propagules to effectively corner the market on earth as well as adjacent planets in our solar system.) Separation of these small tubers while the plants are dormant is an easy method of propagation for *R. ficaria*. These are early spring ephemerals and will slip into early dormancy by the end of May in most years.

A far cry from the several border-worthy species of *Ranunculus*, the tiny, encrusted mats of *Ranunculus yakusimensis* provide a textural groundcover quite unlike any other plant I have grown. The strikingly white-mottled leathery leaves are presented on prostrate stems that spread to make healthy, noninvasive colo-

Ranunculus ficaria 'Brazen Hussy' (Photo by Lynne Harrison)

Ranunculus ficaria 'Collarette' (Photo by Lynne Harrison)

nies. In June, bright, albeit tiny, yellow flowers sit flush to the foliage. It is a little-known yet useful perennial for the rock garden in moist but well-drained sites in zones 6–10.

I collected seed of a charming buttercup species in the alpine meadows surrounding Volcano Puyehue in the Lakes District of southern Chile in 1998. Identified as *Ranunculus peduncularis*, it formed short tufts of deeply cut, orbicular foliage, to 1 in. (2.5 cm) in length, and solitary, bright golden flowers rising to 6 in. (15 cm). The plant grew in very well-drained volcanic soils, offering its lovely flowers through dense, evergreen, and heavily fruited mats of *Gaultheria pumila*. Since the seed has only recently germinated, I am unable to comment on hardiness, although I will grow the seedlings in very well-drained soils in full sun.

Hardiness: As noted for individual species.

Cultivation: As noted for individual species.

Propagation: As noted for individual species.

Trollius

For simple brilliance of flower in a shaded garden, few botanical riches are more treasured than the globeflowers; I have in my garden numerous plants that I have raised from seed exchanges of many societies. Like so many garden-worthy plants, however, the genus *Trollius* has many problems surrounding the taxonomy of its lesser-known species. This is one reason why re-collection of species from the wild, with known provenance, is so important, allowing us to regain confidence in the true identity of the plants that we study and grow. Nevertheless, I think of this genus as much like a good book: something to slowly, methodically experience and embrace, without any hurry to reach the last pages.

While in China in 1996, I collected seed of *Trollius yunnanensis* in a deciduous woods at elevations of approximately 10,000 ft. (3000 m), above the Wenchuan Wolong Nature Reserve in Sichuan Province. The species offers flowers that are the antithesis of what one might expect from a genus collectively known as the globeflowers. Golden-yellow flowers are produced on 2-ft. (0.6-m) stems in early summer, with colorful sepals that extend fully open, in fact reflex slightly away from the core of twelve narrow petals, longer stamens, and the knobby green receptacle of numerous pistils. I find this to be a rather pretty species, but I am often more smitten by plants that hold little doubt as to their identity, compared to those that leave a smudge of doubt on my brow.

Trollius pumilus is similar in many ways to *T. yunnanensis*, though it is smaller in all regards. It is an excellent choice for the well-drained rock garden in full sun.

Trollius pumilus occurs naturally in the grassy alpine meadows of the Himalayas, where I collected seed in the autumn of 1995 at elevations of 9500 ft. (2850 m) along the Milke Danda mountain ridge in eastern Nepal. The flowering stems grow to a mere 10 in. (25 cm) and carry golden cups of petaloid sepals surrounding many narrow petals and deep orange stamens.

Further to the north and east of where I collected *Trollius pumilus* grows the top-notch species *T. chinensis*. This is an extremely ornamental species in cultivation, though often overlooked in lieu of the European and hybrid globeflowers. It provides clear-enough clues to its identity that most plants in cultivation under this name are indeed correct. The dazzling orange flowers are produced in early summer on stems rising to 2 ft. (0.6 m) above clumps of deeply dissected, orbicular leaves. Each flower is composed of five broad, golden-orange sepals encircling a boss of extremely narrow, upright petals (known as nectary petals), which are longer than the stamens. The intensity of color and the size of the flowers are exceptionally variable among individual clones of *T. chinensis*, though to my knowledge no named cultivars of this species exist.

I have never grown the unadulterated version of *Trollius europaeus*, whose unopened globes of orange-yellow gave rise to the common name of the genus. Instead, I have cultivated several named forms of the hybrid globeflower, *Trollius* ×*cultorum*, an interplay between *T. europaeus*, *T. asiaticus*, and *T. chinensis*. The flowers of *T.* ×*cultorum* 'Helios' are the largest and the richest gold of the plethora of European selections. 'Helios' blossoms in late April through May, offering superb orange cups atop upright stems rising to 2 ft. (0.6 m) and handsome mounds of deeply dissected foliage. *Trollius* ×*cultorum* 'Alabaster' has been all the rage for a number of years, with its small globes of ivory sepals and petals atop stems to 15 in. (38 cm). Though I do grow this plant, it is weak in growth and extremely slow to bulk up for sale in our nursery. Better choices are *T.* ×*cultorum* 'Cheddar', which has somewhat larger flowers of ivory-yellow produced from extremely vigorous mounds of filigree foliage, and *T.* ×*cultorum* 'Taleggio', with numerous flowers of near creamy white that open from tight orbs of pastel-yellow. The latter was selected and given to me by my friend Coen Jansen of Ankun, the Netherlands.

Much closer to home grows *Trollius laxus* var. *albiflorus*, the white form of a native species. The pure white flowers are produced in spring as the snow melts from the subalpine areas of the Olympic Mountains and the Cascade Range. I successfully collected seed along a small lake at the base of Mount Townsend a few years ago, and the plant has established well in my garden, where it has proven to be an eager self sower. Interestingly, it responds very well to the summer heat

Trollius chinensis (Photo by Lynne Harrison)

Trollius ×*cultorum* 'Helios' flowers (Photo by Lynne Harrison)

Trollius laxus var. *albiflorus* (Photo by Daniel J. Hinkley)

and humidity of the mid-Atlantic states, despite its cool and moist heritage in the Pacific Northwest.

Hardiness: All globeflowers will be exceptionally hardy in zones 4–9.

Cultivation: Best in moist, humus-rich soils in bright shade or full sun. I cultivate *Trollius chinensis* in full sun and in regular garden loam, and though this continues to blossom quite well, the clumps of foliage sulk by late summer if not provided with a great deal of supplemental water.

Propagation: Named forms must be divided in spring or directly after flowering. The species sets copious quantities of seed, which is easy to germinate if sown fresh. Plants raised from seed collected from nonisolated garden plants should not be considered pure.

Glaucidium

While exploring the slopes of the northern shores of Lake Towada in northern Japan in 1997, I came upon curious dried, two-lobed seed capsules that looked vaguely familiar. As the frosts of autumn had already settled hard upon the landscape, the foliage was completely absent, and I was left to ponder the identity of my find with but one clue.

A moment that I will not soon forget is when it dawned on me that I was walking amidst a rather sizable colony of *Glaucidium palmatum*. It delivered the same impact as would, perhaps, remembering the answer to Final Jeopardy after having bid all your savings. Never being one who could be considered remotely restrained, and certainly outside the protocol of Japanese understatement, I whooped with joy. I had come across another friend on its home ground, and I took every opportunity to study its environment. Not only a friend, I might add, but one of the loveliest of the woodland perennials that I grow in my garden. The genus has made the taxonomic rounds, bouncing between the families Paeoniaceae, Glaucidiaceae, and Ranunculaceae.

In midspring, robust mounds of bright green, lobed, maplelike leaves are formed along stout, 2-ft. (0.6-m) stems. The leaves grow to 6 in. (15 cm) across, becoming progressively smaller and less lobed as they ascend the stem. Directly above the last leaf, atop the remaining inch of stem, slightly nodding, silken lavender flowers are produced in May and June. When backlit by morning or late-evening sun and glistening with a wash of dew or recent rain, a scene is created that even the most jaded must stop to behold. A white-flowered form, *Glaucidium palmatum* 'Album', exists naturally in the wild and can occasionally be encountered in the trade or through seed exchanges; it should be sought out.

Hardiness: Zones 4–8, perhaps colder if mulched in late autumn. Will not tolerate arid or humid climates.

Cultivation: *Glaucidium palmatum* grew naturally in Japan in cool, moist, humus-rich soils on a steep slope beneath a high overstory of *Cercidiphyllum japon-*

Glaucidium palmatum (Photo by Lynne Harrison)

Glaucidium palmatum flowers (Photo by Lynne Harrison)

icum. The katsura and the hill may be disregarded, but heed the edaphic requirements and provide shelter from hot, desiccating winds.

Propagation: Seed is readily produced in cultivation where more than one clone is grown together. It should be sown as fresh as possible and will take two years to germinate. Though a few seedlings might emerge the first spring, leave the seed pots intact for an additional year to ensure complete germination. Plants can be divided in late winter and will offer a number of dormant buds along a woody rootstock; use a sharp knife to remove these along with a substantial part of the root.

CHAPTER 2

On the Vine:
The Climbing Aconites

The genus *Aconitum* has a long tradition in cultivation. It was among the early pioneers that formed the bridge between growing plants for utilitarian purposes and growing plants solely for ornament. As with many poisonous plants—and indeed all parts of this plant are poisonous—aconites contain alkaloids that were found to be useful for medicinal purposes when used in minute quantities. The most potent of these alkaloides is aconitine, and this lethal alkaloid was the drug of choice among the ancients for poisoning arrow tips used in combat. Though we have come to a decidedly less-brutal appreciation for the 100 or more species of *Aconitum* that exist, the fact that they pose a certain threat to inquisitive toddlers is not forgotten in our nursery and perennial borders.

In my garden, one of the first aconites—or monkshoods, as they are commonly known—to blossom is certainly one of the most beautiful. *Aconitum* 'Ivorine', which rises to only 2 ft. (0.6 m) in height, presents its white-hooded flowers with greenish overtones on sturdy stems in late April. As the gardening season continues, the torch is handed from one species to the next, offering flowers mostly in the rich violet-blues associated with the genus.

My collection of nonvining *Aconitum* species has come mostly from seed that was sent from various botanical gardens and plant societies worldwide. As is often and unfortunately the case with seed from such sources, these plants may carry illegitimate names or may be the result of spontaneous hybrids that occurred in cultivation. Though a gardener can choose to relax and enjoy a superb plant no matter what its true identification, a gardener who is also a nurseryman must strive for correct nomenclature. In my opinion, the genus as it is represented under cultivation is hopelessly muddled, with the majority of species and hybrids bearing improper names. This is another reason why I support a continual program of introduction and reintroduction of all species from the wild, at least those that have proven noninvasive under cultivation.

My emphasis here is on the vining species of *Aconitum*, which are largely underappreciated in general cultivation. *Aconitum hemsleyanum* has been available through specialist nurseries for some time, primarily under the name *A. volubile*, and it is the most commonly grown vining monkshood worldwide. I first observed this species in the mountains of South Korea in 1993. It was twining through small maples, lilacs, and weigelas in full sun throughout most of the sites that I explored on the vast Korean Peninsula. The stems rose to 8 ft. (2.4 m) or more in height, which is precisely the size and vigor that it possesses growing in fully exposed areas of my garden. Clusters of lavender hooded flowers are produced in mid-August to mid-September, complementing the golden foliage of selected forms of *Sambucus* and *Weigela*. *Aconitum hemsleyanum*, like other aconites, produces clumps of moderately sized tubers that can be easily separated in spring to produce new plants.

Aconitum episcopale also grows in my garden as a result of collections made in China during the Alpine Garden Society's 1994 expedition to Yunnan and Sichuan Provinces, and I observed this magnificent species there myself in the autumn of 1996. The deeply and finely lobed leaves, which grow to 6 in. (15 cm) across, are carried along 10- to 20-ft. (3- to 6-m) long, vigorous herbaceous stems that rake through the limbs of trees and shrubs in bright situations with adequate moisture. The large, late-summer flowers, to 1½ in. (3.8 cm) in length, are borne in axillary clusters of up to 10 flowers in rich violet tones, appearing nearly red when backlit by late-afternoon sun.

Near Shuduhu Lake, slightly northwest of Zhongdian in Yunnan Province, I observed and collected a most distinctive species growing in fairly damp and shaded areas alongside the monocarpic, yellow-flowered *Meconopsis integrifolia* and dramatic stands of *Smilacina forrestii*. *Aconitum* sp. DJHC 363 seemingly grew as both a vine and a sturdy upright perennial, depending on the support available. Specimens that did not grow near support of any kind produced stems to 4 ft. (1.2 m), from which scandent axillary branches grew in search of support. The foliage was very handsomely and finely dissected, more so than on any other species of *Aconitum* that I have come across. Nearby, specimens that found initial support had begun climbing immediately, and the axillary branches gracefully tumbled downward. I gathered sufficient seed to observe this curious habit under cultivation. I presume this species will make a good addition to those already in cultivation.

In the Wenchuan Wolong Nature Reserve of Sichuan Province, I spotted a most extraordinary cascading aconite growing on wet limestone walls alongside a small unidentified species of *Primula* and *Epimedium davidii*. The rather limp 3-ft. (0.9-m) stems, which carried lobed, maplelike foliage and blue-purple axillary flowers, behaved as if this was its niche of choice, and indeed I did not find this species, designated as *Aconitum* sp. DJHC 664A, growing in any other habitat.

Aconitum hemsleyanum growing through *Acer carpinifolium* at Heronswood (Photo by Lynne Harrison)

Aconitum episcopale makes a nice complement to the golden foliage of *Chamaecyparis obtusa* 'Crippsii' (Photo by Lynne Harrison)

Later, nearing the top of the sacred Emei Shan—a veritable botanical paradise—I found *Aconitum vilmorinianum* quite common. It was growing in densely shaded areas among the branches of *Lonicera*, *Dipelta*, and *Sorbus*. The flowers that remained were deep violet-blue, growing in extremely large axillary clusters along herbaceous twining stems rising to 15 ft. (4.5 m) or more. This species is rare in cultivation, if in fact it has ever been introduced before. I am currently growing in my garden a single specimen of a species that was also collected on Emei Shan and was given to me by an English nurseryman. This specimen possesses a deeper saturation of red in its vivid flowers and, though it may belong to the same species, is a supremely better form than that which I collected; it is definitely worthy of my continued attention and evaluation. The late-summer to early autumn blossoms provide a second season of interest to spring-blossoming shrubs or small trees through which it can be grown.

In 1993, I collected seed of a monkshood species on Mount Kaibang in the northeast corner of South Korea. Not aware at that time of the breadth of climbing species within this genus, I imprudently assumed it was *Aconitum hemsleyanum* and germinated the seed under that name in 1994. In the summer of 1997, the plants blossomed for the first time in my garden. They produced quantities of upright racemes of white flowers, each kissed with violet. The vigorous vining stems grew to 15 ft. (4.5 m), bearing handsome deeply dissected foliage. (Interestingly, in the first three years after germination, this plant grew as a clump-forming, nonvining, herbaceous perennial.) I subsequently concluded that this is a rare (in commerce) species known as *A. albo-violaceum*. It is truly spectacular in blossom, and for many years to come it will be a cherished component of my garden, recalling my first encounter with Mount Kaibang on an exquisite autumn day during my first journey to South Korea.

Hardiness: The jury is still out on many of these species with regard to hardiness. Following initial trials, there seems to be an overall optimism that they will be hardy throughout much of the United States, perhaps requiring an extra layer of protective mulch in areas of zones 4–6.

Cultivation: Full sun or light shade in well-drained, humus-rich soil seem

A deeply saturated color form of *Aconitum vilmorinianum* that I collected in Yunnan Province in 1996 (Photo by Daniel J. Hinkley)

to be the best conditions. The climbing species of *Aconitum* will not tolerate summer dryness for extended periods. Provide ample support for the vines and choose an appropriate-sized shrub or tree if you wish to have them ramble through the stems. A moderately sized specimen of *Betula utilis* at Heronswood was rather destroyed by allowing *Aconitum episcopale* to swamp its structure, and this species had to be moved to the vine arbor.

Propagation: Easy by seed sown fresh in autumn or by division of the tubers in early spring once growth has resumed.

CHAPTER 3

Berries and Bugbanes:
Actaea, Beesia, and *Cimicifuga*

Upon moving to the property that houses our present-day garden in Washington State, we first set about clearing the woodland floor, which was choked in nettles, elderberries, brambles, and salal. The following spring, I was surprised to find a contingent of choice native perennials appear, though in none-too-robust condition due to the dense growth of the aforementioned and now-eliminated understory. Two years later, large colonies of *Trillium ovatum, Viola sempervirens,* and *Actaea rubra* were again thriving. It is the latter plant and its Ranunculaceae relatives that will occupy our time in this chapter.

Baneberries: The Genus *Actaea*

The genus *Actaea* is a member of the buttercup family (Ranunculaceae), which possesses a long and distinguished horticultural heritage and embraces the likes of *Anemone, Aquilegia, Cimicifuga, Delphinium,* and *Ranunculus* among its members. *Actaea* shows its greatest affinity to *Cimicifuga,* the only difference being that the fruit of *Cimicifuga* are dry follicles whereas those of *Actaea* are fleshy berries—but more on that later. The name of the genus comes from the ancient Greek word for elderberry, *aktaia,* suggesting the similarity in the compound leaves of *Actaea* and those of the elderberries of the genus *Sambucus.*

The species that occupy the genus *Actaea*—which number four to six depending on the taxonomist—are closely allied to one another, thus clouding the nomenclature. *Actaea pachypoda,* the white baneberry, is one of two species native to North America and is commonly encountered throughout the eastern part of the continent. It produces handsome mounds of bipinnately compound foliage. Short, terminal racemes of white flowers are formed in early spring and are followed by striking loose clusters of pure white berries, each with a small blackened dot and held on thick, bright red pedicels, offering a superb season of interest in late summer. The species also bears the common name of doll's eyes, which seems too attractive for children, who should be taught to avoid the poisonous fruit; the fruit of all baneberries contain the compound protoanemonin, which when ingested in minute amounts will paralyze the respiratory system.

With its exquisite clusters of glossy scarlet fruit held atop 2- to 3-ft. (0.6- to 0.9-m) stems, the red baneberry (*Actaea rubra*) is the species that I found growing on my property, and it has provided a decade of late-summer fruitful ornament as well as countless seedling-raised offspring for the nursery. Occurring throughout the western half of North America, the species offers racemes of white flowers emerging from handsome clumps of dissected, pinnately compound foliage. Except for the pedicels, which are somewhat less ample on *A. rubra* than those of *A. pachypoda*, few differences exist between the two species. Add to this the fact that there is a red-fruited form of white baneberry (*A. pachypoda* f. *rubrocarpa*) and a white-fruited form of red baneberry (*A. rubra* f. *neglecta*), each often growing side by side with their typical-colored counterparts in the wild, and one can begin to understand the dilemma that taxonomists face when

The white fruit of doll's eyes, *Actaea pachypoda* (Photo by Lynne Harrison)

Actaea rubra fruit (Photo by Lynne Harrison)

studying this genus—to lump or not to lump. Nevertheless, I find both species and their aberrant color forms equal in ornamental effect and certainly deserving of more use in woodland gardens of zones 4–9.

The diminutive *Actaea asiatica* has caught my eye each time I witnessed it growing in the shaded, moist ravines of its native South Korea and Japan. It offers small mounds of ternately compound foliage and exquisite shiny black fruit held on thick, pinkish red pedicels; a white-fruited variant has also been reported. This species is most closely allied to *A. pachypoda* and possesses similarly beefy pedicels. In the Yunnan and Sichuan Provinces of China, I collected a taller and more robust species, which may prove to be *A. spicata*, with small pinkish pedicels carrying handsome shiny black fruit. Interestingly, this plant grows both in perpetually moist soils in shaded ravines and in more exposed, sunny sites throughout the Chinese provinces. I have also become aware that a white-fruited variety of the species is known to occur (*A. spicata* var. *leucocarpa*), though I have not encountered it in the wild or in cultivation.

Hardiness: All *Actaea* species are hardy in zones 4–10. High heat and humidity, as is found in the South, may be a stumbling block in cultivation.

Cultivation: Few ornamental plants can tolerate dank shade and still thrive as the species of *Actaea* can, though that is not to say that baneberries are depen-

An indigenous specimen of *Actaea rubra* uncovered in my garden (Photo by Daniel J. Hinkley)

The black fruit of *Actaea asiatica* (Photo by Daniel J. Hinkley)

dent on such low light to thrive—they happily blossom and fruit in full-sun situations if given adequate moisture. They perform best in a rich edaphic environment of humusy soils and plenty of moisture.

Propagation: Generally performed by seed, which is copiously provided on mature plants. The seed expresses a double dormancy and most often will require two consecutive warm-cold treatments for germination. Seedlings blossom within two years of germination, though they take several years to achieve mature size and substance. Division can be performed in early spring before or just after the plants begin growth.

Beesia

While in Yunnan Province in 1996, I encountered colonies of a little-known member of the Ranunculaceae growing along Tianchi Lake on the Zhongdian Plateau. Known as *Beesia calthaefolia*, it grew here with *Arisaema elephas*, *Rheum alexandrae*, and a species of *Streptopus* (which I have yet to identify). Indeed, the foliage is remarkably similar to that of a *Caltha*—glossy rounded blades to 5 in. (12.5 cm) across on petioles to 4 in. (10 cm), rising by an apparently vigorous system of rhizomes—but the similarity to the marsh marigold ends there. Relatively large (to ½ in. [1.25 cm] across), star-shaped, white flowers are borne on upright stems to 8 in. (20 cm), appearing quite similar to those of *Tiarella*. Later in the season, follicles ripen to translucent amber before spilling their contents.

I was immediately intrigued by this species, though frustrated by its virtual absence from any reference book. It was with great surprise that, in the spring of 1998, I received a telephone call from James Compton of Reading University in England, inquiring as to the possibility of receiving material from our plant for genetic testing. It is believed that this species is genetically very close to *Actaea* and *Cimicifuga*; results of recent DNA tests have confirmed this preliminary assessment.

Regardless of where the genus is ultimately placed within the Ranunculaceae, I will cherish *Beesia* as a highly textural component of the moist woodland, where it will transport me back to that remarkable day at Tianchi, with a host of friends under blue skies and cool breezes amidst a landscape of rarities.

Hardiness: Probably zones 5–8, in cool summer climates only.

Cultivation: Moist, humus-rich soils in partial to full shade.

Propagation: My seed successfully germinated in a single season, from which I will be able to propagate by division in the future.

Bugbanes: The Once and Fading Genus *Cimicifuga*

The genus *Cimicifuga*, known in the vernacular as bugbane or snakeroot, represents the ideal collector's plant: it offers sufficient breadth and diversity to be interesting yet is not so mammoth as to be forbidding. The nomenclature is exasperatingly confused, which provides the challenge of detective work. Meanwhile, and most importantly, the plants themselves provide garden interest with their vertical stature, elegant flowers, and in some species overwhelming fragrance, over a long period from early summer to very late autumn. Found solely in the north temperate areas of the Northern Hemisphere, the natural distribution of the species is quite fascinating. Thirteen Asiatic species are met by a contingent of six North American species. Interestingly, and largely against the norm, the three species that are native to eastern North America are balanced by three western North American species, two of which are local endemics and are currently classified as endangered.

I first became truly cognizant of what this genus can offer the gardener when I was traveling in Korea with James Compton in the autumn of 1993. I was already cultivating a number of species in my garden, and I knew them somewhat superficially by an array of mostly invalid names. Fortunately for me, James was in Korea explicitly to observe *Cimicifuga* in the wild for his doctoral thesis at Reading University. In late September and early October, we saw the lovely late-blossoming white spires of *Cimicifuga heracleifolia* while collecting seed of *C. dahurica* and *C. simplex*. As is often the case, seeing these species in the wild precipitated a complete reevaluation and closer inspection of the species that I already had under cultivation, as well as sparking interest in expanding my assemblage of *Cimicifuga* as a whole.

Through my association with Compton, as well as with Colston Burrell, I have also become acutely aware of the taxonomic difficulties associated with this genus. Few genera of such diminutive size (*Cimicifuga* is estimated to include fewer than 20 species and varieties) present as many taxonomic glitches as this one. Plant taxonomy, being the fluid and adaptive system that it is, should be able to take this problem in stride and ultimately rectify the situation. Bear with me while I tackle this genus and introduce you to its members, describing many identifying characteristics that may seem a bit esoteric—I feel this is the most responsible approach, rather than contributing to further nomenclatural confusion. That being said, it is important to note that if the current tide of thought continues without resistance, the genus *Cimicifuga* will soon lose its identity by subsumption under the umbrella name *Actaea*. As mentioned before, the only major difference between the two genera seems to be the fruit type: dry follicles in *Cimicifuga* and fleshy berries in *Actaea*. Many genera in the plant kingdom possess closely related species bearing different fruit types, so this distinction is not sufficient to support two different genera. In any case, the bottom line is that this genus, collective or otherwise, comprises a large number of extremely ornamental plants that deserve a place in gardens throughout North America and Europe.

Cimicifuga racemosa, known as the black snakeroot, has a colorful past in folk medicine and, until recently, has been the most commonly cultivated species for its ornamental traits as well. The Latin root of the genus name, which means "to chase away," is based on the plant's ability to repel bugs, and black snakeroot historically was used with mattress straw to prevent infestation of bedbugs. The vernacular name of *C. dahurica*, from northeastern Asia, is bug chaser dahurian, showing an ethnobotanical co-evolution of two species from the same genus in two separate geographical regions. A tincture made from *C. racemosa* was also used in the southern Appalachians as an antidote for copperhead and water-moccasin bites. It is native from southern Ontario to southern Georgia and east to Missouri, growing in shaded and moist sites under an overstory of beech and maple. *Cimicifuga racemosa* is a beautiful ornamental species worthy of inclusion in any woodland. It is also the first in my collection of *Cimicifuga* to blossom, producing erect and narrow racemes of creamy white flowers in very early summer. The flowering stems rise to 5 ft. (1.5 m) from a basal mound of leaves, which are twice or thrice ternately compound. (A variety with four-ternately compound leaves, *Cimicifuga racemosa* var. *dissecta*, is possibly extinct.) Black snakeroot is said to be somewhat malodorous when in flower, though I have never experienced anything but joy when seeing this in flower in my garden, where it rises from a shaded area occupied by *Helleborus* ×*hybridus* and assorted ferns.

Cimicifuga americana also hails from eastern North America, but unlike *C. racemosa*, which is more adapted to the lower coastal plains, this species has exploited the mountain and intermontane regions from Pennsylvania and West Virginia south to Georgia and Tennessee. Ornamentally, its later flowering date (August) and somewhat more elegant ivorine floral qualities provide a strong case for inclusion in the garden along with *C. racemosa*. Unfortunately, the two species are hopelessly muddled under cultivation, and this will likely continue for some time. To verify which species you have, examine the seed pods that form in autumn after flowering: each flower cluster along the stem of *C. americana* will result in three to eight (normally three to four) long-stalked follicles, whereas the flowers of *C. racemosa*, possessing a single stalkless pistil, will result in only one. In foliage, the presence of a U-shaped ridge along the entire leaf rachis on *C. americana* further distinguishes it from *C. racemosa*, although this is more a matter for the botanist than for those with an untrained eye.

Cimicifuga rubifolia, once classified as *C. racemosa* var. *cordifolia*, blossoms slightly later than *C. americana*, displaying its whitish flowers in late August when

The flowering stalks of *Cimicifuga racemosa* rise above a rich assemblage of shade-loving herbaceous perennials in the woodland garden in late May (Photo by Daniel J. Hinkley)

the days become noticeably shorter and one first detects autumnal crispness in the early morning air. This species, which hails from the mountains of Tennessee, forms low, compact mounds of glossy foliage. The biternately compound leaves possess relatively few leaflets (9, compared to the 36 typical in other species), which are much larger than the norm, providing easy distinction from the other species. From the handsome foliage mounds arise many-branched racemes of creamy white or ivorine, two-pistiled flowers to 4 ft. (1.2 m) in late summer. The specific epithet, in this case, refers to the superficial resemblance of the foliage to that of some brambles (*Rubus*), not to the foliage's rich ruby color, as we with active imaginations might wish.

Cimicifuga elata is the only species of bugbane commonly encountered in the wilds of the Pacific Northwest, though I have found it to be truly common only in the Columbia River Gorge of southern Washington and northern Oregon. In this picturesque setting, I admired the apetalous flowers that appear in midsummer along 4- to 5-ft. (1.2- to 1.5-m) panicles; the flowers later result in black glandular follicles. Its leaflets are palmate and covered in fine hairs, most noticeably in early spring when the foliage first emerges. *Cimicifuga elata* grows naturally in rather open shaded sites under Douglas firs (*Pseudotsuga menziesii*)

Cimicifuga rubifolia (Photo by Lynne Harrison)

and bigleaf maples (*Acer macrophyllum*) in soils that are moderately moist during winter and drier in summer. Rarely encountered in gardens, it has yet to set the horticultural community afire; other than the appeal of nativity and obvious success with the dry summer climate of the Pacific Northwest, there is little to recommend it over the eastern species.

Slightly south of the Columbia River in Oregon, an extremely rare endemic known as *Cimicifuga laciniata* grows at the base of Mount Hood, which rises jagged and raw above a pristine and rich terrain of plants. I visited this area with James Compton one late September day expressly to see this species in blossom. There it grew in standing water or extremely saturated soils along a lake, representing one of a handful of populations of the plant in Oregon and southern Washington. The species name accurately conveys this plant's laciniate foliage, the individual leaflets being sharply and unevenly lobed. The flowers, which appear on tomentose racemes rising to 6 ft. (1.8 m), usually possess petals, distinguishing it from the apetalous flowers of the less-rare *C. elata*. And unlike *C. elata*, this species's ability to withstand airless soils might recommend it for certain circumstances over any other bugbane, native or otherwise. Unfortunately, *C. laciniata* is extremely rare in cultivation and commerce, and it is currently protected under the Federal Endangered Species Act.

Another rarity from this genus exists isolated from the other species, growing in the shaded, moist draws of the southern Rocky Mountains at elevations of 5000–6000 ft. (1500–1800 m). Completing a triad of species native to western North American, *Cimicifuga arizonica* grows surprisingly well in my garden, though my experience cultivating it is as limited as its geographic distribution. In midsummer, 3-ft. (0.9-m) racemes bearing clean white, petalous flowers are produced from mounds of bi- or triternately compound foliage and result in two to three follicles per flower. The Arizona bugbane has proven to be quite at home in my Pacific Northwest garden, tackling the lack of summer warmth without any noticeable difficulties.

Seven (or perhaps more) species of *Cimicifuga* are found within the borders of China; two of these, *Cimicifuga japonica* and *C. simplex*, are discussed with the Korean and Japanese species. The remaining five species native to China are obscure in cultivation and virtually absent in popular literature. *Cimicifuga mairei* was very common throughout the high meadows of Yunnan and Sichuan Provinces in southwestern China when I visited there in the autumn of 1996. Handsome erect panicles to 8 ft. (2.4 m) carried lovely ripening green follicles throughout October and November. These had followed a nearly simultaneous flowering of all the individual flowers along the inflorescence. I have yet to cultivate this bold and statuesque species in my garden, though it will be provided a place of prominence now that, two years later, the seed has finally germinated.

Cimicifuga brachycarpa occurs at lower altitudes than *C. mairei* in Sichuan, particularly on the lower slopes of Emei Shan and the outlying mountains. The inflorescence of yellow flowers is multibranched and results in very short, almost oval or rounded fruit with scaleless seeds. (*Cimicifuga mairei* bears oblong fruit and seeds with scales around the circumference.) Another yellow-flowered species, *C. yunnanensis*, is found only at elevations above 10,000 ft. (3000 m) and possesses unbranched inflorescences. The leaves of this species are composed of up to 200 small leaflets. Eastward from Sichuan to Hubei or Guizhou Provinces, the extremely rare *C. purpurea* is found inhabiting the same areas as *C. japonica*, though the former is known only by herbarium specimens and has never been in cultivation. It bears black-purple flowers along erect branched racemes.

The fifth Chinese species, *Cimicifuga foetida*, occurs naturally across Siberia to Mongolia and the eastern Himalayas, and for many years it was thought to be the only species that possessed truly yellow flowers. Graham Stuart Thomas refers to the fragrance as that of the brandy bottle (*Nuphar lutea*), though having had an utterly unpleasant experience with brandy as a teenager, I would prefer to associate its fragrance with something much, much less distasteful. This species is represented in my garden from a wild collection of Bleddyn and Sue Wynn-Jones from Sikkim in 1994.

A late-blossoming and dioecious species native to eastern Asia, *Cimicifuga dahurica* produces dramatically branched, somewhat lax flowering stems to 6 ft. (1.8 m) in very late summer and early autumn. I observed this species frequently in the mountains of South Korea in 1993, where I successfully gathered sufficient seed as well as a small division from a plant growing in the wild. Though the seedlings have grown to sizable specimens, only the divided plant has successfully blossomed thus far, and it receives rave reviews from those who observe it in our woodland in early September. Male specimens offer a better flower effect than the females, the inflorescences of which are fewer branched and fewer flowered. The leaves of *C. dahurica* are bi- or triternately compound and grow to 2 ft. (0.6 m) in length, making large and handsome mounds of foliage in bright shade or full sun in moderately moist but well-drained soil.

I can always count on *Cimicifuga biternata* to be in full blossom for Labor Day weekend in early September. The somewhat pink-suffused, scentless blossoms, on numerous 3-ft. (0.9-m) racemes, are not only exceedingly lovely but also highly adaptive to the smaller semishaded garden. As its name implies, *C. biternata* has biternate leaves, with up to nine palmately lobed leaflets, each leaf-

A male specimen of *Cimicifuga dahurica* (Photo by Lynne Harrison)

let possessing serrate margins and a narrow zone of hairs on the veins of the upper surface. The foliage forms handsome, dense mounds that are themselves a welcome component of the summer garden. This species is often sold as *C. japonica* var. *acerina* or *C. acerina*, both of which are invalid names.

Cimicifuga japonica* does exist, in two varietal forms, though I have had little experience with them in my garden. I first observed *C. japonica* var. *japonica* in 1997 on Cheju-do, an island off the southern coast of South Korea, where it produced Lilliputian clumps, no more than 6 in. (15 cm) long, of biternate foliage

Cimicifuga biternata (Photo by Lynne Harrison)

and demure spikes of flowers rising to 8 in. (20 cm). I was surprised to find this species in such a diminutive state, and I will not know for some time whether this compactness is based on genetics or site. Later that autumn, on the Kii Peninsula of Japan, I observed the much larger *C. japonica* var. *acutiloba*, with its glossy divided foliage to 2 ft. (0.6 m) in length and rather large leaflets, growing in densely wooded sites with immense colonies of *Deinanthe bifida*. Lovely spikes of densely arranged white flowers were carried above the mounds of superb foliage—fortunately there was sufficient ripened seed to collect. Both of these bugbane varieties are new additions to my woodland, and I look forward to evaluating their performance in the Pacific Northwest and beyond.

Cimicifuga heracleifolia var. *heracleifolia* is a stunning late-blossoming perennial also native to Korea, where I found it growing under a light overstory of Japanese black pines (*Pinus thunbergii*) on the dryish hills overlooking the China Sea. The vigor of this variety translates well to the garden setting. Ethereal white flowers are produced in late September on sturdy spires to 8 ft. (2.4 m) or more, though it blossoms somewhat earlier under cultivation in my garden. The substantial and leathery foliage is two or three times ternately compound, with each leaflet trilobed. On Mount Sorak in northeastern South Korea, I encountered the species in its rare variety *C. heracleifolia* var. *bifida* growing on a steep, shaded, north-facing rocky slope beneath a dense overstory of *Magnolia sieboldii* and *Acer tegmentosum*. It too made for a striking, late-blossoming specimen, which differed from the typical form by possessing only three leaflets (rarely more) and a notched apex on each flower petal. This rare variant has only recently been introduced into cultivation.

It was also in South Korea that I first observed *Cimicifuga simplex* var. *simplex* growing in the wild, though I initially cultivated it in my garden under the name of *C. ramosa*, which is an invalid name that has been difficult to rectify in the trade as well as in the literature. In short, *C. simplex* var. *simplex* is the variant from northern Japan and Korea from which has arisen the seedling strain "Atropurpurea" and the cultivars 'Brunette', 'Prichard's Giant', 'Scimitar', and most recently, 'Hillside Black Beauty'. 'Brunette' and the purple-foliaged seedlings of *C. simplex* var. *simplex* Atropurpurea Group are perhaps the most celebrated of all bugbanes, at least among the lay gardening community. Unfortunately, 'Brunette' is still erroneously offered as a selection of *C. racemosa* as well as the aforementioned *C. ramosa*. The highly fretted foliage of this cultivar appears in spring in shades of plum-purple and remains in rich, somber tones throughout the summer, when the heavily fragrant flowers emerge on dark stems rising to 6 ft. (1.8 m) in early September. Though the foliage remains effective in shaded sites, its full potential is brought forth in situations of full sun. Planting it with the

Cimicifuga heracleifolia var. *heracleifolia* (Photo by Lynne Harrison)

Cimicifuga simplex var. *simplex* 'Brunette' in the woodland garden (Photo by Lynne Harrison)

The black-purple foliage of *Cimicifuga simplex* var. *simplex* 'Brunette' (Photo by Lynne Harrison)

Cimicifuga simplex var. *simplex* 'Brunette' flowers (Photo by Lynne Harrison)

golden strands of *Hakonechloa macra* 'Aureola' or the lime-green foliage of *Rubus cockburnianus* 'Aureus' creates a memorable scene in the summer and autumn garden. The dark-foliaged seedlings of *Cimicifuga simplex*, properly grown under the seedling strain name of "Atropurpurea," can provide good folial effects similar to that of the dark purple-foliaged cultivars, although it takes a few seasons before maximum color potential is achieved, as the first-year foliage of seedlings will be totally green, developing the richer tones in subsequent seasons. Fred McGourty's introduction, 'Hillside Black Beauty', retains its striking black-purple foliage throughout the hot and humid summers of the eastern U.S., which is normally a bane to all purple-foliaged plants. Although the problem of color fading does not rear its ugly head in the cooler climates of the Pacific Northwest, the gardeners of the Southeast are particularly fortunate to finally have a cultivar available that better retains its folial charms. 'Prichard's Giant' is a tall-blossoming, equally fragrant selection from the same botanical variety as 'Brunette', *C. simplex* var. *simplex*. The foliage of 'Prichard's Giant', however, is rich green rather than purple, quite handsome nonetheless.

From southern Japan, *Cimicifuga simplex* var. *matsumurae* is similar to the variety *simplex*, though it flowers noticeably later. Notable selections from this variety include the lovely 'White Pearl', with large, globular buds of white that open in mid-September to fragrant, starry clusters of flowers along stems to only 4 ft. (1.2 m). 'Elstead' is closely allied and highly desirable; along purple-stained 5-ft. (1.5-m) stems, purplish buds open to pure white, offering the same pervading scent as the other *C. simplex* selections. *Cimicifuga simplex* var. *matsumurae* 'Frau Herms' is the latest of the bugbanes to blossom in my garden, often losing the race to ripen its seed before the first hard frosts of early November.

Hardiness: Fortunately for gardeners across North America and the colder regions of Europe, nearly all *Cimicifuga* species are remarkably hardy, with most rated for zones 3–8. They are generally slow to establish, which is also an excellent indicator that the plants will need infrequent division or care once fully established.

Cultivation: In essence, all these bugbanes are woodland plants and are ideally sited in a semishaded border or woodland garden. In areas with summer heat, protection from afternoon sun is advisable, though my experience in cooler climates has taught me that they will tolerate a full-sun regimen; in fact, the purple-foliaged forms of *Cimicifuga simplex* are more intensely colored under these situations. Folial nematodes have been reported on the East Coast of North America, which can be identified by irregular lesions of necrotic tissue on the leaf blades. I have not observed this on the West Coast. Nematicides can be employed, although I would advise that you simply dispose of the plants and try reestablishing nematode-free stock after a year or two.

Propagation: The propagation of *Cimicifuga* is performed mostly by seed, except for the named selections of *Cimicifuga simplex*. Seed should be gathered and sown as fresh as possible in autumn and exposed to the rigors of low temperatures during the winter months. Germination may occur the following spring, but in all likelihood it will take an additional year. *Cimicifuga simplex* var. *simplex* 'Brunette', which for years passed slowly and expensively through the horticultural circles of the United States and Europe, is now successfully produced through tissue culture and has become more affordable and available. Other named forms of *C. simplex* can be divided in early spring, just as growth resumes.

CHAPTER 4

Hepatica:
Liverworts and Island Treasures

Just as one can often tell a person by the company he keeps, one can also tell a gardener by the plants he tends. The deeper one becomes embedded in the gentle art of collecting and cultivating plants, the more the flocks of one's garden become increasingly esoteric and sophisticated. I count the genus *Hepatica* among a select group of indicator plants for an advanced horticulturist. And oddly enough, this has nothing to do with how difficult the plants are to grow; in fact, *Hepatica* presents few challenges to the gardener of the North Temperate Zone. It is the simple task of finding the plants to cultivate that seems to edit these from the collections of most gardeners—all but those who stay the course in the search for elusive, rare, or simply good plants.

I became familiar with this genus in the deciduous woods of northern Michigan, where I witnessed the endearing powdery blue flowers of *Hepatica nobilis* subsp. *americana* opening during the last days of winter. Tawny fallen leaves of beech, maple, and oak covered much of the plants as the star-shaped blossoms emerged.

My odyssey into further exploring this genus of the Ranunculaceae has been slow and frustrating, as very few modern garden writers have devoted much attention to the cultivation of these woodland gems. The reasons may be twofold: first, the taxonomy of the genus is extremely muddied and difficult to grasp, even by a professional horticulturist; and second, *Hepatica* species, hybrids, and cultivars are slow to propagate and are rarely sold commercially in the United States. Since I am not interested in writing a taxonomic treatise, I need not be threatened by the fact that the names I apply to these species may be invalid in a year's time. Hopefully, with more keen gardeners becoming aware of the elegance these plants bring to the early spring garden, energetic people at specialty nurseries will be spurred into action and will make more of these generally available.

The best-known of the *Hepatica* species is probably *Hepatica nobilis*, mostly due to the fact that, according to some taxonomists, the one species occurs in North America, in Europe, and in Japan and Korea. It must be said that not everyone agrees with this nomenclatural assessment, and it remains a hot topic of debate among those who have time for such arguments. I have used the most recent studies of the genus for my treatment here, but exactly where the taxonomic chips will ultimately fall is anybody's guess.

The three geographical variants of *Hepatica nobilis* have each been assigned subspecies names, and each has somewhat different expressions in leaf shape and flower color. *Hepatica nobilis* subsp. *americana* is said to occur from Nova Scotia to Minnesota and is the type that I admired in earliest spring in the acidic deciduous woodlands of Michigan, a habitat where it has effectively carved its niche. Quite variable in flower color, from pure white to deep blue and rose, *H. nobilis* subsp. *americana* puts on a tremendous but often short-lived floral show in early to mid-March in my garden. The trilobed evergreen foliage also exhibits a great deal of variability, with strong pewter or purple marbling that extends the plant's season of interest throughout the year. The flowering stems rise to 5 in. (12.5 cm).

Hepatica nobilis subsp. *nobilis* (Photo by Lynne Harrison)

Hepatica nobilis subsp. *nobilis* is the subspecies that occurs throughout continental Europe. It too expresses a great deal of variability in leaf shape, leaf mottling, and flower color and shape, and it has not escaped the notice of the continent's long tradition of talented horticulturists. I have purchased from specialty nurseries in Europe selected, unnamed clones based on flower color as well as double-flowered cultivars, the latter bringing a very dear price due to the accompanying difficulties in propagation. In my garden, rich blue *H. nobilis* subsp. *nobilis* grows almost side by side with its American counterpart, and other than the American's slightly larger leaf, it is nearly impossible to tell the two apart even with more elaborate investigation. Breeders associated with the European variant are few and far between, although I have made the acquaintance of one fellow obsessive-compulsive from Sweden by the name of Severin Schlyter. The plants arising from his breeding program represent nothing short of unadulterated, chlorophyllic lust. Flowers of vibrant lipstick-pinks, double whites, or baritone blues as deep as a fresh bruise are offset by foliage that is unrecognizable as that of *Hepatica*. The rounded, ruffled, silver-splashed foliage is more representative of *Heuchera* than *Hepatica*. Even if I am seemingly comfortable with these bizarre aberrations, I still find myself emotionally jerked when observing them in the garden. What is this—can this be? I know it's *Hepatica*, but its language is suddenly incoherent gibberish. And so melodic.

Hepatica nobilis subsp. *japonica* is a much-celebrated plant among Japan's gardening elite, with a dizzying array of color forms and foliage types available commercially. That *H. nobilis* subsp. *japonica* is commonly available for sale does not suggest that the Japanese have mastered the art of vegetative propagation as much as they have the vagaries of pricing horticultural rarities. In nurseries, some of which are devoted entirely to this genus, it is more common to find plants priced in the range of several hundreds to several thousands of U.S. dollars than it is to find any priced in what we, in the U.S., believe to be within driving range of sanity. In the autumn of 1995, I was offered a three-plant, "special price" collection of double-flowered named clones in white, blue, and pink for just over $100 from a nursery near Tokyo. All are still alive in my garden (Buddha exists), and these clones put on a good showing in the spring of 1998, with the white-flowered form thus far exhibiting the greatest vigor of the triad.

In my travels throughout the Korean Peninsula in 1993 and 1997, I became aware of how widespread and seemingly inexhaustible were the natural populations of *Hepatica nobilis* subsp. *japonica*. Korean botanists regard this as a species in its own right, *H. asiatica*, as they do with many of their native plants that have been denied full species rank and are considered mere varieties of species originally described from the Japanese Archipelago. I am supremely unqualified to make the call on this matter, and also politically unwilling to offend a group of personal, somewhat patriotic, friends from South Korea. Nevertheless, I am as impressed with the folial and floral variation in these profuse wild populations as I am with their garden worthiness in the Pacific Northwest. Resultant progeny have now blossomed, creating a multitalented collection of pure white, deep pink, as well as sky-blue flowers held amidst 2-in. (5-cm), three-lobed leaves handsomely mottled in silver and plum.

The only other species of *Hepatica* to occur in North America, *Hepatica acutiloba*, has been assigned, by nature, to shady limestone forests from Quebec to Missouri, though its dependence on lime in the wild does not seem to prevent successful cultivation of this species under more acidic conditions. As one might guess from the species name, the three-lobed leaves of *H. acutiloba* extend to a narrow, acuminate leaf tip, in contrast to the more blunt-tipped foliage of *H. nobilis* subsp. *americana*. The flowers are most often white, but good blue- and pink-flowered forms have been selected from native populations. In areas where the natural range of this species overlaps with populations of the American subspecies of *H. nobilis*, intermediate hybrid populations are observed, indicating a close affinity between the two, while also tempting some taxonomists to simply dump this species into the large shake-and-bake bag of *H. nobilis*.

Hepatica transsilvanica is found in the botanically rich areas of eastern Europe and, in my opinion, represents the most lovely and garden worthy of *Hepatica* species. The foliage is very distinctive, with each of the three to five major leaf lobes somewhat further lobed, providing a rather rounded-leaf effect. In contrast to the semi-clumping nature of the other species, *H. transsilvanica* produces longer rhizomes, which allows for larger colonies in shorter periods as well as increasing the ease of asexual propagation. In mid-March, multitudes of powdery blue to pink flowers are produced in a crowded mass, arising on 5-in. (12.5-cm) stems. As with the two promiscuous American taxa, *H. transsilvanica* will readily cross with the European subspecies of *H. nobilis*, which it does without the aid of human hand in Romania, where the two taxa's ranges overlap. A deliberate cross between selected color forms of *H. transsilvanica* and *H. nobilis* subsp. *nobilis*, made in the early 1900s in England, resulted in a superb hybrid known as *H.* ×*media* 'Ballardii'. With flower color described as "glowing lavender-blue" and foliage and form that show much similarity to that of its *H. transsilvanica* parent, this hybrid is considered to be among the finest of all

Hepatica transsilvanica flower (Photo by Lynne Harrison)

hepaticas and is much sought after. It is interesting to note that the late Lincoln Foster, a well-known gardener from Falls City, Connecticut, crossed *H. transsilvanica* with *H. nobilis* subsp. *americana*, resulting in a selection that he called 'Millstream Merlin'. This deep purplish blue hybrid is still regarded as "*Hepatica nirvana*" among circles of keen gardeners and is used regularly as legal tender in trade for botanical treasures. *Hepatica transsilvanica* 'Elison Spence' is a vigorous clone with outstanding fully double, spode-blue flowers produced in abundance in early spring. This was given to me by Frank Cabot and Caroline Burgess of Stonecrop, New York, though it has not yet fully established in my garden. However, I have observed this pageant queen in other gardens, and it is a plant that I can imagine growing old with, offering bits and pieces to young upstarts as they come to watch me slaver and stumble about my garden.

In the autumn of 1998, I observed *Hepatica yamatutai* in a narrow altitudinal band at 5500 ft. (1650 m) on the slopes of Emei Shan in Sichuan Province. The trilobed leaves, to 3 in. (7.5 cm) long by 3 in. (7.5 cm) wide, displayed great

diversity in the degree of purple diffusion on the undersurface. It grew in sharp-draining limestone formations in rather shaded positions. I look forward to returning to Emei at a future date to witness this species in blossom and observe the variation in flower color that exists within the population. (The only specimens that I have seen in blossom produce extremely large white flowers, though I am unqualified to say whether this represents the type form.) This species is rare in cultivation, and information regarding its natural range of distribution is somewhat sketchy. It is similar to *H. transsilvanica* in foliage and probably represents an easterly continuum of that eastern European species (in association with the following species, *H. henryi*). As with the genus as a whole, *H. yamatutai* requires additional study by botanists to determine its taxonomic standing, though little observation is needed by horticulturists to realize its ornamental potential.

Hepatica yamatutai at Asiatica Nursery, Pennsylvania (Photo by Daniel J. Hinkley)

Closely allied to *Hepatica yamatutai* and superficially resembling that species in foliage is *H. henryi*, which has a brief history in cultivation. I received specimens of this species from China, and they are under evaluation in my nursery. The foliage consists of several rounded lobes, while the flowers thus far produced by my plants are rather small, in shades of light lavender to near white. As a garden plant, *H. henryi* may prove to possess limited appeal, but certainly it may be useful for breeding purposes while providing additional data for an improved taxonomic treatment of the genus.

The story of *Hepatica* does not stop with the brief discussions of the aforementioned species. Other garden-worthy species, though decidedly more rare and elusive, provide sufficient grounds for inclusion in the garden.

During my first trip to South Korea, in 1993, I visited many of the countless islands that surround that nation's coastline. Traveling with a contingent of British horticulturists, I decided to venture alone to the island of Ullung-do in the Sea of Japan while my new friends made their way southward to Cheju-do. When we reunited two weeks later at Chollipo Arboretum on the west coast of South Korea, we discovered that we each had experienced close encounters of the third kind with *Hepatica*, but with extremely distinctive species.

My fellow traveling horticulturists had collected *Hepatica insularis* on Cheju Island, and in the autumn of 1997 I ventured to this remarkable island myself for a firsthand look —and I will never regret that decision. This remarkable species was quite common on the forest floor beneath the rich deciduous woods that cover the slopes of Mount Halla, an extinct but primary volcanic peak that dominates the island's landscape. I was immediately struck by the modest size of the species: diminutive plants with individual leaves less than 1 in. (2.5 cm) in length and width. They grew in the general vicinity of *Hosta venusta* and *Aruncus aethusifolius*, which is interesting when you consider that these plants, both endemic to Cheju-do, share the Lilliputian charms of this *Hepatica* and are in fact the smallest representatives of their respective genera. *Hepatica insularis*, which now thrives

My collections of *Hepatica insularis* from the island of Cheju-do in South Korea growing in small square pots at Heronswood (Photo by Lynne Harrison)

in my woodland, possesses great variation in the degree of silver mottling on the upper surface of the leaves as well as in the saturation of purple on the undersides. I expect that, as with the exceptional, albeit tiny, foliage, the floral coloring will exhibit a great deal of variation, from pure white to blue, as my seedlings mature to procreative age.

While my friends botanized Cheju Island during my 1993 visit to Korea, my experiences on Ullung Island were extraordinary in terms of both the rich endemic flora and the rich culture that remains distinct from the mainland. This remarkable island lies approximately 100 miles (161 km) off the eastern coast of Korea in the Sea of Japan, with the jagged, emerald peaks of Mount Songinbong rising magnificently to 3257 ft. (987 m). The island's economy is based almost solely on an immense squid fishery that is omnipresent during the autumn season. Racks of pungent, drying squid, harvested at night from brilliantly illuminated boats that light the ocean like fallen stars, hang on racks erected along virtually every available piece of island earth.

The plants here have remained sufficiently isolated from the flora of the Korean Peninsula and Japanese Archipelago to develop a personality of their own. In some instances, these variants are adequately distinct to be provided species rank (*Campanula takesimana* and *Sedum takesimense*, for example), while many others are regarded as subspecies, varieties, or forms of their mainland counterparts (such as *Acer mono* subsp. *okamotoanum*, *Acer pseudosieboldianum* subsp. *takesimense*, and *Arisaema angustatum* var. *peninsulae* f. *variegata*). Regardless of where the taxonomic axe may fall with regard to another island endemic, *Hepatica maxima*, this little-known plant will always be a most distinctive member of the genus. Producing 1-ft. (0.3-m) mounds of large, leathery, deep green leaves to 5 in. (12.5 cm) across, each with an underside of rich purple, *H. maxima* is profoundly different from any other *Hepatica* species. It occurs only on the northern slopes of Ullung-do, where it exists in bountiful numbers, exhibiting some variation in leaf color, particularly in the color of the leaf undersides. In my experience, this variation has not been echoed in the intensity of flower color in spring, nor have the flowers been as equally imposing in size as the foliage, as might be assumed for plants of this stature. I have grown on many of my seedlings for evaluation, but so far my specimens have produced flowers of washy lilac and of standard size; perhaps the flowers appear even smaller in association with such magnificent foliage, which tends to obscure the floral display. Nonetheless, *H. maxima* is an extremely worthy species for the effects of the foliage alone, and it may prove instrumental in the breeding of hepaticas for both good foliage and flower. When I returned to Ullung-do in the autumn of 1997, I wondered:

Was it mere imagination and an overexuberant memory that had made this plant so lusty and immense? This second encounter indeed showed that, at least in this matter, my cerebral capacities of conjuring untruths had been held in check.

Hardiness: Most of the *Hepatica* species respond well in zones 4–10 and will tolerate the heat and humidity of the deep South. *Hepatica maxima* has an extremely limited history in cultivation, but thus far it has shown itself to be very adaptable to the cool maritime climate of the Pacific Northwest.

Cultivation: If deep, humusy, rich loam that has adequate moisture but remains well drained actually exists somewhere, I would be glad to know so that I might purchase some. Nearly every reference to *Hepatica* recommends such a soil. My hepaticas thrive in our woodland, in moderate light and in soils that can best be described as sandy loam. Though the plants in my garden receive a standard yearly application of 20-20-20 fertilizer, the most important garden additive is patience, as seedlings or divisions will take several years to grow to sizable colonies. We often remove the spent foliage from clumps in midwinter before the flowers appear so as to tidy the mounds, though I would refrain from doing so until the plants are sufficiently established.

Folial nematodes have been a serious problem and can be identified by irregular, necrotic patches that appear on the foliage during the growing season. To combat, first try removing and disposing of the foliage from infected plants during autumn cleanup. Effective but quite toxic nematicides are available and will

Hepatica maxima (Photo by Lynne Harrison)

control the problem, but simple removal of the plants might better be considered if the problem becomes severe.

Propagation: Propagation by seed is rather tedious and tenuous, especially if the seed is harvested and grown in pots. Seedlings must remain in the pots for up to four years until they are large enough to survive the shock and tribulations of transplanting. It is much easier to just sow the fresh seed directly under the foliage of the mother plant (or simply do nothing at all, since this is what the plant will do naturally) and allow the young plants to mature to a moveable size in situ. When sufficiently large, they can be easily divided in early spring as growth resumes.

CHAPTER 5

Beyond Frilly Filler:
The Genus *Thalictrum*

Of the many perennials that I nurture in my garden, few are admired more than *Thalictrum*. With the collective punch of a multitude of flowers provided by each plant, the ornamental attributes of this genus come not from reliance on an individual flower, as in its larger-flowered kin, garden stalwarts such as peonies, trollius, columbines, and clematis. Before and after flowering, *Thalictrum* offers ferny foliage that provides substance, while extending the plant's contribution to the summer garden. The all-inclusive common name of meadow rue is based on the resemblance of the foliage to that of common rue (*Ruta graveolens*). In reality, gardeners will more likely find themselves confusing a nonblossoming *Thalictrum* with an *Aquilegia*, which has nearly identical foliage (as noted by the specific epithet of *Thalictrum* aquilegi*folium*).

With more than 130 species of *Thalictrum* native to the North Temperate Zone, the taxonomy of the genus can be difficult to grasp, and undoubtedly a great befuddlement of nomenclature exists in cultivation. I have sifted through my experience with the meadow rues and can offer a distilled collection of those most worthy for integration in the garden.

Of the 35 species and cultivars (or at least the 35 different names) that I have included in my garden at one time or another, most are used best as secondary components in the border, rock garden, or woodland. Collectively, they lend an airy presence of color to the garden, adding polish and continuity to an arrangement without smothering the intended effect. By careful selection, one can glean months of utility from late spring through early autumn. In most instances, the color of the individual flowers is provided by a feathery bundle of dangling stamens that, unlike the colorful and nectar-rich flowers of other members of the ranunculus family, engage the wind rather than insects to deliver pollen to nearby plants.

Individual specimens slowly increase in size each year, but meadow rues are among the least demanding plants that I have incorporated into my borders. The flowering stems of the more diminutive species do not require staking and, in fact, remain upright and sturdy long after the flowers fade. The taller species, however, especially if grown in rich, moist soil, will easily reach 8 ft. (2.4 m) in height and will begin to topple when the flowers expand. While some gardeners may find this trait objectionable and will wish to provide support, I find charm in the fallen stems of these flowers, as they provide a pastel, frothy union with nearby blossoms or foliage of sturdier flowering shrubs or perennials. I will discuss here a handful of species, cultivars, and hybrids, several of which I have had the opportunity to observe in their native habitats.

Five species of *Thalictrum* are well suited to the rock garden and can be useful as low, albeit deciduous, groundcovers in the woodland. *Thalictrum kiusianum* is a carpeting species that produces 4- to 6-in. (10- to 15-cm) stems of finely textured foliage and slowly increases by stolons. Lilac flowers held just above the foliage emerge from May through August. Content in full sun as well as in the semi-shade of the woodland garden, it can be propagated by division in early spring just as growth resumes. *Thalictrum kiusianum* is perhaps better understood under cultivation than it is understood by taxonomists. Though it is often cited in Western literature as occurring in Japan, there is nothing in Japanese or Korean literature to suggest that it actually is part and parcel to their flora.

While in South Korea in 1997, I collected seed of a species that has great affinity to the form of *Thalictrum kiusianum* that I currently cultivate. Collected under the name *T. taquetii*, which is recognized in the floras of both Korea and Japan, the plant grew on a damp stone ledge along a waterfall in the area adjacent to Chuwangshan National Park. The stems rose to a mere 4 in. (10 cm), with bipinnate leaves to 3 in. (7.5 m) and ovate leaflets to ¼ in. (0.6 cm). Whether this will ultimately lead to helping to clarify the mysteries I have conjured regarding *T. kiusianum* (real or imagined), only time will tell.

From the drier sites of Greece and Turkey, another low-growing species, *Thalictrum orientale*, has gained notoriety as being quite desirable as well as somewhat miffy under cultivation. The colonizing stems, to 4 in. (10 cm) in height, sport early and comparatively large flowers of light pink or white. I have successfully established this species in a bright, shaded position in the well-drained, humus-rich soils of our woodland, where it slips into dormancy in midsummer. Less demanding under cultivation, *T. tuberosum* hails from southwestern Europe and bears somewhat larger leaves and even larger flowers of ivory white on 10-

in. (25-cm) stems. I have received seed of this species from numerous society seed exchanges and from plant listings of botanic gardens (index seminum) but, alas, have never received the real McCoy. When I locate this species I will incorporate it in the same bright but somewhat sheltered location where I now cultivate the former species.

Thalictrum ichangense has distinctively broad and oval, shiny green leaflets that are deceptively similar to the foliage of *Epimedium*. In May, pale pink flowers are produced on 6-in. (15-cm) stems on the plants growing in full sun in our scree garden, though the stems stretch to 8 in. (20 cm) on those planted in the woodland. If both sexes are present, seed will be freely produced, though as with other *Thalictrum* species, the clumps are easily divided.

A plant I currently cultivate under the name of *Thalictrum* sp. "Taiwan" is becoming increasingly available in the United Kingdom as well as in nurseries in Japan, where I originally obtained the plant in 1995. It is a charming, long-blossoming species that forms small tufts of foliage and produces a bountiful display of rather large, pure white flowers on stems to 8 in. (20 cm) from early April through May. It possesses an intriguing similarity to *Anemonella thalictroides*, and I am curious as to whether there is close affinity between the two.

For many years I have grown a species of *Thalictrum* that was first collected in Afghanistan and subsequently made the horticultural rounds throughout the United States and Europe as *Thalictrum* sp. "Afghanistan." Recently confirmed as *Thalictrum isopyroides*, it will continue to be one of the most beautiful meadow rues in my collection. Delicate tiny leaves of intense steely blue cloak stems rising to 15 in. (38 cm); small, greenish yellow flowers are produced in early summer. *Thalictrum isopyroides* should be grown in the sunny rock garden or front border with sharp drainage. I have used it to great advantage in a border devoted to blue and yellow, with a low carpet of *Stachys byzantina* 'Primrose Heron' in front and the slightly taller *Veronica peduncularis* 'Georgia Blue' flanking one side. Though the dark blue, starry eyed flowers of the veronica are long since faded by the time the flowers of the thalictrum appear, annually planted *Lathyrus sativus* snakes through the meadow rue's foliage and produces its electric-blue pea flowers concurrently.

While visiting the Kunming Botanical Garden in 1996, I observed trial beds of a large, 4-ft. (1.2-m) hybrid meadow rue with extraordinarily intense blue foliage. I was unable to decipher whether *Thalictrum isopyroides* was indeed one of the parents, but it would not be surprising if that is in fact the case. Seed given to me by the staff of the garden is now growing at Heronswood, and we will continue to select the best of the progeny before settling on a superior clone to introduce to the trade.

In South Korea, I collected seed of *Thalictrum actaeifolium* and *T. filamentosum*, both of which provide an air of distinction to the garden. The former species grows to 2 ft. (0.6 m) in height and is the second longest blossoming meadow rue in my collection. The broad, jagged-edged, and blue-green foliage sufficiently warrants this plant's specific epithet, appearing *Actaea*-like when first emerging. In early summer, masses of apetalous flowers composed of rosy red stamens (lighter pink in the variety *brevistylum*) create a festive scene that entertains the gardener for weeks on end. *Thalictrum filamentosum* offers one of the longest flowering seasons of any plant in the garden. I planted seedlings of *T. filamentosum* var. *tenerum* on the north side of our house in 1994, after having collected it on South Korea's Mount Sorak the previous year. As this is a dioecious plant (male and female flowers are produced on separate plants), and as I had inadvertently planted only females, the flowers, which consist of pure white pistils atop 15-in. (38-cm) stems, continue unfertilized and none the worse for wear for nearly four solid months. It brightens a dark corner of the foundation bed near the front door, associating with hostas and hellebores.

The common meadow rue, *Thalictrum aquilegifolium*, from Europe, is perhaps the best-known of the cultivated species, and with good reason. In early summer, 3- to 4-ft. (0.9- to 1.2-m) stems of ethereal lilac-pink flowers are produced from ferny clumps of foliage. I have planted this species at the base of a dark red-foliaged *Acer palmatum* with which it contrasts delightfully. The nearly black flowers of *Iris chrysographes* rise into and mingle with the feathery flowers of the common meadow rue to create a composition of singular beauty. The flower color of *T. aquilegifolium* is quite variable, from pure white ('Album') through deep rose-pink ('Purpureum'). The flowers of *T. aquilegifolium* 'Album' open in late spring from purplish buds atop stems to 4 ft. (1.2 m). I have used this white-flowered form effectively in a mixed planting with a dark red, double-flowered columbine backed by red-foliaged barberries and the steely blue-flushed-pink foliage of *Rosa glauca*.

In early spring, the purple-mauve young stems and foliage of *Thalictrum flavum* var. *glaucum*, also from Europe, begin their thrust upward from the soil, soon to intensify to a striking silvery blue color. It is not until early summer that pastel flowers of soft yellow float above the lovely 6-ft. (1.8-m) columns of foliage. The brawny stems are initially upright and strong, but soon after the flowers expand, they gracefully (at first) lean over or into other garden components. In my garden, these pastel feather-dusters are in perfect combination with the dark black-purple foliage of *Cotinus coggygria* 'Purpureus', which partially holds the stems upright even after rains. *Thalictrum flavum* var. *glaucum* crossed with *T. rochebrunianum* has given rise to *Thalictrum* 'Elin', by far the most striking of

Thalictrum actaeifolium (Photo by Lynne Harrison)

The pure white flowers of *Thalictrum aquilegifolium* 'Album' strongly contrast with the adjacent *Berberis vulgaris* 'Royal Cloak' at Heronswood (Photo by Lynne Harrison)

Thalictrum 'Elin' (Photo by Lynne Harrison)

the tall thalictrums that I have grown and among the most distinctive new herbaceous perennials to come our way in many years. Robust and sturdy purple stems rise in early spring bearing glorious steely blue foliage; the stems ultimately reach 12 ft. (3.6 m), carrying airy panicles of soft yellow and lavender flowers even higher. We have not yet had to stake this new addition to our garden. As this is a sterile hybrid, propagation must be carried out by division.

I also cultivate an unnamed folial variant of *Thalictrum flavum* that was brought to us by Seattle gardener Marian Raitz. Steely blue foliage is suffused with golden yellow as it emerges in spring. Though the color more or less disperses by the time flowering occurs, the plant is a sight to behold in the early days of spring.

By the time midsummer comes along, I still await the flowers of two species that are among the most beautiful of their genus: *Thalictrum delavayi* and *T. rochebrunianum*. *Thalictrum delavayi* (also offered as *T. dipterocarpum*) sports beautiful, finely textured foliage that is acutely distinct from that of other species. Rather than emerging in dense and fluffy terminal heads, the flowers are displayed in long airy panicles on stems rising to 5 ft. (1.5 m). The individual flowers are a two-tone delight of lavender sepals surrounding creamy yellow stamens, resembling a clematis of most minute proportions. Collecting seed of this species near the town of Lichang in Yunnan Province brought a sense of awe in knowing that I was in the very same landscape where the French missionary and botanist Pierre Jean Marie Delavay first saw and collected this plant in the nineteenth century.

Thalictrum delavayi offers a superb, pure white-flowered variant as well as a selection with fully double flowers in the typical lavender color. A sizable stand of *T. delavayi* 'Album' at the well-known white garden at Sissinghurst Castle in Kent provides a striking late-summer frosty haze that swarms over other garden inhabitants. *Thalictrum delavayi* 'Hewitt's Double' sacrifices the inner guts of yellow stamens for a double dose of lavender sepals. Because the double flowers do not set seed, the flowers are extremely long-lived and will easily provide eight weeks of color, making it ideal for cutting. I have generously interplanted 'Hewitt's Double' amongst a good-sized planting of *Hydrangea macrophylla* 'Blue Prince', which has resulted in a colorful harmony while providing airy textural relief to the planting.

Thalictrum rochebrunianum is the most commonly cultivated of a quartet of relatively large-flowered meadow rues, including the less frequently encountered and highly coveted *T. chelidonii* and *T. diffusiflorum*. References to these three species in the literature are so profoundly contradictory as to their appearance

The floriferous *Thalictrum delavayi* 'Hewitt's Double' (Photo by Lynne Harrison)

that they are very likely caught up in a taxonomic muddle that may take years to sort out. With that caveat aside, the large pink and white flowers of *T. rochebrunianum* in my garden are presented in sprays similar in fashion to those of *T. delavayi* but on substantial stems of dark purple. Unlike other species that I have grown, *T. rochebrunianum* is slow to establish, but it appears happy in the partially shaded condition that it occupies on the margin of the woodland garden.

I collected seed of *Thalictrum finetii* DJHC 473 in Yunnan Province in 1996, and the seedlings thus far have been exceptionally garden worthy. It is among the tallest of meadow rue species, rising to nearly 10 ft. (3 m) in the shaded, somewhat moist environment in which it grew. The extremely large, mauve flowers open from tantalizing inflated buds to reveal a lovely central boss of yellow stamens. When these came into blossom in the spring of 1998, creating quite a stir among our patrons, I selfishly whisked the entire flat away from the nursery to my private stash in order to observe each seedling and collect the resultant seed. This species will surely be an outstanding addition to North American gardens, and I look forward to sharing it when I have again built up sufficient stock.

In the summer of 1993, the astounding blossoms of *Thalictrum diffusiflorum*, the largest of the genus, appeared for the first time on a plant that I had brought from England. Quarter-sized (1-in. [2.5-cm]) lavender blossoms centered with yellow stamens were produced, albeit sparingly, atop 2- to 3-ft. (0.6-

to 0.9-m) wiry stems cloaked with finely textured, steely blue foliage; the blossoms generated considerable excitement from the nursery staff and visitors alike. Despite its delicate appearance, *T. diffusiflorum* has proven to be a durable garden plant—although it is exceedingly cranky in nursery containers.

Thalictrum chelidonii has also produced flowers in our collection at Heronswood, although the blue and yellow flowers, while relatively large, opened on 6-in. (15-cm) stems, which made viewing enjoyment difficult at best. The large flowers of these four species truly allows one to see the genus's close relationship with *Aquilegia* and *Clematis*.

The ever-growing list of perennials available for use in our gardens is astonishingly immense, as is that of plants that remain unknown and await discovery by the garden enthusiast. The numerous and distinctly charming thalictrums are among those many perennials that merit more interest by American horticulturists in years to come.

Hardiness: By North American standards, *Thalictrum* is very hardy, and nearly all species will thrive in USDA zones 4–8, with several species thriving in even lower temperatures.

Cultivation: I have found most of the species to be tolerant of partially shaded conditions; indeed, many grow in their native lands as woodland herbs. The taller, border-worthy species respond best in full-sun situations.

Propagation: Nearly half of all *Thalictrum* species are dioecious. Thus, unless both sexes are present in the garden, viable seed will not be produced. Color variants of each species generally come true to seed, although named cultivars must, of course, be divided to insure that new plants are true to type. When seed is formed, it can be easily gathered and sown in pots of compost or directly in the ground in autumn. Germination occurs in early spring, and if the seedlings are transplanted early, ensuring adequate plant development throughout the growing season, then flowering normally occurs the following spring or summer. Never a nuisance, self-sown plants can be found in the garden, and these may be transplanted to a permanent site or shared with gardening friends. Plants can also be increased by dividing in early spring. Tissue culture has proven to be a viable alternative for bulking up hybrids and cultivars to salable levels.

Thalictrum diffusiflorum (Photo by Lynne Harrison)

CHAPTER 6

Berberidaceous Botany

It is perhaps because gardeners and horticulturists are so familiar with the woody contingent of the barberry family (*Berberis*, *Mahonia*, and *Nandina*) that it generally comes as a surprise to learn that the Berberidaceae by and large consist of choice woodland perennials. In fact, the family houses a virtual treasure-trove of genera that are currently highly regarded and exuberantly sought by gardeners worldwide.

I have chosen to cover in this chapter only those genera that have general application to gardeners of North America, eliminating a clan of tuberous-rooted genera, namely *Bongardia*, *Gymnospermium*, and *Leontice*, that would be appropriate for cultivation only in the arid regions of the Southwest.

Epimedium:
Barrenworts, Bishops Hats, and Horny Goat Weed

Fashions in gardening and garden style come and go, and with these ebbs and flows, genera of plants become discovered or rediscovered, celebrated, molded to seeming perfection, and then routinely dismissed until it is their turn again in the spotlight. With a sophisticated and quiet demeanor, the genus *Epimedium* has yet to experience the skyrocket to fame and fortune in mainstream horticulture. Instead it has inspired a slow but steady acceptance over the centuries, relying on the conversion of one gardener at a time exposed to and smitten by understated, delicate charm tempered by concrete demeanor.

Renewed interest in this genus, however, is gaining momentum across the gardening world, which ultimately will elevate these highly adaptable, utilitarian, and elegant plants to celebrity status with all the associated trappings. This unsolicited enthusiasm has resulted largely from the introduction of numerous and extraordinary species from the mountains of China, which have in many ways rewritten our perceptions of the effects this genus brings forth to the garden. Of the 44 species currently recognized worldwide, 36 have been discovered and described since 1975 from the remote areas of this vast and still underexplored country. Undoubtedly many species still await discovery in China's rugged and isolated mountain valleys.

Though my current enthusiasm for *Epimedium* is based generally on those species that have been recently introduced, a large assemblage of species and hybrids from Europe and Asia Minor have long brought an enormous range of utility and beauty to the garden. Over the past decade, I have come to appreciate these qualities in my zone 8 garden. *Epimedium ×rubrum* never fails to impress me with the quality of its crimson-margined foliage as it unfurls in late spring, ultimately enveloping the early spring show of red flowers. The sturdy evergreen colonies of *E. pinnatum* subsp. *colchicum* remain among the best for groundcover in the shaded woodland, while adding a dazzling show of yellow, red-stained flowers in spring before a new flush of handsome leathery foliage. *Epimedium grandiflorum*, a deciduous species from Japan and Korea, is held in high regard at Heronswood, with a large number of distinctive cultivars that are considered the most lovely for flower effect; *E. grandiflorum* 'White Queen' is among the best, with very large, pristine white flowers held on 15-in. (38-cm) stems above handsome foliage. The *Epimedium* species just discussed, and many others that have long been in cultivation, are time-honored additions to any garden and should not be dismissed as old hat.

My garden experience with the more recently discovered species is limited, though each year I find my enthusiasm and passion for the genus growing, as does my understanding of the differences between the species and the cultural conditions they require. Much of this information has been extracted from conversations with and materials prepared by my friend Darrell Probst, whom I was in company with when I observed my first *Epimedium* in the wilds of China—a long-awaited experience that I will not soon forget. Darrell's enthusiasm and passion has also played a central role in this genus's increasingly celebrated status in the United States; he alone has been instrumental in bringing 18 or more Chinese species into cultivation. In addition, I am indebted to Sue and Robin White of Blackthorn Nursery in Hampshire, England, who have, as with many other garden-worthy genera, prompted my exploration of these plants in greater detail.

Before examining those species that are most responsible for this impending commotion, perhaps a few words on anatomy and culture are in order. In de-

Epimedium grandiflorum 'White Queen' (Photo by Lynne Harrison)

scribing individual species, *Epimedium* flowers demand close examination, as the floral interest of the various species is not always determined by the same flower part. Without exception, all *Epimedium* species possess two sets of four sepals and four petals. The outer sepals, similar to bud scales, protect the flower in bud and are shed upon opening. In some species, the inner sepals are expanded and colorful (rarely spurred), whereas the petals are quite small. In others, the sepals are small while the petals are large and colorful, possessing a distinctive spur- or horn-shaped appendage that entices pollinating insects to the nectar produced inside.

If one species could be fingered for acting as the catalyst for the current wave of fascination with the genus, it would be *Epimedium acuminatum*. Hailing from Yunnan and Sichuan Provinces, *E. acuminatum* was first discovered in 1858 by the French missionary and naturalist Paul Hubert Perny, though it would be more than another 120 years before the species was firmly established in Western cultivation. Until recently, only two clones of this striking species were available in general cultivation: Roy Lancaster's clone from Emei Shan in Sichuan, with large, pale lavender petals and lighter lilac sepals, and Mikinori Ogisu's collection from the same mountain, which possesses larger and deeper colored petals and which I find to be the better garden plant. Forms of *E. acuminatum* bearing white or pale pink flowers have also been recorded. The evergreen foliage is extremely handsome on all forms, emerging in spring mottled with red and maturing to glossy, spiny edged spears with a long and elegant leaf apex.

In my garden, these forms have settled in quite happily in partially shaded conditions and often will blossom throughout the summer. The clones of *Epimedium acuminatum* that I collected in Sichuan Province in 1996 (DJHC 734, 840, 841, 842) thrilled us here at the nursery when they blossomed for the first time in the spring of 1998. Of the four clones, the best in foliage and flower was DJHC 842, with its large flowers of nearly white inner sepals and purple-fading-to-lavender petals. The elegant foliage emerged in tones of dark red and faded to hot pink and finally to deep green with ruddy mottling.

Epimedium acuminatum is among the handful of species that I have observed in their wild state, having witnessed it growing in western Sichuan on damp, limestone ledges at elevations of 4000–6000 ft. (1200–1800 m). Seeing the diversity in form and size in the wild—some plants possessing 6-in. (15-cm) leaves on stems to 18 in. (45 cm) and flowering scapes to 2 ft. (0.6 m)—I was disturbed by the amount of pressure that is put upon the species by collection for medicinal uses. Countless vendors along the lower reaches of Emei Shan had urns filled to the brim with dried root of this and other species, which is dispensed for the treatment of male sexual dysfunction. When contemplating the number of animal and plant species that are now endangered due to man's quest for timeless virility, it makes one hope that no truly effective cure is ever found.

Still rare in cultivation, *Epimedium brachyrrhizum* was collected on Mount Fanjing in Guizhou Province by the Beijing Botanical Garden. It was initially collected under the name *E. leptorrhizum*, and as I have cultivated the latter species myself, I can understand the

The mottled foliage of *Epimedium acuminatum* DJHC 842, one of the clones brought back from my 1996 expedition to Sichuan (Photo by Daniel J. Hinkley)

Vendors along the lower reaches of Emei Shan in Sichuan Province sell vats of dried rhizomes from wild-collected *Epimedium* as an aphrodisiac (Photo by Daniel J. Hinkley)

Epimedium brachyrrhizum (Photo by Lynne Harrison)

initial confusion since the two have a close affinity. The greatest difference is in the long rhizomes of *E. leptorrhizum*, as compared to the short, congested rhizomes of *E. brachyrrhizum*. The evergreen leaves of *E. brachyrrhizum* are formed on petioles rising to 1 ft. (0.3 m). Large, 2-in. (5-cm) bicolor flowers of blushed white inner sepals and rather long-spurred, rose-pink petals are produced in April and May in copious quantities. The plant will benefit from some overstory protection against late-spring frosts, though it has been found to be perfectly hardy in zone 5.

In my limited experience with *Epimedium brevicornu* I have noted a superficial resemblance to *E. stellulatum*, although *E. brevicornu*, which was introduced into cultivation by Mikinori Ogisu from northwestern Sichuan Province, has extremely thin deciduous foliage, with up to 27 leaflets per leaf, transforming to good autumn tints of gold if grown in areas with sufficient sun. It is one of three deciduous species of *Epimedium* currently known from China. The small, starry, white flowers with reflexed spurs are produced in abundance along 15-in. (38-cm) stems arising from compact clumps of foliage. It is a very hardy species. A form known as *E. brevicornu* f. *rotundatum* simply possesses foliage that is more orbicular than that of the type.

In 1996, on rocky slopes along a small creek below Baoxing in Sichuan, we found an epimedium that Darrell Probst originally identified as *Epimedium latisepalum*, but which later proved to be a different but then-unnamed species; it was assigned the name *E. chlorandrum* a year later, in 1997, and our collection provided the first successful introduction of this species into western cultivation. (Interestingly, Ogisu originally collected this species in the same area of Sichuan also under the name *E. latisepalum*.) The plant blossomed at Heronswood in the spring of 1998 with sprays of numerous large flowers of creamy inner sepals and spurred petals of pastel-yellow. Magnificent narrow foliage held in threes emerges with sensational reddish mottling. Even beyond associating the blossoms with remarkable days in Sichuan, I still find this species the most handsome in flower among those that I currently have in my collection.

Although *Epimedium davidii* has been firmly established in horticulture for more than a decade, it is surprising how infrequently it is encountered outside of collectors' gardens. The species was first collected by the French missionary Père David on limestone cliffs above Baoxing, and it was from this same locality that the British plantsman Martyn Rix reintroduced the species in 1985. The clones collected by Rix, *E. davidii* EMR 4125, are the forms that constitute most of the plants currently in cultivation. They have large, pure yellow, spur-shaped petals and shorter inner sepals of dark red. In 1996, I observed the species growing on wet and shaded limestone walls slightly below the Wenchuan Wolong Nature Reserve at an elevation of 3500 ft. (1050 m), as well as in moist, mossy areas

Epimedium chlorandrum (Photo by Daniel J. Hinkley)

along a river at the valley bottom. *Epimedium davidii* creates demure evergreen plants with compact rhizomes and sprays of large, yellow flowers in spring and, in the cool maritime climate of the Pacific Northwest, throughout the summer. My newly collected clones of the species blossomed in the spring of 1997, and their inner sepals were much smaller than those of the Rix collection, giving the flowers the appearance of being completely yellow. This species benefits from yearly applications of lime to the soil, and though the leaves are evergreen, it is best to tidy the clump by shearing the foliage in late winter on a yearly basis.

Epimedium dolichostemon is another handsome species discovered by Mikinori Ogisu in eastern Sichuan. It is similar in appearance to *E. sagittatum*, though the airy flowers of white inner sepals and rose-red petals, emerging along 15-in. (38-cm) stems, are somewhat larger than those of *E. sagittatum*. The foliage of *E. dolichostemon* is mottled in liver tones upon emergence, later fading to dark green. This species has been slow to establish in my garden and may be resentful of the acidic conditions under which it grows. In the spring of 1997, I applied lime to the soil, and the plant's appearance has greatly improved, though this may be more a product of time than soil pH. It grows in partial shade.

Epimedium davidii (Photo by Lynne Harrison)

Epimedium dolichostemon crossed with *E. acuminatum* has resulted in two lovely hybrid selections made in Japan. *Epimedium* 'Amanogowa' forms vigorous, compact clumps of evergreen foliage that emerges mottled red. In late spring, 2-ft. (0.6-m) stems carry dozens of relatively large flowers with broad, white inner sepals and coppery colored, spurred petals, which are shorter than the inner sepals. *Epimedium* 'Kaguyahime' is a lovely plant that also produces mounds of evergreen foliage that picks up pinkish red tones in winter. Panicles of flowers rise to 2 ft. (0.6 m) or taller, brandishing pink inner sepals and rich purple, spur-shaped petals.

Even those horticulturists who are currently unsmitten with this genus cannot deny the distinctiveness of the flower shape of *Epimedium ecalcaratum*, which is also certain to influence future hybridization efforts. Superficially resembling a miniature *Kirengeshoma*, *E. ecalcaratum* produces bell-shaped and spurless, rich yellow flowers along 15-in. (38-cm) stems arising from clumps of handsome evergreen foliage that displays intense tints throughout winter. The species was first described in 1991 after being discovered by G. Y. Zhong in western Sichuan. In its raw state, it is as hardy as *E. davidii*, and the hybrid progeny that are sure to roll down the pike will undoubtedly add enormous breadth to the floral intrigue offered by this marvelous group of plants.

Epimedium epsteinii was named in 1997 by William T. Stearn to honor the late, great plantsman Harold Epstein of Larchmont, New York. It is a striking species, with evergreen foliage arising from long, creeping rhizomes. The lovely large flowers have broad, white inner sepals, often streaked with purple, and reddish purple, long-spurred petals.

Epimedium fangii is one of four species to occur on Emei Shan in western Sichuan Province, and it was named in honor of the botanist Wen-pei Fang, who dedicated much of his life to exploring and describing the diverse flora of this remarkable mountain. It was Fang's son, now a retired professor of botany, who arranged our visit to the herbarium at Sichuan University in Chengdu as we prepared for our time in the surrounding mountains in the autumn of 1996. The lovely *E. fangii* possesses few but large flowers, with elegantly narrow and spreading petals of yellow, produced along 15-in. (38-cm) stems from clumps of evergreen foliage.

Epimedium flavum is a low-growing evergreen species similar to *E. davidii* in many respects, though the flowers of *E. flavum* are substantially larger, to $1\frac{1}{4}$ in. (3.1 cm) in diameter, and a pale yellow color. The species was named in 1995 by William Stearn, who authored the first monograph on this genus in 1938. *Epimedium flavum* grows in western Sichuan Province.

I originally received *Epimedium franchetii* under the pretense of it being a yellow-flowered form of *E. acuminatum*, and this description is indeed appropriate, as both its elegant evergreen foliage, which emerges a bronzed green, and its large flowers of soft pastel-yellow are very similar in shape and size to those of *E. acuminatum*. *Epimedium franchetii* performs admirably in the garden in light shade and appears tolerant of our acidic conditions. I am currently cultivating a clone of this species called 'Brimstone Butterfly', which was raised and named by Robin White in England; its inner sepals of rusty red are in lovely contrast to the yellow petals.

While in northern Honshu, Japan, in 1997, my traveling companions and I encountered expansive hillsides of *Epimedium grandiflorum* subsp. *koreanum* in moist, shaded sites. It is among the largest of the epimediums that I have witnessed, with some stems rising to nearly 3 ft. (0.9 m) in height. This subspecies is also known to occur on the Korean Peninsula and north to Manchuria, though we failed to locate it in South Korea, where it is now considered quite rare. Light yellow to greenish white flowers are produced among the deciduous leaves in early spring. Because of the large numbers of plants naturally growing in a single locale, it would be quite thrilling indeed to visit the native habitat during spring blossoming to observe the variation in flower color. Farther south, I observed a small population of *E. grandiflorum* subsp. *higoense* growing along a hot, dry, rocky outcropping on Shikoku Island. Despite this severe natural environment, the plant has translated well in cultivation to moist, humus-rich soil in partial shade. Compared to the previous subspecies, *E. grandiflorum* subsp. *higoense* creates much smaller plants, reaching to only 6 in. (15 cm) or slightly more and producing sprays of medium-sized white flowers above the foliage in spring.

A close look-alike to *Epimedium brachyrrhizum*, *E. leptorrhizum* possesses a short history in the West, although it has already proven useful in breeding work through the efforts of Elizabeth Strangman of Washfield Nursery in Kent, England. From Sichuan and Guizhou Provinces, the species has shown itself to be vigorous under cultivation, producing robust stands of low, evergreen, leathery foliage that emerges reddish bronze in spring. Large rose flowers, elegantly spurred, are produced in April on 1-ft. (0.3-m) stems. *Epimedium leptorrhizum* should be grown in a moist and humus-rich soil that does not become exceedingly dry during the summer months. This species crossed with *E. dolichostemon* resulted in *Epimedium* 'Enchantress'. The hybrid produces vigorous clumps of evergreen, corrugated foliage that is dark glabrous green above and near white beneath. The flowers of 'Enchantress' are similar in shade and size to those of *E. leptorrhizum*, though the flowering stems may rise to 16 in. (40 cm) and possess many more flowers.

Epimedium grandiflorum subsp. *higoense*, showing its ephemeral dark leaf margin
(Photo by Lynne Harrison)

Epimedium leptorrhizum (Photo by Lynne Harrison)

Epimedium myrianthum is represented in my garden by a clone that was collected on Tianping Shan in Hunan Province, and it is among the most floriferous of all the species that I currently grow. Arising from handsome evergreen clumps of foliage, which emerge mottled red in spring, 2-ft. (0.6-m) stems carry up to 100 tiny flowers with white inner sepals and small yellow petals. It blossoms throughout the growing season, from early spring through late autumn. The extraordinary number of flowers as well as the long flowering season will add greatly to future breeding programs involving this species.

Described in the early 1990s, *Epimedium ogisui* was named in honor of the legendary Japanese plant explorer Mikinori Ogisu, who is undoubtedly the person most responsible for the resurgence of interest in this genus of plants. It was this species that we most wanted to find during our expedition in the mountains above Baoxing, where the species was first discovered by its namesake along limestone rocks close to waterfalls. We eventually found it far below Baoxing in a valley rich in a wide assortment of plants. The wild species's exacting cultural conditions may be difficult to duplicate in cultivation, but if successful, the horticulturist will be rewarded with 3 to 12 large, pristine white flowers produced on horizontally held stems and clumps of evergreen foliage that emerges bronzy green in spring.

Though we failed to locate *Epimedium fangii* in the wilds of Sichuan Province in 1996, we did successfully collect its hybrid with *E. acuminatum*, *E. ×omeiense*, which is the only known naturally occurring hybrid in China. The variable-sized flowers, borne on robust 2- to 3-ft. (0.6- to 0.9-m) panicles, range in color from a dark murky purple to light lavender with yellow-tipped spurs. Of the two original clones of *E. ×omeiense* collected by Ogisu on Emei Shan, one was described as the type, while the other was given the clonal name 'Storm Cloud', which Blackthorn Nursery introduced in 1997. The latter has already settled into our garden quite happily. When it blossoms, 'Storm Cloud' produces compound inflorescences of flowers with inner sepals of various sizes and shapes and large, spurred petals, both in tones of copper-purple. My collections of *E. ×omeiense* blossomed in the spring of 1998, and the flowers were similar in size to those of *E. acuminatum* but with less contrast in color between the petals and sepals. Though I would be hard pressed to declare this plant unworthy of cultivation, it does not compare favorably with the clones of *E. acuminatum* that I grow.

Epimedium pubescens, which is native to northwestern and central China, grows contentedly in an open position in my garden and is among the longest blossoming of all species in my collection. The evergreen foliage emerges handsomely mottled, and a continuous progression of small flowers with pure white inner sepals and deep yellow petals is produced along 2-ft. (0.6-m) stems from late spring until midautumn. This long blossoming sequence may be a product of our cool summer temperatures in the Pacific Northwest. It has proven to be hardy only in zones 6 or above.

Epimedium sagittatum is a fine evergreen species from northwestern Hubei Province, with large and heavily textured, leathery foliage. One of the oldest and most widely cultivated of the Chinese species, *E. sagittatum* is collected for use in traditional medicine in China and Japan, though I find its absence in Western cultivation quite puzzling. The flowers are composed of white sepals and diminutive, cupped, bronzed petals. The mounds of elegant spear-shaped, 6-in. (15-cm) foliage makes *E. sagittatum* a most beautiful species in my estimation.

Easily grown under cultivation, *Epimedium stellulatum* is currently represented in the West by a single clone known as 'Wudang Star'. It was collected on Wudang Shan in Hubei Province by Roy Lancaster in 1983 and was subsequently described as a new species by William Stearn in 1992. This superb plant produces 12-in. (30-cm) mounds of evergreen foliage that transforms to burgundy tones during the winter. In early spring, 18-in. (45-cm) panicles carry profuse starlike flowers of pure white inner sepals and short, bronze petals, resembling the haze-like blossoms of *Saxifraga stolonifera*. *Epimedium stellulatum* 'Wudang Star' thrives in the acidic soils of my woodland, where in just three years' time it has produced robust clumps.

I remember first gazing upon *Epimedium wushanense* in full blossom at Robin White's Blackthorn Nursery and feeling awestruck that such a plant was only just then becoming known to Western horticulture. First consider its compound evergreen leaves, with elegantly long and narrow spearlike leaflets extending to 8 in. (20 cm) in length, marvelously mottled in purple when young. Add to this airy panicles that carry up to 100 large, light pink to yellow to rusty orange flowers rising to 4 ft. (1.2 m) high. In flower and foliage, *E. wushanense* is rewriting the book on what we think of as an *Epimedium*. The general hardiness of this species is not currently known, as only a handful of specimens are in cultivation outside of its native range in northeastern Sichuan Province. Darrell Probst, of Garden Visions nursery in

An arresting tangerine-yellow flower of *Epimedium wushanense* (Photo by Lynne Harrison)

Massachusetts, has germinated seedlings that resulted from crosses between *E. wushanense* and *E. epsteinii*, which surely will set the horticultural world on fire while leading to subsequent pairings with other species.

I certainly am not alone in feeling the excitement brought forth by these epimediums, whether new introductions or well-known garden regulars, as well as by the prospect of the many unknown species still waiting to be discovered. Nevertheless, there are still too many keen gardeners who have yet to make the acquaintance of this fine genus, and it is with great pleasure that I anticipate watching as gardeners across North America come to know and appreciate all that *Epimedium* has to offer.

Hardiness: One of the truly appealing characteristics of the epimediums as a whole is their adaptability to numerous climatic conditions. Though a large number of the newly introduced Chinese species are not fully tested in gardens throughout North America, most are hardy in zones 5–10. Exceptions have been noted in the preceding descriptions of individual species.

Cultivation: Most *Epimedium* species will colonize easily in well-drained but moist, humus-rich soil in somewhat sheltered locations. Some, such as *Epimedium pinnatum* subsp. *colchicum*, show exceptional drought tolerance once fully established. Other than *E. grandiflorum*, which is unforgiving of alkaline conditions, most species embrace a wide range of acceptable pH levels. All epimediums respond best if shorn to the ground in late winter, both to renew the foliage, which may appear weather-beaten by winter's end, and to allow fuller enjoyment of their blossoming, free from folial interference. This is one garden chore for which procrastination will simply not do, because once the succulent flowering stems have begun to emerge from the ground, they are easily damaged during the shearing process.

Propagation: All epimediums tend to be rhizomatous, though some are much more vigorous in this regard than others. Propagation is generally best done by division in early spring or late summer when the plants are in active root growth. More painstakingly, plants can also be raised from seed, which is a difficult process at best. Seed is discharged when still green, and extreme care must be taken to collect it just before dispersal. Like that of *Helleborus* and *Cyclamen*, the seed of *Epimedium* possesses an oil-rich appendage that aids in dissemination by ants. Seed is produced in abundance if different species or different clones of the same species are grown together. The resultant seedlings, many of which will likely be hybrids, often will blossom within a year of germination.

Achlys

Achlys triphylla var. *triphylla* is commonly encountered throughout the Cascade and Olympic Mountain ranges of the Pacific Northwest, at moderate elevations and on both the eastern and western slopes, and it is one of the few solely western North American plant species that is complemented by an Asian counterpart. As implied by the specific epithet (which translates as "three-leaved"), *A. triphylla* has leaves that are divided into three triangular lobes, with the middle one somewhat more broadly obovate than the laterals and each possessing an irregular margin. The flowering stems emerge in late spring from ground level, producing airy spikes of white flowers composed entirely of stamens and pistils. In fact, the plant's genus name comes from the Greek word for mist, referring to the translucence of these flowers. The common name vanilla leaf refers to the practice among early Northwest pioneers of drying the foliage for its pleasant vanillalike fragrance. (It is also known in the vernacular as sweet-after-death.) The Asian version of the species, *A. triphylla* var. *japonica*, occurs in both Korea and the northern areas of Japan, most notably on Hokkaido. It is nearly identi-

Achlys triphylla var. *triphylla* alongside a hybrid rhododendron (Photo by Lynne Harrison)

cal to its Western counterpart, though it possesses somewhat smaller features in all regards. I have not observed this variety in the wild, but I do have plants established in my garden that I purchased at a nursery in Japan some years ago.

Hardiness: Probably zones 5–9 for both varieties, though *Achlys triphylla* var. *japonica* is thoroughly untested in North American gardens.

Cultivation: Both varieties require shade and rather moist, well-drained soils, where they will colonize quite easily by rhizomes to form dastardly good groundcovers. I lost a colony of *Achlys triphylla* var. *triphylla* in my woodland for unknown reasons, but I suspect that it may have resulted from over-fertilization.

Propagation: Once established, a healthy expanse of this species will provide an abundance of rhizomes for propagation, which should be done in early spring as growth is resuming. I have collected seed of our native variety in the Olympic Mountains and found it to be quite easy to germinate if sown fresh. The seed did not demonstrate a double dormancy, germinating the following spring.

Caulophyllum

I first admired the startling fruit of the blue cohosh (*Caulophyllum thalictroides* var. *thalictroides*) while traveling along the East Coast in autumn, specifically during a visit to the Mount Cuba Center for the Study of Piedmont Flora, Delaware. Clusters of lovely blue fruit with a whitish bloom were illuminated above a folial melange of the forest floor by the low-angled autumn sun. The scene spoke to the richness of the eastern deciduous woods as well as to how we often disregard the ornamental fruit produced by numerous herbaceous species. In early spring, from New Brunswick to Tennessee, the coppery colored, compound triternate foliage of *C. thalictroides* var. *thalictroides* emerges with each leaflet showing variable lobing, from none to three lobes. The flowers are relatively insignificant, composed of bronzy or greenish yellow sepals and reduced petals, held in clusters on 18-in. (45-cm) stems. In Korea and Japan, I observed and collected seed of *C. thalictroides* var. *robustum*, which was also exceedingly handsome in fruit. The umbels of large, whitish blue fruit held atop 2-ft. (0.6-m) stems were commonly encountered in rather dry deciduous oak woods, especially throughout Mount Odae National Park on the east coast of South Korea. Although I have not observed this plant in foliage in the wild, as it had long since died off when I saw it, seedlings from my 1993 trip are now transplanted into my garden and are demonstrating a remarkable similarity to its North American counterpart.

Hardiness: Both varieties of blue cohosh are hardy to at least zones 4–9, perhaps into cooler zones if provided some overstory protection.

Cultivation: The natural habitats of this species's two varieties indicate that these are denizens of the light woodland in moist but well-drained soils. In Korea, *Caulophyllum thalictroides* var. *robustum* grows with *Disporum uniflorum* and *Smilacina japonica* at moderate elevations under deciduous trees. I have successfully grown the American variety in my woodland with a dense overstory of Douglas firs, but I have not yet had good fruit set. This may be due to insufficient light or the absence of sufficient heat in our maritime climate.

Propagation: The best option is division of the rootstock in late winter or early spring. Propagation by seed is abysmally slow, at least in the Pacific Northwest where there is little heat during the growing season. Even when sown fresh, the seed will take at least two years, perhaps three, to germinate.

Caulophyllum thalictroides var. *thalictroides* (Photo by Lynne Harrison)

Diphylleia

With each year that the colony of *Diphylleia cymosa* in my garden matures, my infatuation with the genus grows. I was first exposed to this Appalachian native in a Seattle garden in early autumn, when the plant is in its finest season. Striking umbels of blackish blue fruit covered with whitish bloom ripen in late summer on electric-pink stems. These pedicels rise from atop the 2-ft. (0.6-m) leaf petiole, which, like that of the closely allied genus *Podophyllum*, is branched with a pair of leaves. Though this was the effect that I was seeking when I included the plant in my garden, I have since come to greatly appreciate the large, two-lobed, bright green, peltate leaves and the clean white flowers produced above the foliage in late April and early May.

For those gardeners who have equal affection for plants from eastern North America as well as the exotics from Japan and China, the fascinating similarity between the two floras has probably not gone unnoticed. In nearly every genus native to eastern North America, woody and herbaceous alike, a closely related East Asian counterpart generally exists, and considering a disjunction of more than 5000 miles and an expansive ocean between, that is quite remarkable. Such is the case with *Diphylleia*, with the Japanese and Chinese counterpart described as simply a variety of the American species. *Diphylleia cymosa* var. *grayi* occurs in mountainous regions of Honshu and Hokkaido in Japan as well as in Yunnan Province of China. The foliage of the variety is somewhat smaller than that of the species type and has a less-jagged margin. From seed collected along a forest stream on northern Honshu, I have young plants now established in my garden. I eagerly await their maturation so that I can observe more closely the differences between the American and Asian cousins.

Hardiness: Zones 5–9. This genus is restricted to cool mountainous regions in its distribution and may resent excessive summer heat and humidity.

Cultivation: Best cultivated in sheltered sites with humus-rich soils and adequate summer moisture. This is a long-lived, clumping perennial and patience is required to achieve its full stature.

Propagation: Easily produced by seed if sown fresh in autumn. If seed is allowed to dry, a double dormancy may develop and a second season of stratification will be required for germination. Division in early spring is quite easy.

Diphylleia cymosa (Photo by Lynne Harrison)

The striking blue fruit of *Diphylleia cymosa* (Photo by Daniel J. Hinkley)

Jeffersonia

In the historic curated gardens of Monticello, Thomas Jefferson's elegant and restored estate, grows a plant that was named in Jefferson's honor while he was Secretary of State in George Washington's first administration. *Jeffersonia diphylla* ranks among the most distinctive and cherished of American wildflowers, with extraordinary foliage and exquisite albeit ephemeral flowers in early spring. The elegant leaves have two deeply dentate lobes, which emerge in late winter like folded hands in prayer holding a single-stemmed flower rising to 10 in. (25 cm). The flowers are composed of eight white petals surrounding an equal number of yellow stamens and a green pistil, resulting in a curious flat-topped capsule that opens like a jack-in-the-box to expose the rounded, golden seed within. *Jeffersonia diphylla* is native from the eastern Canadian provinces south to Alabama and west to Wisconsin, where it is frequently found associated with limestone formations in shade. A double-flowered form of this species is mentioned in literature, though I have not encountered it nor do I know of anyone who has.

Jeffersonia dubia is the Asiatic counterpart of *J. diphylla* and the only other species in the genus. Though the two are certainly recognizable as close relatives, the two-lobed foliage of *J. dubia* emerges in spring with a distinctive violet blush, and the flowers, produced in early to midspring before the foliage is fully expanded, are lavender-blue and possess fewer petals than the flowers of *J. diphylla*. I observed this species in its native South Korea growing in a densely shaded site in the rich deciduous woods surrounding Mount Chuwang north of Pohang. Its natural distribution is centered farther to the northeast in Manchuria as well as eastern Russia. A pure white form of this species, *J. dubia* f. *alba*, is naturally occurring, although it currently has limited availability in commerce. The form is indeed quite lovely in blossom and deserving of procuring if encountered, though I am partial to the type color.

Hardiness: Both *Jeffersonia* species show exceptional hardiness in zones 4–10 and tolerate the warm summer areas of the southern states.

Cultivation: Though *Jeffersonia diphylla* often grows naturally in alkaline soil environments, this does not seem to be a prerequisite for good growth; this species thrives in our slightly acidic woodland. *Jeffersonia dubia* is more demure and seemingly less robust than its American cousin, and it requires more time for establishment. Once it settles in, however, *J. dubia* will demonstrate a greater tendency toward stoloniferous growth. Both species are well adapted to light woodland conditions.

Propagation: Seed is generously produced on both species, and propagation by this method is quite dependable, as long as the seed is sown fresh. The

Jeffersonia diphylla (Photo by Lynne Harrison)

Jeffersonia dubia (Photo by Lynne Harrison)

seedlings are fragile and may benefit from an extra year in the seedling tray before transplanting. I have raised seed received as *Jeffersonia dubia* f. *alba* only to
have the progeny blossom with type color. As I have never actually collected seed
of the white form and raised the resultant seedling to flowering size, I am reticent
to say that this does not come true to form. I have divided both species in autumn
with good success, though I feel better recommending early spring division just
as growth resumes.

Podophyllum

I was introduced to the genus *Podophyllum* in the deciduous woods of northern
Michigan, where *Podophyllum peltatum* is commonly found growing in moist,
humus-rich soils with *Trillium grandiflorum*, *Sanguinaria canadensis*, and *Dicentra cucullaria*. More work remains to be done on this genus to fully comprehend
both the number of species that actually exist and the variation within each species. The literature cites 10 species in addition to those that I will discuss here,
though many are known only from a single specimen and may prove to be synonymous following additional study. It has been suggested that the genus *Podophyllum* be split into three genera; only *Podophyllum peltatum* would retain the old
genus name, while *P. hexandrum* would adopt the name *Sinopodophyllum* and the
other Asiatic species would take on the genus name *Dysosma*. Currently the momentum appears to be in favor of retaining *Podophyllum* as the all-inclusive
name, and I have thus followed the traditional classification of the genera. I am
indebted to Julian Shaw for his help in sorting out the intricacies of the genus.

A typical *Podophyllum* plant consists of a rhizome from which arises a two-
branched petiole, each branch topped by an always peltate though not always
lobed leaf blade. The anatomy of *Podophyllum peltatum*, or the mayapple as it is
commonly called, does not depart from this norm: two 12-in. (30-cm), umbrella-
like, deeply lobed leaf blades top 2-ft. (0.6-m), branched petioles. The species is
vigorously stoloniferous, and the terminal leaf, which occurs at the apex of the
stolon, is carried on a simple, nonforked petiole. Collectively, the two leaf types
make for a lush and striking groundcover, which is perhaps the only reason for
including the mayapple in the garden. Nine-petaled, 1½-in. (3.8-cm) white flowers emerge on short peduncles from the juncture of the two leaves, though this
occurs after the leaves have fully expanded, eliminating any chance for enjoyment of the flower. *Podophyllum peltatum* does have a pink-flowered form, but just
how regularly this occurs, I am unsure. While visiting the Henry Foundation
near Philadelphia, Pennsylvania, I observed pink-flowered individuals of this

species that had been collected in Texas under the name *P. peltatum* var. *deamii*. The rose-red buds opened to a soft pink flower. The 2-in. (5-cm), egg-shaped, yellow fruit of this species, or red in the variant, is edible when fully ripened and is reported to taste very similar to guava.

Podophyllum hexandrum, native from Asia Minor through the Himalayas and into central China, has greater ornamental impact than its American cousin. Though the foliage effect is not nearly as bold as that of *P. peltatum*, *P. hexandrum* offers patterned leaves that emerge in spring deeply glossed with variable amounts of black-purple mottling. The flowers, which vary from pure white to deep rose, are produced with the foliage, allowing for full appreciation of the floral effect. In late summer, striking scarlet-red, egg-shaped fruit hang on short peduncles from the axils of the leaf petioles, providing a second season of ornament to the woodland garden. I encountered *P. hexandrum* frequently in open areas of northwestern Yunnan Province, the brilliant scarlet fruit still attached to stems that had long withered, but supported by the stems of barberries, roses, lilacs, and lyonias, at the base of which they grew.

The exact position of the flower clusters on the leaf petiole seems to be the feature most often used to differentiate the other Asiatic species of *Podophyllum*, and these species are among the most dramatic foliage plants that I currently have in my garden. *Podophyllum pleianthum* carries leathery and glossy 15-in. (38-cm) leaves in pairs atop 18-in. (45-cm) stems. The leaves, which have five to nine shallow lobes, provide a distinctive starfish-like shape and a textural quality unlike any

Podophyllum hexandrum (Photo by Lynne Harrison)

Podophyllum hexandrum in fruit (Photo by Lynne Harrison)

other plant I know, remaining unblemished well into late summer. In late spring, rather odoriferous flowers with narrow, elongated, blood-red petals to 2 in. (5 cm) are produced in clusters of five to nine. The location of the flower cluster is variable from plant to plant: either from the juncture of the two leaves or slightly above the juncture on the petiole of the largest leaf. Fortunately, the carrion fragrance cannot be detected in the garden, though it makes itself readily known when brought into an enclosed space. This and numerous other species of *Podophyllum* are pollinated by flies.

The only major difference between *Podophyllum versipelle* and the previous species, other than its somewhat smaller and more prominently lobed leaves, is

Podophyllum pleianthum (Photo by Lynne Harrison)

the position of the flower cluster. In the case of *P. versipelle*, the cluster is attached to the leaf petiole directly under the larger of the two leaves; before the leaf blade fully expands, the clusters of squat, burgundy flowers appear above the foliage. I recently received specimens from China (under the name *P. veitchii*) that fit the description of this species, and to the best of my knowledge, these will be the first introduction of true *P. versipelle* into cultivation. Up to this point, what has traveled about under the name *P.*

Podophyllum pleianthum showing its silvery fruit clusters (Photo by Daniel J. Hinkley)

The flowers and subsequent fruit of *Podophyllum versipelle* are borne on the leaf stem at or directly below the juncture of the leaf blade (Photo by Lynne Harrison)

versipelle in both Europe and the United States has most definitely been *P. pleianthum*. The fruit of the two species is quite similar, as both form striking clusters of large, silvery gray fleshy pods that ripen to yellow.

Podophyllum difforme is a striking member of the genus, and I shall not soon forget the day I first encountered it. It was growing in some quantity in a nursery near the city of Aomori in Japan, on the northern end of Honshu, though the species is native to Hubei Province in China. I was caught off guard by its extraordinary large, leathery leaves, not unlike those of *P. pleianthum*, centrally blotched with pewter, blackish purple, or a combination of both. I have since grown a sizable number of seedlings of *P. difforme*, and I find that each one possesses a striking individuality all its own. The petioles are densely coated with white hairs, though these are seemingly ephemeral in nature, with older leaf stems being quite glabrous. Salmon-pink flowers are borne from the leaf petiole directly below the largest leaf, followed by clusters of yellowish green, plum-sized fruit. This may prove to be a difficult species to maintain in temperate climates due to its propensity to begin growth in autumn when rains commence.

During our trip to Sichuan Province in the autumn of 1996, while I lingered on the upper slopes of Emei Shan, at an elevation of 9500 ft. (2850 m), quite spellbound by the incredible diversity of plant species, my colleague, Darrell Probst, dropped in elevation to explore the steep, rocky cliffs 1000 ft. (300 m) below. It was there that he happened upon a sizable colony of what we now believe to be *Podophyllum delavayi* (treated as *P. veitchii* by Chinese botanists). The irregular

Podophyllum difforme (Photo by Daniel J. Hinkley)

peltate foliage, to 1 ft. (0.3 m) across, was composed of six lobes, each lobe itself divided into three lobes. The lobing extends around three-quarters of each leaf, while the remaining unlobed quarter possesses an extremely dentate margin. Sadly, the seed had long since dissipated, but with permission we were able to collect a small piece from this colony. The foliage was quite decrepit, and although it was obvious even then that the foliage featured a distinctive variegated pattern, nothing could have prepared me for its arrival the following spring. The young foliage emerged in tones of black-purple, transforming to a satiny green mottled in rich plum. The deep red inflorescences, to 1 in. (2.5 cm), are produced in small clusters of two to three flowers at the leaf juncture.

Hardiness: All the *Podophyllum* species discussed here are hardy in at least zones 6–10, though the information is incomplete for hardiness in colder areas.

A silver-variegated color form of *Podophyllum difforme* (Photo by Lynne Harrison)

The exquisite variegated foliage of *Podophyllum delavayi* (Photo by Lynne Harrison)

We mulch the plantings of *Podophyllum pleianthum* with sawdust in exposed areas of our garden, while those in the woodland have not required protection.

Cultivation: *Podophyllum* is best grown in humus-rich, well-drained soils provided with adequate moisture during the summer. There is only one flush of growth each season, and it takes several years for small plants to fully establish and mature. Do not be dismayed if younger plants slip into early dormancy; they will return with added vigor the following year and will blossom in three to five years from germination. Fruit will be produced if more than one clone of each species is planted, though there does seem to be some degree of self-compatibility. The possibilities for creating interspecific hybrids have been inadequately explored, but limited trials have brought promising results.

Propagation: The current wisdom says that, under favorable conditions, stoloniferous growth is possible in all Asiatic *Podophyllum* species. This will assuredly increase the availability of flowering-sized plants at affordable costs. For *Podophyllum peltatum*, division is the most acceptable method, if not for producing additional plants, then certainly for controlling its colonization of the garden. Seed propagation of these species offers few challenges. Germination occurs the following year in very early spring; protection from late frosts should be provided. We have successfully entered *Podophyllum delavayi* into tissue culture propagation.

Ranzania japonica

I never feel comfortable writing about plants with which I have not had at least some garden experience; however, I must make an exception with the monospecific genus *Ranzania*, as it is a plant that I certainly will become better acquainted with as time goes on. The genus name commemorates Ono Ranzan, "the Japanese Linnaeus." *Ranzania japonica* is seldom encountered either in cultivation or in its native habitat in the mountains of Honshu; although I have traveled extensively in its native range, I have not had the good fortune to stumble upon it and observe its preferred habitat. A robust specimen grows at the Botanical Garden of the University of British Columbia, where it produces clumps of foliage not dissimilar to that of epimediums, with stems rising to 15 in. (38 cm) terminating in two leaves, each composed of three trilobed leaflets. As the leaves expand, clusters of very pretty, pendulous, blue-violet cups are produced on wiry pedicels to 3 in. (7.5 cm). The flowers of *R. japonica* are superficially reminiscent of the flowers of the lovely *Jeffersonia dubia*. The pedicels stiffen after fertilization, resulting in upright clusters of white berries held above the foliage.

Ranzania japonica is a rare plant in collections, but certainly not difficult to grow. For many years, Harold Epstein had several robust clumps of this species growing in his celebrated garden in Larchmont, New York. My own minute garden specimens appear ridiculously small in comparison, yet I have cultivated the patience to wait for their coming of age.

Hardiness: Within the confines of limited data, I would risk a guess that *Ranzania japonica* is hardy in zones 5–9, perhaps colder if given protection.

Cultivation: In well-drained, humus-rich soils in bright but sheltered positions. Provide supplemental moisture during the growing season as needed.

Propagation: Division is the best method of propagation, which should be done in early spring as growth resumes. Fresh seed is also an option, although it will demonstrate a double dormancy and will not germinate until the second spring after sowing. Seedlings present their inaugural flowering in five to seven years.

Ranzania japonica growing alongside *Primula poissonii* (background) at the University of British Columbia Botanical Garden in Vancouver (Photo by Lynne Harrison)

Vancouveria

The vagaries of plant distribution have always held great fascination for me; what events—be they climatic, geographic, or cataclysmic—took place to bring about the distribution of any given genus of plants, whether extremely limited, widespread, or disjunct (split)? Whereas the genus *Achlys* represents an odd disjunction between western North America and East Asia, its family member and close *Epimedium* ally, *Vancouveria*, is found only along the West Coast from Washington to north-central California. The genus name honors George Vancouver, who in 1789 was the first to sail into the Strait of Juan de Fuca, the body of water separating Vancouver Island from Washington's Olympic Peninsula.

Vancouveria hexandra is the only member of the genus to occur in my home state of Washington, where it is frequently encountered in well-drained, shaded sites, especially to the south of Olympia. As with all three species of this genus, the foliage of *V. hexandra* is triternate, with each of the 27 leaflets being trilobed and growing to 1 in. (2.5 cm) long and ½ in. (1.25 cm) wide. This is also the only species that is deciduous, though it is only partially so in my garden. In this

Vancouveria hexandra (Photo by Lynne Harrison)

and many other cases of plants that are "partially deciduous," a shear-cut during autumn or spring cleanup is all that is demanded; the semiretentive foliage looks quite bedraggled by spring. On erect, branched stalks to 10 in. (25 cm), flowering stems produce in late spring numerous small blossoms of three outer sepals and six each of white inner sepals and petals, all of which are strongly reflexed, and six golden stamens. The overall floral effect is similar to that of an *Epimedium*, in particular *Epimedium stellulatum*, though the six-merous flowers (parts in sixes or multiples thereof) of *Vancouveria* set the genus apart from the four-merous flowers of *Epimedium*.

Farther south, from southern Oregon to northern California, two additional species have natural ranges that overlap. The species that I find most garden worthy, *Vancouveria planipetala*, possesses handsome triternate, leathery evergreen foliage, with leaflets that are decidedly less lobed and more rounded than those of *V. hexandra*. It blossoms in late spring with sprays of ¼-in. (0.6-cm) white flowers produced atop 18-in. (45-cm) stems. *Vancouveria planipetala* creates rather open stoloniferous colonies of stems, as compared to the more aggressive and dense growth habit of *V. hexandra*. It is quite drought tolerant once fully established.

Vancouveria planipetala (Photo by Lynne Harrison)

The lovely, albeit scarce in cultivation, *Vancouveria chrysantha* occupies dry, open sites among scrub on slopes and is the most drought tolerant of the triad of *Vancouveria* species. Like *V. planipetala*, this species creates light, spreading stands of dark green, leathery foliage, perfect for knitting among the creeping stems and rich blue stars of *Omphalodes verna*, with which it will share its lovely blossoming effects of saturated yellow flowers on 10-in. (25-cm) stems. *Vancouveria chrysantha* is the species most infrequently found in commerce, and on several occasions I have purchased this species and transported it over huge distances only to have it re-speciate to *V. hexandra* at blossoming time.

Hardiness: All three species are hardy to at least zones 5–9, though *Vancouveria planipetala* may exhibit leaf scorch in extended temperatures below 15°F (−9°C). Extra mulching with leaf litter will increase hardiness in colder climates.

Cultivation: Best grown in well-drained soils in partial shade, although plants are tolerant of full-sun sites if provided additional water during the growing season. *Vancouveria hexandra* is mildly aggressive and intolerant of diminutive, delicate neighboring plants in my garden. This flaw of character should be taken into account when siting. As with epimediums, removing the foliage in midwinter will rejuvenate the summer appearance of all three *Vancouveria* species, deciduous or evergreen, while allowing for a better enjoyment of the flowers.

Propagation: Division of the rhizomes at any time of the year has been successful, though early spring would be preferable. I have germinated seed of *Vancouveria chrysantha*; each seed is small and possesses a very hard seed coat. Soaking in water for 24 hours before sowing is helpful but, considering the size of the seed, not very practical. Two years may be required for germination, depending on the freshness of the seed sown.

CHAPTER 7

Corydalis:
Jewels in Many Hues

The genus *Corydalis* is hardly new to cultivation in North America or Europe, having been cultivated for years as a cottage garden perennial. The generic name is the Greek word for the crested lark, as the tubular flowers can, with some imagination, suggest the appearance of a crested bird's head. As a genus, the 300-odd species can bring to the garden a feisty personality steeped in charm and adaptability. Some are bulbous perennials that tend to be reticent to colonize, while others are fibrous-rooted, short-lived, and more than willing to conquer manicured gardens. In my horticultural endeavors, I continue to make their acquaintance one species at a time. Among these, numerous friendships have been cemented for life, while others have resulted in rather unpalatable personality conflicts. Generally, in the latter cases, any unpleasantness stems from the faults of the other party.

Corydalis lutea is a tough and durable plant that presents multitudes of tubular, spurred, bright yellow flowers on 15-in. (38-cm) stems. Though I can recall being tempted by its handsome ferny foliage and seemingly nonstop flowering habit, I thankfully resisted the initial infatuation. Its propensity to self seed exuberantly was a bit frightful, even to one who has excelled within the precept of "plant first, evaluate second, then eradicate." This plant, though quite lovely, is best enjoyed in others' gardens. To be fair, I have learned that its excesses are not as exuberant in climates with harsher winters, where it is considered a benign self-sowing, short-lived species.

Corydalis ochroleuca is quite similar in its overall demeanor, with pure white flowers on stems arising from finely cut silvery gray foliage. I have planted this in our light woodland at the base of *Viburnum sieboldii*, which coaxes the lax flowering stems of the corydalis up into the lower limbs—adding a spritz of light to the otherwise dull foliage of the viburnum during the summer months. Though I was originally convinced that the penance for my transgressions in regard to this species would be weeks of weeding out its progeny, *C. ochroleuca* has been exceedingly reluctant to self sow, and I have dug and shared with friends only a handful of seedlings in ten years.

I first encountered *Corydalis ochotensis* inhabiting flood plains along several rivers at moderate elevations throughout the northern reaches of South Korea. Like *C. ochroleuca*, *C. ochotensis* appeared quite willing to reseed and form large colonies. Bright green ferny foliage emerges along stems to 18 in. (45 cm), and the bright yellow flowers are produced over a long period of time. This species is obviously adaptable to perpetually saturated soils and should be put to use in gardens where these conditions exist.

Somewhat more intriguing in form is *Corydalis cheilanthifolia*, which makes a dense rosette of very finely dissected, chestnut-toned foliage, from which arise 10-in. (25-cm) spikes of spurred, yellow flowers in midspring. It is well suited to damp soils; under similar conditions in my garden it self sows in a somewhat arrogant manner, though it is more polite in drier locations, especially in summer. As is often the case with plants such as these that I have grown weary of and ban-

Corydalis cheilanthifolia (Photo by Lynne Harrison)

ished from the garden, their reappearance is inevitable and generally in sync with my emerging regrets for having removed them. *Corydalis cheilanthifolia* is considered a perennial, yet I have found the individual plants to exhibit a short-lived nature. In any case, it is unlikely that you will ever bemoan the loss of a single plant.

Corydalis cheilanthifolia is somewhat similar to a plant whose seed I collected in eastern Nepal in 1995. The plant was later identified as *C. chaerophylla*, a long-lived perennial species with mounds of finely fretted, somewhat bronzy foliage on stems rising to 2 ft. (0.6 m). Though this took more than two years from seed to finally produce flowers, patience was rewarded in the spring of 1997 with quantities of small but pleasing yellow flowers produced along 6-in. (15-cm) terminal racemes. This species grew in a moist, open situation in the Himalayas at an elevation slightly above 10,000 ft. (3000 m), and it has settled in quite nicely in our garden in richly amended soil that receives adequate moisture throughout the summer and several hours of direct sunlight each day. Like many of its brethren, *C. chaerophylla* has been nominated for an Excellence in Procreation award by Horticultural Pro-Life, Inc.

An annual *Corydalis* that I have come to greatly admire is *Corydalis sempervirens*, which hails from northeastern North America extending across Canada to British Columbia. It is a wispy plant that grows to 15 in. (38 cm) and possesses striking steely blue leaves and charming lavender and yellow flowers throughout the growing season. *Corydalis sempervirens* has migrated in my garden to the most inhospitable of sites under the eaves of the western foundation, which is generally dusty dry by midsummer—yet it takes these digs in stride, delightfully commingling with other drought-tolerant perennials and shrubs that eke out an existence here. Its shiny black seed is scattered in late summer, just as I begin to tidy the garden and remove the plants that are by now spent of their energy—confident that the offspring will germinate the following spring.

Natively speaking, two species of *Corydalis* are found in the Pacific Northwest, one of which has become admired in collectors' gardens throughout Western horticulture. *Corydalis scouleri* is a bold, stoloniferous perennial that thrives in rich moist soils at moderate elevations in the Cascade and Olympic Mountain ranges, from British Columbia to northern Oregon. Of the many *Corydalis* species that I cultivate, I find *C. scouleri* to be among the finest. The acid-green ferny foliage, thrice divided, is produced on stems to 5 ft. (1.5 m) that sport racemes of up to 30 lovely rose-lavender flowers in midspring. In a moist bed in our light woodland, this species provides luxuriant foliage early in the season in concert with the flowers of *Meconopsis betonicifolia* and *Primula japonica*, with which it shares its bed, and later carries the bed on its own in the quiet of late summer. Slowly increasing in breadth, the clumps of this species are easily contained by reducing them in size in early spring.

Whether for its general elusiveness or its intrinsic beauty, *Corydalis aquae-gelidae* is a rarity that I cherish highly in the garden. Strangely, the sole seed that I germinated of this native North American species came from an established plant in Germany—it having originally been collected as seed from one of the few known populations in northwestern Oregon and southwestern Washington. The rich green, ferny foliage of *Corydalis aquae-gelidae* grows in basal clumps to 4 ft. (1.2 m) and is crowned in June and July with many-flowered racemes of creamy white flowers blushed with rosy lavender. As its species name implies, this plant's preferred growing conditions are along cold streams and springs. It grows near *C. scouleri* in rich, perennially moist soils in my woodland garden.

Corydalis solida is widely grown in European gardens and deserves greater attention in North America outside of the gardens of plant collectors. There are few more lovely early spring-blossoming bulbous perennials, and it combines ex-

Corydalis scouleri (Photo by Lynne Harrison)

ceptionally well with numerous other spring ephemerals. In relative terms, *C. solida* is more diminutive than others in the genus, with grayish green, twice- or thrice-divided foliage rising to 8 in. (20 cm) high. Soon after the foliage appears in March and April, dense spikes of spurred flowers emerge with a spectral diversity of flower color and quality, mainly in shades of lavender to salmon—I have heard the flower color of seedling-grown plants described as ranging from pasty flesh to murky puce, though I have seen many unnamed clones growing in close proximity and find the range of colors quite lovely in mass. For many years, *C. solida* f. *transsylvanica* was the most sought-after form of the species due to its rich red color, but it has proven to be exceedingly difficult to propagate and as difficult to find in nurseries. Although it is not known exactly where *C. solida* 'George Baker' originated, this cultivar is suspected to be a better seedling of f. *transsylvanica* that possesses greater ease of propagation, and it has become widely available, though certainly not commonly encountered. 'George Baker', named to honor a superb British collector of bulbs, has rich brick-red flowers and is a more acceptable selection for cultivation. Additional named forms of this species should be added to one's lust list and ultimately to one's garden when sources are found. I have gathered two choice pink forms from Europe, 'Beth Evans' and 'Nettleton Pink', as well as a sky blue form from Russia, 'Blue Pearl'. Closer to home, from Mount Tahoma Nursery in Washington, I received a Ukrainian selection that is particularly heavy blooming with stems of rich blue-violet

Corydalis solida f. *transsylvanica* 'George Baker' (Photo by Lynne Harrison)

flowers; it is known as *C. solida* 'Harkov'. Shining in blossom in early spring, the white form of the species, *C. solida* 'Alba', is indeed a lovely plant and should be sought out. *Corydalis solida* subsp. *incisa*, as one might guess from the name, possesses foliage that is incised in its secondary divisions rather than delineated entirely into separate leaflets. The subspecies's striking red-violet flowers make it certainly worthy of the hunt. Spreading over time to form sizable colonies, *C. solida* thrives in semishaded conditions in soils that have adequate spring moisture but dry out completely by midsummer. The plants totally retreat at this time, hunkering down during the hot and dry months of summer and autumn.

Another bulbous species, similar to the previous one but larger on all fronts, *Corydalis malkensis* comes from the Caucasus in southeastern Europe. For years it made the horticultural rounds as *C. caucasica* var. *alba*, and it was under this name that I first obtained the species from Gisela Schmeimann of Cologne, Germany. In her lovely garden, as well as in other collectors' gardens in Germany and the Netherlands, I admired the plant's upright stems, to 8 in. (20 cm), carrying dazzling, quite large and pure white, spurred flowers. In just three years' time, *C. malkensis* has settled in nicely in my bright woodland, offering numerous flowering stems in late March and disappearing completely by the first of June.

The white-flowered form of a closely related species from south-central Europe is the only form of *Corydalis cava* that I have experience in cultivating. *Corydalis cava* 'Albiflora' was given to me by plantsman extraordinaire Jack Elliot of England, and I enjoy the pure white flowers densely held in racemes to 6 in. (15 cm) above broad, bluish green foliage. *Corydalis cava* can be distinguished from *C. solida* by the absence of bracts on the base of its flowering stem.

In our woodland, in well-drained and droughty soils, we successfully cultivate *Corydalis decipiens*, a species that I have come to greatly appreciate. An early spring ephemeral, *C. decipiens* is a bulbous species from southeastern Europe. In early to mid-March, large, floriferous racemes of spurred mauve flowers with violet overtones rise to 10 in. (25 cm) from ever-increasing tuberous clumps of foliage to 6 in. (15 cm). We grow *C. decipiens* adjacent to a clump of *Ajuga reptans* 'Burgundy Glow' that in foliage embraces the same color as the *Corydalis*; together they shine for three weeks in late February and March.

Corydalis paczoskii, which I obtained from seed provided by the Royal Horticultural Society in England, grows near *C. decipiens* in light shade and well-drained, organic soils. Like *C. decipiens*, it is a bulbous spring ephemeral, retreating to dormancy by late spring after offering a very pretty display of rose-lavender flowers.

While visiting Rosemary Verey in her garden at Barnsley House in England, I noticed a rather distinctive *Corydalis* species, of which Ms. Verey offered me a

Corydalis decipiens (Photo by Lynne Harrison)

piece to take home. Later, the species was identified as *Corydalis linstowiana*, which, interestingly, had been collected in China by the staff of Quarry Hill Botanical Garden of northern California and subsequently shared with the gardeners at Barnsley. This jet-setting species has made a good home for itself at Heronswood, producing a large woody bulb from which arise short tufts of finely dissected, blue-gray leaves and stems to 5 in. (12.5 cm) carrying a long progression of purple-blue flowers from early June through July.

Somewhat similar in effect to *Corydalis linstowiana*, *C. smithiana* is a recent introduction to cultivation made by the Alpine Garden Society's expedition to Yunnan and Sichuan in 1994. Collected under the number of ACE 154, it was growing in quarry rubble above Napa Hai near Zhongdian, where I was to visit two years later. It is a short-lived, fibrous-rooted perennial in cultivation, but it eagerly self sows, creating low mounds of grayish green, highly fretted foliage and lavender-pink flowers tipped in purple on stems to 8 in. (20 cm).

It wasn't until recent collections of a blue-flowered *Corydalis* species from China that an interest in the genus approached a crescendo, the reverberations of which haven't come close to abating. Of course, that a blue *Corydalis* exists is not earth-shaking news to many gardeners, especially those hardy, knowledgeable folks known as rock garden enthusiasts who have tried and tried again to cultivate the cagey *Corydalis cashmeriana* in their gardens—though with few successes, I suspect. Before the Chinese collections, this bulbous blue-flowered species had been tried the most, and its reputation of being difficult under cultivation was, for the most part, justified. *Corydalis cashmeriana* is assuredly a spectacular species in full blossom, with deep blue, tubular flowers arising on 8-in. (20-cm) stems from clumps of glaucous blue-green, ferny foliage. Although I have not observed it in cultivation outside of my own garden, I might venture a guess that even at its best this species would never be an exceptional garden-worthy perennial—speaking in terms of the traditional herbaceous border. I generally can coax a single flowering stem from the ground in early summer, which, much to my distress, has become an effulgent dinner bell to seemingly every slug in the greater Puget Sound region. Seldom have I obtained an open flower before the stem is consumed at ground level. Hailing from high elevations of the Himalayas, *C. cashmeriana* requires rich soil in semishade that will dry out somewhat in summer when this and nearly all other bulbous species slip into complete dormancy immediately after flowering.

In the horticultural equivalent of attention deficit disorder, the ultimate prize is seldom cherished when finally possessed by the true plant collector. Even before the latest acquisition is firmly established in the garden, sights are set on that which is far and beyond: extraordinary, exquisite, unobtainable. How thoroughly strange that one such mission of lust—the celebrated blue *Corydalis*, hidden in remote mountainous valleys of China—has made its horticultural debut with no less attention than that paid a Barbra Streisand concert. And unlike many rarities that remain established only in the gardens of the rich and selfish, this plant is destined to become mainstreamed into American borders. Six years after I received my first fibrous-rooted blue *Corydalis*, I am as enamored with its performance as those who collected it are proud of its stalk and capture.

In 1985, Ruben Hatch of Vancouver, Washington, collected a scaly-stemmed species of blue-flowered *Corydalis* in the Wenchuan Wolong Nature Reserve of Sichuan Province. He later dubbed the plant *Corydalis* 'Blue Panda' (for reasons discussed below, 'Blue Panda' has not been assigned to a distinct species), and Ruben began propagating and distributing it over the next five years, but the demand was ridiculously high and the supply exasperatingly low. When I visited the panda reserve in Wolong in 1996, I too found this species quite common in extremely wet sites, often growing in wet seeps and heavily eroded soils. My collection, *Corydalis* sp. DJHC 625, has blossomed with lovely purple-blue flowers atop blue-green foliage, though it does not possess the same icy blue flowers of the former.

I purchased 25 plants of 'Blue Panda' in the early spring of 1992 for a princely sum, and I planted more than half of them into my garden in well-amended soil in partial shade. Within weeks the plants had established and were burgeoning in growth, making sizable clumps of very pretty, finely dissected, delicate foliage. By the middle of March, each clump was sporting hundreds of tubular, spurred flowers of electric blue on stems to 15 in. (38 cm), the blossoms offering a delicate but substantial fragrance. And the effects continued. With the increasing heat of summer, by late July the plants faltered, and I thought the show had come to a close. I sheared each plant back to the base, hoping to achieve a tidier clump of foliage to enjoy for the remaining season. Within a matter of weeks, however, the plants were back in high gear with obvious intentions to continue the floral performance. And this they did until the first hard frosts of mid-November.

Whereas some may subscribe to the notion that such an electrifying blue is a bit weighty, there is no denying that it is unrivaled by any other plant currently grown in temperate gardens. 'Blue Panda' grows in several areas of our garden and creates superb compositions. Its flowering stems rake through the golden fluid strands of *Hakonechloa macra* 'Aureola', providing a richness in contrast not exceeded by any other pair of plants in the garden. Complementing pinks must be of equal value in order to contend with the intensity of blue in the *Corydalis*. I initially tried combining 'Blue Panda' with *Diascia* 'Salmon Supreme' near a deck planting on the east side of the house, but the typical richness of the *Diascia* was deflated when planted in tandem. Later, a more successful duo performance was orchestrated with the more concentrated pink of *Diascia* 'Ruby Field' and the bronze erect strands of *Carex buchananii*.

Three years after Ruben Hatch visited the Wenchuan Wolong Nature Reserve, James Compton, John Darcy, and Martyn Rix introduced into England collections of *Corydalis flexuosa* from the Wolong and Baoxing valleys in western Sichuan. Because the native populations of this species show remarkable variety of intensity and hue in flower, each of the introduced clones was given a name: *C. flexuosa* 'Père David', *C. flexuosa* 'China Blue', and *C. flexuosa* 'Purple Leaf'.

'Père David' has long-lasting, rich blue flowers, with just the slightest dash of purple thrown in. The flowering stems grow to 12 in. (30 cm) from a ferny colony of green foliage. In our light woodland, it grows with *Astrantia major* 'Buckland', the purple tones of the *Corydalis* amplifying the slight pinkish cast of the *Astrantia*. Rising above are the stems of *Lathyrus venetus*, a clumping sweet pea with rich cerise flowers that fade to blue as they age, making an effective combination.

Corydalis flexuosa 'China Blue' has fragrant, light (nearly white) blue flowers and bright green foliage. At Heronswood, 'China Blue' offers its ethereal flowers

Corydalis flexuosa 'Père David' (Photo by Lynne Harrison)

Corydalis flexuosa 'China Blue', growing at Heronswood with *Primula japonica* (Photo by Lynne Harrison)

for a long period in early spring to early summer in a rather moist area of the bright woodland. Here its wiry stems gather about the stems of *Primula japonica*, whose 3-ft. (0.9-m) candelabras of magenta flowers rise stiffly above. The superlative powdery blue flowers of this *Corydalis* selection add a complementary and long-lasting foil to the scene. Unfortunately, 'China Blue' has been the weakest form in constitution in my garden, but for reasons that may be due more to the cultivator than the cultivated.

Corydalis flexuosa 'Purple Leaf' emerges in early spring with each leaf deeply blotched with black-purple in remarkable complement to the vivid purple-blue flowers. In a less-than-subtle combination, I have interplanted this among the gleaming golden foliage of *Aquilegia vulgaris* 'Variegata', a white-flowered selection that I grow only for its brilliant golden-mottled foliage. In midseason, when I rejuvenate the *Corydalis* by cutting it to the ground, I do the same to the columbine, prompting an encore duet for the remaining months of the summer garden. 'Purple Leaf' also serves to provide an effective foil for the lime-colored flowers of *Helleborus viridis* in January and February.

Though the Compton, Darcy, and Rix collections appear superficially quite similar to *Corydalis* 'Blue Panda' in foliage and flower, the dissimilarities may

Corydalis flexuosa 'Purple Leaf' (Photo by Lynne Harrison)

prove that more than one species is at play. The three named clones of *Corydalis flexuosa* are all stoloniferous, which adds to their overall marketability. A single plant of 'Purple Leaf' or 'Père David', if given adequate moisture and fertility during the growing season, will cover 1½ sq. ft. (1400 cm²). *Corydalis* 'Blue Panda' is clumping and does not travel. Additionally, the flowering sequence of the verified *C. flexuosa* clones is by far earlier and shorter. My clones of *C. flexuosa* first begin showing flowers by late February, whereas 'Blue Panda' is not in blossom until late March. Numerous new cultivars of this species are popping up in commerce in England, some with flower colors distinct enough to justify their naming. Christopher Grey-Wilson recently introduced 'Balang Mist', which has very pale flowers and glossy pewter foliage. I am currently evaluating a clone that I brought back from England under the name of *C. flexuosa* 'Nightshade', and I find it to be quite remarkable. The spurred flowers possess two distinct shades—mauve and a rather iridescent purple—and together provide a striking effect for a long period of time. With this said, I suspect that over time the original clones of *C. flexuosa* currently in general cultivation will be lost due to self-sown seedlings establishing within propagating stock. These will ultimately dilute the clonal material to a somewhat indistinguishable, but still remarkable, selection of plants.

A spectacular species closely allied to *Corydalis flexuosa* is known as *C. elata*, which also hails from China. Robust clumps of bright green foliage emerge in early spring, providing an excellent background for the indigo-blue flowers that are produced throughout June along stems to 2 ft. (0.6 m). Like *C. flexuosa*, this is a nonbulbous species and quickly establishes in somewhat moist soils, better if amended with organic matter. *Corydalis elata* grows on the north side of our home adjacent to and superbly paired with the golden evergreen foliage of *Lonicera nitida* 'Baggesen's Gold'.

Hardiness: Most of the *Corydalis* species mentioned are hardy in zones 4–9, although summer heat will more than likely be their demise. The genus has been successfully grown in the grueling climate of Colorado as well as in partial shade in the frigid areas of New England. Initial reports from the eastern seaboard indicate that the plants may be early blossoming there, with a temporary retreat in the heat of summer. If you are able to grow the more common *Corydalis lutea* or *C. ochroleuca*, you probably will also be able to cultivate the blue species discussed, though auspicious siting may be the ultimate key.

Cultivation: Generally, the fibrous-rooted *Corydalis* species are tolerant of full sun or partial shade and, as one would expect, are less lanky when grown under brighter conditions. Temporary drought conditions will not kill the plants, but they will begin to slip into dormancy if allowed to dry out. A spring and midsummer application of a well-balanced fertilizer adds flowering stamina to the plants. In our garden, we shear the blue-flowered species to the ground after initial flowering has ceased, encouraging a reflush of foliage and flower while preventing an overabundance of self-sown seedlings.

The bulbous species appreciate well-drained soils in full sun or partial shade with adequate spring moisture. These slip into complete dormancy by late spring and tolerate summer drought.

Propagation: The nonbulbous, scaly-stemmed blue species have proven to be exceptionally unchallenging. At Heronswood, we have discovered the importance of removing all debris from the potting table after dividing *Corydalis* in late summer: hundreds of our trees, shrubs, and vines growing in pots now share their digs with strong growing *Corydalis* plants, the result of minute stem scales that have contaminated the potting soil.

The bulbous species are certainly more challenging in regard to propagation. They do produce bulb offsets on a yearly basis, and these can be removed and replanted at any time, though propagation is most successful once the plants begin to slip into dormancy in early summer.

Propagation by seed for most *Corydalis* species is more a matter of prevention than skill. If seed is required, as can be the case in some rarer species, care must be taken to harvest the pods as they approach maturity, or secure a cloth bag around the stems bearing the seed capsules and collect after dispersal. The small, shiny black seed, which has a high-protein membrane to encourage "takeout" by ants, is dispersed quickly and without warning. We raise *Corydalis paczoskii* and *C. decipiens* from seed and find that it is best to leave the seedlings undisturbed in their seed pots for three years before transplanting.

CHAPTER 8

Woodland Poppies

Few plant names are more evocative than "poppy." The name brings forth first and foremost—especially for those of us who were raised with a yearly dose of the adventures of Dorothy, her clutch of comrades, and Toto, too—the image of wide-open and sunny meadows of sleepy, pastel flowers. Those who were exposed as children to even the most superficial attempt at gardening add the ephemeral orange goblets of the oriental poppy (*Papaver orientale*) to those associations. The oriental poppy was the one perennial that I can remember as a child returning every May, emerging from a weedy patch of an attempted garden by my mother, a mother of four, which needs no further explanation.

Hidden, however, from an unfortunate majority of gardeners and would-be gardeners is a fascinating world of hinterland poppies that thrive under cool, moist, and shaded conditions. Among these are the most fabled and cosseted of all garden plants: the blue Himalayan poppies of the genus *Meconopsis*, which live above the clouds but translate well to a cool-climate garden with considerably more oxygen. Also not to be ignored are a gathering of less-celebrated relatives that, in foliage and flower, bring a lively congestion to the woodland throughout spring and most of summer.

Meconopsis

The royal clan of the family Papaveraceae is indeed the genus *Meconopsis*, which is primarily of Asiatic origin, though there is one New World representative, the annual *Meconopsis heterophyllum* (*Stylomecon heterophyllum*), as well as a western European member, *Meconopsis cambrica*, the well-known Welsh poppy. *Meconop-*

137

sis cambrica is cultivated in many forms, in its typical single yellow as well as single and double forms in shades of orange-red, which make exceedingly handsome additions to the wild border or cottage garden in full sun or partial shade in nearly any soil type.

To imply that *Meconopsis* is best suited to the woodland requires some creative footwork that allows me to cover all bases. I have observed many of the garden-worthy species of *Meconopsis* growing in their native haunts, most of which I would not consider remotely woodland-like, although I witnessed the lovely yellow-flowered monocarpic species, *Meconopsis integrifolia*, growing in a rather damp, shaded draw at 12,000 ft. (3600 m) in extreme northwestern Yunnan Province. The truly spectacular blue-flowered perennial species, *M. grandis* and *M. betonicifolia*, however, grow in their native Himalayas in a fully exposed, rocky habitat in well-drained soils with adequate subsurface moisture.

At high elevations of eastern Nepal, lusty perennial mounds of *Meconopsis grandis* grew with stems rising to 3 ft. (0.9 m), each capped by a single ovary brimming in seed. My seed collections of this Himalayan species blossomed at Heronswood for the first time in the spring of 1998, offering enormous and exquisite flowers of purple-blue centered with a striking central boss of golden stamens. From this first experience in successfully bringing this species to blossom, I have come to the realization that it may be difficult to maintain long term in low-elevation gardens. Nearly half of the plants that blossomed expired shortly thereafter—not exactly a standing ovation for my efforts in coddling them.

In a garden setting, however, I have had a much different experience with

Meconopsis ×sheldonii (Photo by Lynne Harrison)

Meconopsis betonicifolia and *M. ×sheldonii*, a spectacular hybrid of *M. grandis* and *M. betonicifolia*. (Within this hybrid, the seedling strain "Ryovan," developed in Scotland, stands apart as the largest, most luscious, and certainly most carefree.) In the beginning days of my garden, *M. betonicifolia* contentedly self sowed in a well-drained, acidic bed on the eastern side of a shed in our back garden, where the plants received supplemental water throughout the growing season and a half day of full sun. This population was lost during a summer of extreme heat, and I retreated to our woodland with their progeny that I had raised from seed.

I have now planted a substantial colony of both *Meconopsis betonicifolia* and the *M. ×sheldonii* Ryovan Group in a moist and rich woodland border. There they perform quite well indeed, although there seems to be nothing, in truth, perennial about them at all, offering three or four years of an exceptional showing and then expiring; the hybrid has proven to be the longer living of the two. Undoubtedly, removing their inaugural attempt at flowering during the first spring will stave off a swift demise. This painful decapitation (painful, at least, for the decapitator) allows for sufficient basal growth to ultimately permit full flowering as well as to encourage survival for at least an additional year. During the blossoming period, offshoots for the following season's growth will already be visible at the base of the flowering stem—the equation is quite simple: lack of basal growth at time of flowering equals completed life cycle, and it's time to busy yourself collecting the seed when it ripens. This is exactly the approach that I take in my garden, setting out sufficient numbers each year to replace those that we assume will falter. In May to mid-June, these plants reward us with a scene that is unparalleled by any other perennial—like a flock of turquoise macaws sweeping into the landscape, bringing with them pieces of the sky to

Meconopsis betonicifolia alongside *Aruncus dioicus* in the woodland at Heronswood
(Photo by Lynne Harrison)

The lovely turquoise blossoms of *Meconopsis betonicifolia* (Photo by Lynne Harrison)

place among the garden, the silken buds opening in rich shades of lavender, fading quickly to ethereal blue.

Meconopsis paniculata and *M. napaulensis* are considered truly monocarpic, but as they often will not blossom for three or four years, I garner as much, if not more, effect from these species as I do from the perennial species. The *M. paniculata* and *M. napaulensis* thriving in our light woodland came from wild seed that I collected in 1995 along the Milke Danda and Jajale Himal, extended mountain ridges in Nepal, where mats of woolly, golden and silver, felted foliage intermingled among spent plants that had finished blossoming, rife with seed in many-flowered panicles to 6 ft. (1.8 m) or taller. One might think that because our stock is of varied wild-collected origin, we would know precisely what species we are dealing with, but in fact the nomenclature of the two species is muddled, and the confusion is made even worse by the fact that the species frequently interbreed even in nature, presenting diverse and multicolored hybrid swarms. It is as a superb folial groundcover, however, that I most wish to use these plants. When the evergreen rosettes are lit by the low-angled rays of winter sun in our light woodland, no plant shines as brilliantly. *Meconopsis napaulensis*, with felted platinum rosettes to 1 ft. (0.3 m) across, ultimately produces blue flowers along 4- to 6-ft. (1.2- to 1.8-m) stems in three to six years, whereas *M. paniculata* blos-

The golden-haired foliage of *Meconopsis paniculata*, growing in eastern Nepal (Photo by Daniel J. Hinkley)

Meconopsis paniculata in flower (Photo by Lynne Harrison)

soms somewhat sooner, with flowers produced from striking gilded mounds along 4-ft. (1.2-m) stems in two to four years' time. The flowers of the latter species can range from yellow to red to blue. Though these species grow at moderate elevations in the Himalayas, they successfully make the transition to garden use throughout cool summer areas of North America.

Another Chinese species perhaps most resembles *Meconopsis cambrica* in blossom, although the flowers are larger, more richly hued, and produced much later in the season. *Meconopsis chelidoniifolia* possesses the deeply lobed foliage reminiscent of the greater celandine (*Chelidonium majus*), but the similarities stop there. The stems of *M. chelidoniifolia* cagily rake through the stems of small trees and shrubs in our rather dark woodland, illuminating the branches with the enlightening qualities of its yellow flowers in July and August, just when the woodland sorely desires more floral companionship. After flowering, small plantlets form at the tips of the branches at the leaf-stem juncture. As these will ultimately fall to the ground and grow, we are presented with an easy and ideal method of propagating the plants, free from the uncertainty of sowing seed.

I collected seed of *Meconopsis prattii* in 1996 in its native Yunnan Province, where it grows in areas that represent the antithesis of what most would consider good *Meconopsis* territory. Amidst rocks and baking slopes, the remains of this somewhat monocarpic species were offering copious quantities of seed. Two years later, these collections blossomed for me in cultivation, creating spiny foliaged rosettes from which emerge elegant 2-ft. (0.6-m) spikes of rich blue flowers. These spikes are determinate in nature: the terminal flowers are presented first, followed by flowers lower on the stem, and finally, nearly two months later, result in blossoms directly at the soil surface. With such an enormously long season of flowering, any concerns regarding its short-lived nature are dismissed; I am committed to continuing to collect seed of this species and include it in a full-sun, droughty area of the garden, amidst a small colony of *Helleborus* ×*sternii*.

Hardiness: Cool summer climates only in zones 3–8. The best garden specimens of *Meconopsis betonicifolia* and *M.* ×*sheldonii* that I have ever seen were in collections in Anchorage, Alaska, and the surrounding areas.

Cultivation: As noted for individual species. On most non-monocarpic *Meconopsis* species, one can easily observe the following year's growth at the base of the flowering stem. To encourage these buds to develop fully, one should block the first attempt at flowering as soon as the buds appear. This will allow for development of the dormant buds, effectively transforming a notoriously short-lived species into a longer lived perennial. Simply removing the flowering stems as soon as they appear has proven to be more effective in making the plants quasi-perennial than the perfect soil medium, moisture, pH, or light exposure.

Propagation: Propagation of *Meconopsis* may be performed by division in early spring, though seed is the best bet. Successful germination of *Meconopsis* seed first and foremost depends upon its freshness when sown; many a gardener has ordered seed through catalogs and seed exchanges only to be crestfallen when nothing ultimately emerges. We sow our seed at Heronswood in large flats,

Meconopsis chelidoniifolia (Photo by Lynne Harrison)

Meconopsis prattii flowers (Photo by Lynne Harrison)

generally on the day that we harvest the seed in midsummer, and will have full germination in the flats the following spring, after exposure to the rigors of winter weather. The seedlings are pricked out and transplanted when sufficiently large to handle the shock of transplanting, and they are treated with sufficient water and food during the first growing season. By autumn, a large crown develops on the seedlings, and at this stage they should be set out into the garden.

"Poppies, My Lovely, Poppies"

Eastern North America holds its own in hosting a large number of species from the poppy family that are either counterparts to the Asian flora or are singular to this continent. *Stylophorum diphyllum* occurs in partially shaded sites from western Pennsylvania south to Tennessee and west to Missouri. The deeply lobed, somewhat felted leaves to 8 in. (20 cm) in length form distinctive mounds, from which are produced a long succession of bright yellow, four-petaled poppies throughout spring and into early summer. The fruit that follows grabs at least as much interest as the flowers, with quantities of silvery haired, ovoid capsules held on nodding stems above the foliage. Though its leaves are much less deeply lobed, the Chinese counterpart, *S. lasiocarpum*, can be easily distinguished from the American species by its narrow, long fruit held stiffly upright following a long display of bright orange-yellow flowers. The root of *S. lasiocarpum* possesses a red juice that is used medicinally in China, which brings to mind a monospecific genus in Papaveraceae found only on the North American continent—*Sanguinaria*, the bloodroot. Both *Stylophorum* species are exceedingly useful throughout the summer for effects of flower as well as fruit, and they take the hardships of summer drought in stride once fully established. They are hardy to at least zone 4 and are easily propagated by seed. Some consider the American species to be overly exuberant in self sowing, though this has not been a problem in my garden.

The bloodroot, *Sanguinaria canadensis*, is a distinctive spring ephemeral that I would come upon as a child while chasing morel mushrooms in late spring in the deciduous woodlands of northern Michigan. The foliage of *Sanguinaria* emerges from the ground in pairs, like unopened wings of a luna moth, or a pair of frail, folded hands clutching a precious, single white flower. The flowers rise to 6 in. (15 cm) above the foliage. We learned as children that the root of this species would paint our hands and faces with a red stain—just as it did the faces of warring or celebrating aboriginal tribesmen that inhabited the eastern half of the continent. The native peoples also used bloodroot for a host of medicinal purposes, uses that were adopted by European settlers arriving on the scene. *San-*

Stylophorum diphyllum (Photo by Lynne Harrison)

Stylophorum diphyllum flower (Photo by Lynne Harrison)

Stylophorum lasiocarpum (Photo by Lynne Harrison)

guinaria canadensis 'Multiplex' is a somewhat more garden-worthy form, as it possesses fully double, though equally short-lived flowers, while the rarely encountered *S. canadensis* 'Peter Harrison' is a pink-flowered compeer. The species as well as its two cultivars are simply too ephemeral in flower to be considered top-notch woodland components for floral effects; though, to be sure, a certain sorrowful charm is evoked when one comes across the remaining shards of shattered flowers, with petals in ethereal white scattered across the forest floor, seemingly only hours after they first unfurled. The rounded, lobed leaves are reason enough to include bloodroot in our gardens; they expand ultimately to 8 in. (20 cm) across and are produced atop ever-increasing colonies of rhizomes. *Sanguinaria* is hardy in zones 4–9.

Closely allied to *Sanguinaria*, the snow poppy (*Eomecon chionantha*) from eastern China has similarly shaped, succulent, somewhat waxy foliage that arises from vigorously spreading rhizomes, which also possess a reddish orange sap. The pure white flowers, centered with a bundle of golden-yellow stamens, are borne sporadically from May through July on 15-in. (38-cm) branched pani-

Sanguinaria canadensis (Photo by Lynne Harrison)

Sanguinaria canadensis 'Multiplex' (Photo by Lynne Harrison)

cles. If given a rich and moist area in shade or partial shade, *Eomecon chionantha* displays an ebullient spreading habit that can delight or disgruntle the gardener, depending on how much influence of the gardening hand is desired for the space allotted. Add to this the plant's propensity to stow away, in the form of tiny bits of rhizome hidden among the roots of transplanted shrubs or perennials, and the introduction of this species into any garden should be given serious forethought. Though I have been spellbound by the snow poppy's stunning foliage effects when piercing a stand of blue-flowered *Ajuga pyramidalis* in spring, I admittedly have mounted a stringent campaign of total eradication from my garden. The eminently multitalented *Eomecon* currently has the upper hand. It will survive zones 6–9.

Eomecon chionantha, the snow poppy (Photo by Lynne Harrison)

Hylomecon japonicum, from the mountains of Japan, Korea, and northeastern China, is far and away a more polite species, mimicking an elegant golden poppy held above low stands of distinctive pinnate foliage. Blossoming in April to early June, it will make a sizable colony in rich, shaded soils, and it seems quite content to do so in a manner that allows for ease in editing the quantity when necessary. A second species in this genus, *H. vernalis* from eastern Siberia, reportedly exists, but I have not encountered it in the wild or under cultivation. *Hylomecon* is hardy in zones 5–9.

Pteridophyllum racemosum comes from the shaded woodlands of Honshu and Hokkaido in Japan, where it produces low, spreading colonies of ferny leaves that from a distance appear much like the foliage of the dwarf deer fern (*Blechnum penna-marina*). That it is a higher plant is made apparent in early spring, when racemes of charming white, four-petaled bells rise on erect racemes to 15 in. (38 cm) above the foliage. Its scarcity in gar-

Hylomecon japonicum (Photo by Lynne Harrison)

Pteridophyllum racemosum (Photo by Lynne Harrison)

dens of the United States has not permitted the gathering of sufficient data regarding its cultural needs, though it is apparently quite happy in our semishaded woodland in well-drained, but moist, humus-rich soils. Propagation is easily performed by division in late winter or early spring, just as the new growth is appearing.

Chelidonium majus is a widespread herbaceous species extending from Europe eastward into Asia, where the spectral continuum transforms to the recognized variety of the Far East, *C. majus* var. *asiatica*. Generally considered quite weedy, the greater celandine, as *C. majus* is commonly known, offers a double-flowered form that is charming in our woodland, presenting airy sprays of small, perfectly double, yellow poppies throughout most of the summer above 20-in. (50-cm) leafy mounds of finely dissected pinnate foliage. *Chelidonium majus* 'Flore Pleno' will self sow with abandon if provided the opportunity and will come mostly true from seed, though excess seedlings can be removed with ease if the task is performed while they are small. Hardy in zones 6–10.

Hardiness: As noted for individual species.

Cultivation: As noted for individual species.

Propagation: As noted for individual species.

The flowers of *Pteridophyllum racemosum* (Photo by Lynne Harrison)

Chelidonium majus 'Flore Pleno' (Photo by Lynne Harrison)

CHAPTER 9

Rheums with a View:
The Ornamental Rhubarbs

Few gardeners who have cultivated the edible rhubarb (*Rheum ×cultorum*) can deny that they have admired the columns of white flowers unfurling in globular splendor in early summer. But homage to such things in the vegetable garden is generally bittersweet, often but a swan song of yet another spring gone by—the end to a season of freshly picked and eaten produce. As a young gardener, in fact, I was taught to never let the blossoming stems emerge from our rather antique hand-me-down clump of "pie plant" that we grew on the far side of the vegetable patch. Advice well taken but, fortunately, not always heeded.

My admiration for these curious, brawny flowering stems ultimately led me to examine the rhubarb genus in greater detail. There I found a wealth of species and hybrids that convey polished effect to the garden, rather than simple harvest to the kitchen. It can be assumed, however, that the rhubarbs bred for succulent, flavorful leaf stems will bring supremely more ornament to the garden than the ornamental species will bring pleasure to the dining table.

I only recently began growing true *Rheum palmatum*, a species native to China and, in its typical white-flowered form, infrequently cultivated. Having brought this back from a collecting foray to England, I use the plant to good effect in my light woodland, where it produces gigantic, *Gunnera*-like foliage in matte green and erect flowering panicles of white rising to 6 ft. (1.8 m) or higher. Certainly the best-known of the ornamental rhubarbs is this species's red-flowered cultivar, *R. palmatum* 'Atrosanguineum'. With a flair for the dramatic, 'Atrosanguineum' awakens in early spring with ruby-red foliage, which conjures nothing short of pure, unadulterated anticipation for what is to come. As the jagged leaves unfurl to nearly 3 ft. (0.9 m) across, the reddish tints of the upper surfaces take on a patina of aged copper, while the undersurfaces retain an intensity of

Rheum palmatum 'Atrosanguineum' (Photo by Daniel J. Hinkley)

matte rose-red. I am held spellbound in the early days of May when the fresh, up-wardly held leaves, backlit by sun, capture and illuminate a palette of arresting colors and textures. Yet the show has only just begun, as in early June a massive flowering stem heads skyward, carrying large, knobby buds sheathed with scarlet bracts. After the stems reach upward to 7 ft. (2.1 m), the buds unfurl to create an airy spectacle of crimson flowers with cerise overtones. If good seed set occurs, an additional season of interest continues with numerous glossy red, triangular fruit dangling from this treelike inflorescence. Several other selected cultivars of *R. palmatum* are available, including 'Red Herald' and 'Hadspen Crimson' (both by Eric Smith) and 'Red Select'. I should mention that the distinctive foliage shape and color is more a product of patience than of simply acquiring a good clone. Foliage on young plants is less lobed and less colorful than on mature specimens.

Though I am a proponent of using such bold-foliaged plants to interrupt the monotony of more delicately clad perennials, the mammoth proportions offered by *Rheum palmatum* are difficult to incorporate into small-scale landscapes. Fortunately, numerous other species and hybrids lend folial contrast in an altogether more diminutive format. *Rheum australe* emerges in early spring with handsome tawny-pink, rounded leaves that ultimately expand to 1 ft. (0.3 m) or more across while darkening to rich green. From this tidy, low mound of foliage, flowers of creamy white are produced in early summer along a flowering stem to 4 ft. (1.2 m). Native to the Himalayas, *R. australe* grows in my garden adjacent to *Hebe anomala*, which possesses needley evergreen foliage in tones of purplish green, adding textural relief as well as colorful complement to the rhubarb.

In the autumn of 1995, long after my fondness for this genus had ripened to serious infatuation, I found myself among four friends and twenty-four Sherpas traversing a remarkable high ridge in eastern Nepal known as the Jajale Himal. Here, high up in the thin-aired Himalayas, we found two species of rhubarb: one of them I already had in cultivation in my garden, but the other brought a new and unforgettable encounter. The former, *Rheum acuminatum*, is superbly worthy of cultivation for both foliage and flower. The 10-in. (25-cm), glistening green leaves are triangular in shape and have a heavily veined texture. The leaf undersurfaces have a purplish red hue and the petioles are bright cherry-red. In early summer, flowering stems to 3 ft. (0.9 m) carry sprightly panicles of rose-red flowers, followed by, in most years, good crops of red fruit. Though *R. acuminatum* grows naturally in fully exposed alpine meadows at elevations of nearly 12,000 ft. (3600 m), it has settled contentedly in my garden, growing in bright shade under a high overstory of Douglas firs. Sharing this portion of the garden with *Helle-*

Rheum australe (Photo by Lynne Harrison)

The highly textural, purple-backed foliage of *Rheum acuminatum* (Photo by Lynne Harrison)

borus, *Lathyrus vernus*, *Erythronium*, *Asarum*, and *Cyclamen*, the rhubarb alone carries this bed in early to midsummer.

The fabled Tibetan rhubarb, *Rheum nobile*, was the second of the two species that we encountered on Jajale Himal. I came across this fantastical, rather surreal plant growing in large numbers beside an alpine lake at 15,000 ft. (4500 m). Rigid, pyramidal flowering stems to 5 ft. (1.5 m) were cloaked from bottom to top with 10-in. (25-cm), translucent bracts in tones of creamy pink and amber, a remarkable scene reminiscent of a petrified army of curiously clad soldiers. Beneath the bracts, which provide protection from rain and frost alike, short panicles were crowded with seed—literally thousands of seeds on each stem. Storing food reserves over several years, this species will flower and set seed only once before dying. All the seed gathered from this Himalayan site successfully germinated within weeks after I brought it home, though I suspect that the chances of this high-altitude species blossoming under cultivation in the Pacific Northwest are slim at best. It may be more ideally suited to extremely cool and moist climates, such as Scotland or maritime Alaska. Nonetheless, my brief association with *R. nobile* in the wild will not soon be forgotten.

A related species that possesses similarly striking protective bracts along the flowering stems is much better suited to cultivation. *Rheum alexandrae*, from the

Rheum nobile in eastern Nepal, showing its immense, translucent bracts (Photo by Daniel J. Hinkley)

Tibetan Plateau and the mountains of western China, first blossomed in my garden in 1994. It is perfectly perennial, though I have found it to be somewhat biennial in flowering effect. The 2-ft. (0.6-m) flowering stems produced in early June carry a contingent of protective translucent bracts, which resemble creamy white hearts, along their entire length. Like those of *R. nobile*, the flowers of *R. alexandrae* are produced on short panicles hidden beneath. The very low clumps of distinctive lance-shaped, glossy green foliage grow to 10 in. (25 cm) in length. When I observed this species in the mountains of northwestern Yunnan Province in the autumn of 1996, it was growing along the edges of lakes and wet meadows at elevations of 10,000–14,000 ft. (3000–4200 m) in precisely those conditions that are recommended for successful cultivation in the garden: full sun and rich, extremely moist soil. Sizable colonies of the species were growing in near-stand-

Rheum alexandrae (Photo by Daniel J. Hinkley)

Rheum alexandrae in Yunnan Province, providing a late-season display of rich autumn color (Photo by Daniel J. Hinkley)

ing water and adjacent to vast, dreamy blue expanses of *Gentiana sino-ornata*, where the rhubarb's foliage was transformed to rich, glossy clarets and oranges in the crisp October air. Interestingly, in my garden, *R. alexandrae* has been most successful in quite opposite conditions. Having nearly lost this species several times in perpetually moist sites, I finally chanced a slightly raised island bed in full sun that receives supplemental irrigation during the summer. Here it has thrived and blossomed, though the autumn color does not develop to the intensity that I observed in the wilds of China.

Although more demure species exist, *Rheum kialense* is one of the tidiest of the rhubarbs that I cultivate. Ideally suited to the rock garden or near the front of the border in full sun, this endearing plant quickly forms dense, spreading mounds of small, rose-backed, 4-in. (10-cm) triangular leaves. In early summer, small flowers emerge in reddish tones in bud form, later fading to pink and then white as the flowers age. They are densely produced on willowy stems to 8 in. (20 cm) in height. *Rheum kialense* grows in my garden with *Veronica spicata* 'Red Fox' at the very front of a full-sun border, the more fully saturated red of the rhubarb complementing the softer hued veronica. This species is thought to be one of the parents of a hybrid rhubarb that is held in high esteem in our garden—in fact, the hybrid is among the best of any foliage plant ever used in our perennial borders. *Rheum* 'Ace of Hearts' produces substantial but manageable mounds of stiffly upright, heart-shaped foliage, exposing the muted red-burgundy undersurface. Some may say that we overuse 'Ace of Hearts' at Heronswood, as its strong folial presence is found in numerous compositions, but I offer no apologies. The flowers, produced on 5-ft. (1.5-m) branched panicles in midsummer, are a rather dingy white, though this is of no concern to me. Whether paired with the rich lavender spikes of *Salvia pratensis* or flanking the iridescent golden foliage of *Philadelphus coronarius* 'Aureus' in early spring, the contrasting or complementing abilities of 'Ace of Hearts' are too exceptional to be as underused in American horticulture as they are.

Another exceptional species in foliage and flower for the front of the border or as a bold yet diminutive addition to the rock garden is *Rheum persica*. The 10-in. (25-cm), rounded, leathery, and wrinkled leaves are produced in early spring and form a prostrate mound of highly ornamental foliage. A curiously short cluster (to a mere 6 in. [15 cm]) of brick-red buds arises from the center on 18-in. (45-cm) pedicels; the flowers quickly age from red to creamy yellow. It provides a distinctive if not somewhat alien effect to the full-sun, well-drained location where it thrives in our garden. *Rheum persica* anchors a rather droughty bed, which it shares with finely textured companions: *Diascia*, *Gaura*, and the demure, gray-foliaged, powder-blue-flowered *Veronica turrilliana*.

Rheum kialense (Photo by Lynne Harrison)

Rheum 'Ace of Hearts', displaying its remarkable burgundy leaf undersurface (Photo by Daniel J. Hinkley)

Rheum persica (Photo by Lynne Harrison)

I first observed the extremely dwarf rhubarb species known as *Rheum dela-vayi* growing at Savill Gardens in Windsor Great Park, and I immediately knew that I would someday add this species to my rhubarb collection. To my knowl-edge, it is the smallest of the lot, forming low, quickly spreading colonies of glossy green, ovate foliage to 2 in. (5 cm) in length and erect, dusty-pink flower spikes to 5 in. (12.5 cm) in late spring. My garden plant came from the Irish plantswoman Helen Dillon through Bleddyn Wynn-Jones of Wales. *Rheum dela-vayi* is not only scarce in cultivation, but it is equally shy in the literature; I can only assume that this species hails from western China, which is where Delavay primarily collected.

My association with these plants is through tradition, travel, and mostly, un-alloyed enjoyment in my garden. It is a relationship that is far from simple infat-uation or the vagaries of fashion. Culinarily and decoratively, rhubarbs will con-tinue to be a cherished component of Heronswood.

Hardiness: The majority of ornamental rhubarbs are considered hardy in zones 5–9, though their limited use in American gardens has not allowed for a finely tuned assessment of their true potential in gardens throughout the conti-nent. They enjoy the relative coolness of a northern climate and resent the warmth and humidity of the Southeast.

Cultivation: As with the edible rhubarbs in our vegetable gardens, the or-namental species require that somewhat mythical soil often referred to as "deep and rich." Though I find this cliché annoyingly over-applied, nothing could more aptly describe the conditions in which these plants best thrive. Amending a shallow soil with copious amounts of manure or humus will not do. One must excavate a sizable area to the depth of 3 ft. (0.9 m) (shallower for the smaller species) and fill with as much organic matter as possible. The resulting effects will be noticeable and long-lived. To produce such a sizable flowering stem on a yearly basis requires substantial amounts of food reserve as well as adequate moisture. If the plants become stressed from drought or lack of nutrients during the spring season, they will retreat to early dormancy, and the show will come to an early end.

With that said, it is important to understand that a contentedly grown plant will return for an extended encore, but a brief intermission must be expected. After the ordeal of such exuberant flowering, the foliage will show signs of post-mortem stress. Especially in areas that serve up late-spring assaults from hail storms, the once-ethereal folial scene can beg for a make-over. And that is precisely what we do to our rhubarbs at the end of June, removing the flowering stems and foliage alike while applying a handful of high-nitrogen fertilizer to each plant. Within days, the plants respond with new foliage and vigor that will extend until the first frosts. As a nurseryman, I must allow the seed on the flowering stem to fully ripen, but if one can live content without this need, it makes good sense to remove the flowering stem and foliage as soon as the flowers begin to fade.

Propagation: Propagation can be achieved both by division and by seed. The former can present some difficulty to the untrained hand, as the root structure is quite woody and difficult to interpret by the uninitiated. Simply look for dormant buds in early spring before growth resumes, and with a digging fork or sharp knife, remove a single bud with a substantial root piece. Replant at the same depth. Propagation by seed is difficult at best, not due to germination difficulty but to the promiscuous nature of different species planted near each other; seed will rarely come true. Each winged fruit is a single seed; seed should be sown immediately upon harvest, which should be carried out when it begins to fall from the flowering stems in midsummer. Germination is immediate, and no cold stratification is required. Seedlings should be left in their germination trays until the following spring, when they can be transplanted to the garden or containers.

CHAPTER 10

Cuckoo for Cardamine:
Cardamine, Pachyphragma, and *Wasabia*

The Brassicaceae embraces a wealth of horticultural subjects that are mainstays to our gardens and dinner tables alike. From kale and broccoli to sweet alyssum and wallflower, the members of the family are neatly bound together by an easily recognizable floral format: four petals. In fact, the former name of this group of plants was Cruciferae, with the rather apparent Latin root based on the four-parted cross. Of course, other floral characteristics are used to delineate membership to the clan, and the pungent foliage offered by many of the kin is often a useful tool in the field. (Once you master the smell of fresh broccoli, you are well on the way to being able to identify numerous taxa in this enormously odoriferous family.) Held within its ranks are a few highly refined yet underrated genera that deserve closer inspection for possible integration into our gardens. Without any intended disrespect to numerous branches of the family not herewith included, my objects of affection on the following pages are the genera *Cardamine, Pachyphragma,* and *Wasabia.*

Cardamine

The genus *Cardamine* is one I would consider a "tot." I learned this coinage while traveling with the well-known and superb plantswoman Helen Dillon of Dublin, Ireland. Although she does not necessarily consider this particular genus to be a tot—a term of endearment for any plant deserving of affection—without reservation, I do. Collectively known as the lady smocks or cuckoo flowers, the genus *Cardamine* contains a number of polite, highly refined but gutsy species as well as a branch of the clan that is generally not acknowledged by invitations to the family reunion.

If there were an award for a plant's procreational performance, *Cardamine oligosperma*, known commonly as shotweed or common cress, would have already beaten a garden path to the podium. Swollen and charged seed pods, sensitive to the touch, hurl their propagules a respectable distance from the parent. Had I previously been aware that my introduction to *Cardamine* was in spending endless hours weeding this aggressive species from my garden, I might have dismissed outright a worthy genus of little-known, undercultivated perennials. Sometimes it pays to ignore the nomenclature of a plant one is busy killing.

Perhaps the best-known of the lot is *Cardamine pratensis*, a common but cherished meadow wildflower of Europe and the British Isles. In early spring, a leafy rosette of fresh green pinnate foliage delivers many 15-in. (38-cm) tall, erect racemes of pink to lavender, four-petaled flowers. *Cardamine pratensis* thrives in any continually moist garden soil in partial shade or full sun and is effective if underplanted with the early spring blues of *Omphalodes verna* or *Lathyrus vernus* 'Caeruleus'. I delighted in seeing a lovely natural meadow of this cardamine in full blossom on a pristine spring day near Cologne, Germany, in 1997. I was there to observe a collection of hellebores developed by the late Helen Ballard of England, though I must profess that this vibrant meadow of native color created significant diversions from the matter at hand.

In my garden, I cultivate a few named clones of this species, including three that are fully double flowered. *Cardamine pratensis* 'William' possesses charming, long-lasting dark lavender "roses" with purple-tinged foliage, while *C. pratensis* 'Edith' produces short clusters of double white flowers. The more commonly available *C. pratensis* 'Flore Pleno', cultivated in gardens since the mid-1600s, encompasses many different but very acceptable double-flowered clones with a range of colors from white to rose to lavender. I was at one time duped into purchasing a curious clone known as *C. pratensis* 'Improperly Dressed'. With foliage identical to that of common cress (*C. oligosperma*), this cultivar bore flowers that lacked petals as well as any obvious reason to cultivate it. Interestingly, *C. pratensis* can reproduce vegetatively by producing plantlets at the ends of the leaves, especially when in contact with the moist soils in which it thrives. This not only aids in the propagation of named forms but also accounts for the reports of meadows throughout Europe bearing solid stands of double-flowered plants.

In earliest spring, when florets of hoarfrost are still counted among the blossoms of the garden, *Cardamine trifolia* comes into play with white flowers of simple and virginal elegance. The flowers are borne in March and April on 6-in.

Cardamine pratensis 'Flore Pleno' (Photo by Lynne Harrison)

(15-cm) stems that emerge from low, textural, and tidy mounds of somber green foliage. Slowly forming fastidiously neat clumps, *C. trifolia* is not nearly so dependent on the moister conditions that other cardamines prefer; in fact, this species is considered moderately drought tolerant. As an underplanting with *Rhododendron mucronulatum* 'Alba' in the partial shade of our woodland, *C. trifolia* creates a stark and crisp composition that thaws a gardening heart still frozen in dormancy. Long after flowering, indeed throughout the calendar, this evergreen species wins affection for its fortitude, feistiness, and simply good presence. I am continually amazed that it is not more eagerly sought and grown by keen gardeners of Europe and America alike.

Cardamine diphylla, which has been transferred by some taxonomists to the genus *Dentaria*, hails from the East Coast of the United States. Following the early spring blossoms of clean white on 5-in. (12.5-cm) stems, the entire plant disappears by midsummer, with the white, thick, and scaly rhizomes so characteristic of this genus snaking just below the ground surface. After the cool rains of autumn return, the handsome bronze-marbled foliage, composed of a trio of jagged-edged leaflets resembling those of *Pachysandra procumbens*, is renewed to lend substance to the winter garden. *Cardamine diphylla* prefers light woodland conditions and will persist longer into the season if the soil remains moist, yet it is content to rest during the long dry months of summer.

Cardamine trifolia (Photo by Lynne Harrison)

Another species from the eastern U.S., *Cardamine laciniata* is a demure and attractive woodlander that is representative of the paucity of native herbaceous perennials contained in the palette of the American horticulturist. Delicate, slightly nodding lavender to white bells rise above very pretty dissected leaves on 5-in. (12.5-cm) stems in midspring. This species too retreats for the summer months, but it does not reappear, at least not in our Pacific Northwest garden, to accompany the off-season landscape. As with all garden components that hurriedly depart in midseason, take care to mark their staked claims so as not to disturb them while in their dormancy.

Cardamine bulbifera is a taller species, with distinctive whorls of leaves atop 2-ft. (0.6-m) stems. It is native from southern Scotland to France, Iran, and central Russia, where it is dependent on rich, moist soils. The foliage is often dark purple upon emergence, fading to light green as each stem is crowned by heads of soft pink flowers, shyly nodding downward. Unlike other members of the genus, *C. bulbifera* forms bulbils in its leaf axils, making propagation as well as colonization in the garden quite effortless. Caution should be taken when introducing it into your garden, yet I wouldn't be without this species in ours. It is a lovely, albeit prominent, component of the early spring border, matching nicely with unfurling heads of *Muscari latifolium* with which it congregates.

Cardamine waldsteinii is a new addition to the garden and one of many species of this genus that are native to eastern Europe. I was drawn to it immediately in flower, when large blossoms of distilled white are held slightly above handsome 4-in. (10-cm) stands of green foliage. The species spreads over time to form large colonies in well-drained, moisture-retentive soils; at Heronswood, it thrives in the partial shade and rich, humusy soil of our light woodland, making a colony of extraordinary appearance when in flower. Though it departs in winter, *C. waldsteinii* is an ideal companion to *Cyclamen hederifolium* and *Cyclamen coum*, which fill the void with foliage and flower during the cardamine's off-season.

In the autumn of 1995, while trekking in eastern Nepal along the Milke Danda and Jajale Himal, I saw the dying stems of *Cardamine macrophylla* in rich, perennially moist soils. I had already planted this species in my garden, but I sited it in what is now obviously too dry a setting. Its large, bright green, frond-like compound foliage emerges in midspring along 18-in. (45-cm) stems to form a large rosette from which flowering stems grow to 2 ft. (0.6 m) or more. Capped by clusters of fragrant pink flowers in June, *C. macrophylla* will begin an odyssey toward early dormancy if allowed to dry out. Later, in China, I observed this species growing in the perpetually moist soils near Tianchi Lake in Yunnan Province, at an elevation of 12,000 ft. (3600 m).

In contrast, *Cardamine raphanifolia*, a native of southern Europe to Greece and Turkey, remains evergreen throughout the year at Heronswood. Possessing glossy green, pinnate leaves composed of distinctive rounded leaflets, this species will form a large colony if provided a rich, moisture-retentive soil in shade or partial shade alike; in fact, it will thrive in the standing water of a slow creek or seasonal pond. For many weeks in mid- to late spring, clusters of rich pink flowers are held slightly above the foliage on flowering stems to 10 in. (25 cm). In our garden, *C. raphanifolia* is sited with *Polygonatum verticillatum*, *Arisaema thunbergii* var. *urashima*, and a pink-flowered form of *Sanguinaria canadensis*—none of which are thought of as mired minions—and the cardamine thrives in this well-drained site to punctuated perfection. It carries this part of the garden through the off-season with its handsome winter foliage long after its companions have retreated to below the ground surface for the year.

In contention for my *Cardamine* of choice are three eastern European species, each offering handsome foliage in addition to the grandest flowers of the genus: *Cardamine enneaphyllos*, *C. heptaphylla*, and *C. pentaphyllos*.

From Yugoslavia, *Cardamine enneaphyllos* is perhaps the most beautiful of all species that I currently grow. It bears stems and foliage that come forth ruby-red in early spring and later fade to dark green. Large clusters of nodding ivory bells open from fairly saturated yellow buds while the plants still possess their spring

Cardamine waldsteinii (Photo by Lynne Harrison)

Cardamine macrophylla (Photo by Lynne Harrison)

Cardamine raphanifolia (Photo by Lynne Harrison)

finery, making for a superlative union of flower and foliage. Slowly increasing to form sizable colonies in winter-moist, humus-rich soils, this species provides a prideful early addition to the woodland, and it often stumps even the best of visiting plantspeople in its identity.

Cardamine heptaphylla has large pinnate leaves reminiscent of those of a small and finely cloaked hellebore. Large, lilac-white, four-petaled flowers with a satiny texture emerge on stiffly upright, 18-in. (20-cm) stems in early March. Equally bold in foliage, yet with a somewhat more refined mettle, *C. pentaphyllos* has politely nodding flowers in tones of smoky pink that emerge in late winter. Both species are from summer-moist sites in the mountains of southern Europe, and they require similar conditions of humusy, well-drained but perennially moist soils in partial shade. Plants will go dormant early in the season while tolerating the resultant dry soils in early summer. I have interplanted these two species with *Helleborus* ×*nigercors* and *H. torquatus* in my garden, as they pursue the rich theme of the hellebores just as the latter's flower structures lose their effectiveness.

Cardamine enneaphyllos (Photo by Lynne Harrison)

Cardamine heptaphylla (Photo by Lynne Harrison)

Cardamine pentaphyllos (Photo by Lynne Harrison)

Additional species of *Cardamine* are suitable for the garden, but my experience with them is unfortunately too short to provide comment of any merit. These hardy, little-known perennial plants are currently more widely grown in European gardens than in North America. *Cardamine microphylla*, *C. quinquefolia*, and *C. kitaibelii* are all available from time to time through specialty nurseries of the U.K., and they are certainly worth a go for gardeners wanting to explore the breadth of ornament this genus can provide. Other than those few species, the lesser-known cardamines are difficult to find in commerce, though seed may be found through plant society seed exchanges. It is my feeling, however, that any good garden plant eventually will be discovered by a larger gardening audience—and this genus is undoubtedly waiting its turn.

Hardiness: Most of the species discussed are more than likely perfectly hardy in zones 4–10, though there is scant reference to successful, or otherwise, cultivation in colder climates. If uncertain, mulch heavily in late autumn.

Cultivation: Best in light shade in humus-rich, somewhat moist soils, especially in late winter and early spring. The deciduous species often falter and go completely dormant if allowed to dry out during the summer. The evergreen species should be given supplemental water during the growing season.

Propagation: Division is quite easy in late winter. The rhizome, characteristic for many of the deciduous species, is a length of tissue consisting of thick, fleshy, leaflike scales. Each scale has at its base a dormant bud that will ultimately produce a new stem if severed and replanted. It thus becomes quite easy to chop the rhizomes into numerous small pieces, less than 1 in. (2.5 cm) in length, to produce new plants. The fibrous-rooted species, such as *Cardamine pratensis* and *C. trifolia*, are easily divided in early spring; *C. pratensis* will produce plantlets at the tips of its leaves if allowed to come into contact with the soil surface, allowing for easy propagation of the double-flowered forms of this species.

Pachyphragma

Very closely allied to the genus *Cardamine*, within which it was once included, *Pachyphragma* is a monotypic genus with its only species, *P. macrophylla*, occurring naturally in the Caucasus and northeastern Turkey. I first encountered this durable perennial in the garden of Rosemary Verey at Barnsley House in Eng-

Pachyphragma macrophylla (Photo by Lynne Harrison)

land. She had used it brilliantly as a fresh and vibrant groundcover beneath a specimen of *Viburnum henryi*, whose dark, leathery foliage was in striking contrast to the bright green mounds of foliage and ethereally white flowers produced atop 15- to 18-in. (38- to 45-cm) stems. At Heronswood I planted divisions brought back from Barnsley, and this charming plant has proven itself to be durable and extremely adaptive. It is in full blossom in early to late spring, during the high season of hellebores, harmonizing well with the darker flowered forms. Unlike numerous perennials that initially delight and then proceed to swamp the garden in overexuberant growth, *P. macrophylla* slowly, decidedly, gracefully makes a better showing year after year. Though it has already earned a loyal following in Europe, it deserves much greater use across the United States.

Hardiness: Zones 5–9.

Cultivation: As for *Cardamine*, in full sun or light shade in moist, humus-rich soil.

Propagation: Our single clone of *Pachyphragma macrophylla* sets very little seed, though we have found that late-spring cuttings root readily under mist. Division is an acceptable alternative, but very few divisions are provided per plant.

Wasabia

Anyone who has eaten sushi or sashimi and used the pungent, green, horse-radish-like substance to liven its raw flavors has formed a relationship with wasabi, though one probably based on its ability to rotoroot one's nasal passages if overconsumed. Similarly, my appreciation for the genus *Wasabia* has a greater history in its culinary aspects than in its ornamental involvement in my garden, though the latter is gaining momentum on a yearly basis. In the garden, clumps of fresh green, orbicular leaves to 6 in. (15 cm) across provide a superb foil to the bright white, four-petaled flowers that are formed along 10-in. (25-cm) stems. I collected *Wasabia japonica* from deep-shaded areas along streams on Shikoku Island in Japan, although the species is so often cultivated in that country that I am unsure as to whether these represented actual wild clones. The genus's two species occur in Japan (the other one being *W. tenuis*), and both have in the past been placed in the genus *Cardamine*.

Hardiness: As the range of *Wasabia japonica* extends along the entire Japanese Archipelago, from Kyushu to Sakhalin, I suspect that the species possesses

Wasabia japonica (Photo by Lynne Harrison)

a great deal of adaptability as far as cold tolerance, although it is thoroughly untested throughout much of the country.

Cultivation: In perpetually moist soils or shallow water, in shade.

Propagation: Dividing the thick rhizome in early spring is our preferred method of propagating, although it can also be accomplished with freshly sown seed.

CHAPTER 11

Triosteum

Rather than obscurity, rarity, or breathtaking beauty, the quality that I find most appealing in a plant is possession of a unique character—being that one species or genera that simply refuses to fit the mold. Countless times I have learned the characteristics that define a species, genus, or family not by examining the typical members, but instead through simple curiosity about an oddity that does not fit. A case in point is the rather bizarre herbaceous members of the Caprifoliaceae. The family comprises an enormous contingent of common landscape genera: *Abelia*, *Dipelta*, *Heptacodium*, *Kolkwitzia*, *Weigela*, and the vining and shrubby species of *Lonicera*. In the midst of a group so crowded with stardom, a little-known herbaceous genus has sat quietly and sadly unnoticed, until recently. The genus *Triosteum* contains three species, two of which are Asiatic and perhaps more deserving of cultivation.

Triosteum himalayanum produces upright stems to 2 ft. (0.6 m) that bear felted, lime-green foliage to 4 in. (10 cm) in length. Rather nondescript yellowish brown, tubular flowers emerge in terminal racemes in midsummer and result in clusters of large, glossy red fruit, which are retained until the early days of autumn. I first came to know this species through my great friend Gerald Straley, who was curator of collections and research scientist for the Botanical Garden at the University of British Columbia from 1982 to his untimely death in 1997. I later observed *T. himalayanum* firsthand growing in abundance at elevations above 10,000 ft. (3000 m) in the areas surrounding Zhongdian in northwestern Yunnan Province. It shared a similar habitat with *Podophyllum hexandrum*; in fact, in more than thirteen sites that I explored in this area, both species were present in equal numbers even though the overall terrain and vegetation differed significantly. I collected sufficient seed of *T. himalayanum* in China, and I look forward to comparing the resultant plants to the clones that I already possess.

Triosteum pinnatifidum, which I blindly grew from seed offered through the Kunming Botanical Garden in 1992, also hails from China, though the closest I came to encountering it in situ was as an herbarium specimen in a dimly lit museum at the Wenchuan Wolong Nature Reserve in Sichuan Province. It is supreme among the herbaceous plants that I grow for the effects of foliage. Large, jagged-lobed leaves to 8 in. (20 cm) in length are attached in pairs perfoliate to the 18-in. (45-cm) stem. The overall effect is not unlike that of *Hydrangea quercifolia*, though I am personally partial to the effects of the *Triosteum*. *Triosteum pinnatifidum* presents a fairly insignificant display of flowers in 5-in. (12.5-cm) terminal racemes in early summer, followed by large and handsome succulent fruit of white blushed with rosy pink on the sunny side. Its location in the Heronswood woodland has made that area a common destination for keen plantspeople who come for a romp about the garden.

Hardiness: Hardy to at least zone 5, or perhaps lower.

Cultivation: I cultivate *Triosteum himalayanum* as well as *T. pinnatifidum*, and both are exceptional plants for the woodland garden. They are seemingly more content in light shade and moist, humus-rich soils in my garden, though

Triosteum himalayanum (Photo by Daniel J. Hinkley)

Triosteum himalayanum in scarlet fruit (Photo by Daniel J. Hinkley)

Triosteum pinnatifidum (Photo by Lynne Harrison)

The handsome white-blushed-pink fruit of *Triosteum pinnatifidum*
(Photo by Lynne Harrison)

this is somewhat contrary to the conditions in which I found *T. himalayanum* growing in the wild.

Propagation: Accomplished either by seed or by cuttings in early spring before flower initiation occurs. Germination of seed, as with *Viburnum* and other members of the family, may take two years.

CHAPTER 12

The Herbaceous Aralias

Long after I had left the deciduous woods surrounding the family farm in north-central Michigan, I returned to find that, as a lad, I had explored an area that hosted two species of herbaceous aralia, *Aralia nudicaulis* and *A. racemosa*. (It is only possible to go home again when one rediscovers the surroundings that remained unfamiliar in youth.) I now grow both of these species in my woodland garden along with a collection of other herbaceous *Aralia* species that have made my acquaintance in lands far and near. I find all to be sensational, multiseasonal components of the garden, possessing a remarkable adaptability to soil conditions and light.

Unlike the woody members of the genus, the herbaceous species have unarmed stems, though they can be, in some instances, exuberantly stoloniferous. All species produce compound foliage with broad leaflets along stems rising to between 2 and 10 ft. (0.6–3 m) and panicles of compound flowers in tones of cream that result in purple or black fruit; associating these traits with the genus *Aralia* will put one firmly on the road to easy identification of the plants, whether in eastern or western North America as well as East Asia. Each area possesses species that vary slightly in appearance, but all species embrace a commonality of ornamental characteristics. Be aware that these are not "in-your-face" ornamental plants. This nonwoody portion of the genus brings to the garden a subtle and illustrative demeanor that is appreciated by those gardeners who have moved beyond the need for glaring grandiosity.

Aralia nudicaulis, referred to in the vernacular as wild sarsaparilla, is a rather modest plant that rises to less than 2 ft. (0.6 m) in height, and it occurs naturally from the eastern Canadian provinces south to Georgia and west to Colorado. The bipinnate leaves grow to 15 in. (38 cm) in length, and the inflorescence, a panicle composed of multiple umbels, is produced in late spring, later giving way to succulent, blackish purple fruit.

Another species hailing from the eastern coast of North America, *Aralia racemosa*, or life-of-man, is a remarkable and highly textural component of the light woodland. It extends naturally from New Brunswick south to Georgia and west to Utah and New Mexico. More rhizomatous in nature than the other species I have observed, *A. racemosa* makes a sizable colony over time. Herbaceous stems rise to a mere 2 ft. (0.6 m), sporting foliage with a decidedly more bronzy tint upon emergence, which is in lovely contrast to the panicles of creamy white flowers to 3 ft. (0.9 m) presented in June. The stems and foliage of *A. racemosa* have a long history of medicinal use by Native Americans.

Closer to home, *Aralia californica*, commonly called elk clover, is a northern Californian species that extends north to a botanically fantastic east-west blockade known as the Siskiyou Mountains in southern Oregon. I observed this species in its native haunts, growing in dark shade and running water with *Darmera peltata*. From collections made during that initial visit to the Siskiyous (with my close friend Gerald Straley), I have cultivated and appreciated *A. californica* for

numerous years, growing it next to a seasonal pond on our property. In soils that are saturated in winter and dusty dry in summer, this species takes the hardship in stride, rising to nearly 6 ft. (1.8 m) while presenting bright, cascading clusters of creamy white flowers in midsummer. Rich black-purple fruit held on pinkish pedicels form much later, as the foliage transforms to buttery yellow. Interestingly (and to be assigned to the "ones that got away" section of horticultural literature), among my original seed germinations of this species I was granted a lovely yellow-margined variegated mutant that I subsequently abused for several years before losing. It seems that in youth one is not remotely aware of either the rarity of such events or the finite seasons of one's life when such gifts are granted.

I first became familiar with *Aralia continentalis* in South Korea, though the range of this extremely hardy species extends as far north as Vladivostock. This is a superb species

Aralia californica flowers (Photo by Lynne Harrison)

that rises to 5 ft. by 5 ft. (1.5 by 1.5 m), bearing compound leaves to 4 ft. (1.2 m) in length and great pendulous panicles of flowers that droop gracefully downward. The flowers are creamy white, developing a pinkish blush as they age. The masses of purple fruit that follow offer no less exuberance than a massive bevy of ripe, albeit tiny, grapes. I marveled at the spectacular display of *A. continentalis* in the northern reaches of South Korea, where it grows commonly on forest margins in relatively moist but well-drained sites.

I observed and collected seed of *Aralia cordata* in Japan as well as on the island of Ullung-do off the eastern coast of South Korea, where numerous individuals exhibited jet-black stems, a trait that has remained on many of the subsequent seedlings raised at Heronswood. Though quite similar to *A. continentalis*, *A. cordata* is more stiffly upright in flower and fruit, if in the same size and format. The individual leaves of this species are decidedly more cordate (heart-shaped) than those of its continental counterpart—hence the name. In Japan, the shoots are blanched in early spring as they emerge and are considered a delicacy. Not surprisingly, *A. cordata* seems nearly irresistible to slugs in my garden, a propensity that I oddly have not observed with other species. Numerous species of birds that frequent my garden are attracted to the plant's stunning fruit.

Aralia cordata in fruit (Photo by Lynne Harrison)

It was at Knighthayes in England that I first admired the statuesque clumps of bronzy tripinnate foliage of *Aralia cachemirica* rising to nearly 10 ft. (3 m) in height on finely pubescent stems—although I have procured a mere 6 ft. (1.8 m) from this species in my own garden. A few years later, I encountered this species along a trail while dropping in elevation on the last days of our trek in eastern Nepal in 1995. The foliage was transformed to brilliant tints of red, and clusters of purple, succulent fruit hung in pendulous panicles. Disappointingly, my wild collections failed to establish in the garden, even though the species has thrived in a sunny, moist site in my garden for several years. My colony of seven individual clones exhibits great diversity of foliage tinting; several possess rich coppery tones when first emerging in spring, while others are nearly yellow-green. *Aralia cachemirica* is a distinctive and bold herbaceous perennial that deserves wider use in North American gardens.

Hardiness: With the exception of *Aralia cachemirica*, the herbaceous aralia species are hardy to at least zone 5, with *A. nudicaulis* and *A. racemosa* being even hardier; *A. cachemirica* is hardy only in zones 6–9.

Cultivation: Woodland conditions with rich, moist soils are seemingly best, though I have found a great deal of latitude in this regard, with nearly all species tolerating periodic dryness and full-sun conditions, at least in the Pacific Northwest. Protect plants from the sliming mollusks, especially upon emergence in early spring.

Propagation: Though division is certainly appropriate for the more rampant species—that is, *Aralia racemosa*—the other species are more clump forming in nature and do not offer themselves easily to this method. Seed should be collected in late summer and sown immediately; it will germinate readily the following spring.

Aralia cachemirica displaying its burgundy autumn tints in eastern Nepal (Photo by Daniel J. Hinkley)

CHAPTER 13

The Ubiquitous Umbellifers

The umbellifers, now known collectively as the family Apiaceae, have played a long and distinguished role in our horticultural and agricultural heritage. From carrots and dill to bronze fennel and Queen Anne's lace, the family embraces a wealth of species within which we are ethnobotanically entangled. The common thread is the flower type, that of the umbel, designed like a wheel with numerous spokes emanating from the center. Yet, as is frequently the case, this thread must be studied and deciphered in order to fully recognize the unifying characteristics of the plant family. The subtleties are there to behold once we take the time or develop the skill to look. It is precisely these anomalies in the plant kingdom that will forever hold me entranced as I weave a course through its bounty. Boredom and botany may both exist, but never in the same universe.

Angelica

The genus *Angelica* represents an enormous collection of garden-worthy species that, for the most part, have not yet been discovered for wider use in gardens. One species that perhaps has found its moment in the sun is *Angelica gigas*. A bi- or triennial species, it produces mounds of bold, pinnate foliage during its first one or two years, and in its last year, the plant rockets to 5 ft. (1.5 m) with countless heads of black-purple flowers to 8 in. (20 cm) across. These will be swarmed by a flickering contingent of hymenopterids (honey bees, wasps, and other creatures), creating a stunning combination of plant and insect in late summer. I have observed enormous fields of this species cultivated in Korea for

Angelica gigas (Photo by Lynne Harrison)

export to China for medicinal purposes, and I have seen native individuals, generally growing under rather dark and moist conditions. An occasional white-flowered form is encountered.

Much newer on the scene is *Angelica taiwaniana* 'Vicar's Mead', which I brought back from a nursery in England in 1996. That first season the plant grew as a colorful folial component to the border, with large pinnate foliage in arresting blackish purple tones. The following spring, it again emerged in hues of varnished ebony, fading later to plum as it soared skyward to 10 ft. (3 m), offering a full summer of lovely pink umbels to 5 in. (12.5 cm) across. Though 'Vicar's Mead' failed to emerge this spring, verifying my claim that it embraces a lifestyle similar to that of *A. gigas*, we have successfully germinated enough seed at Heronswood to fill even the most exuberant of demands (which generally is only garnered by plants whose seeds don't germinate).

Emerging in my woodland in early spring, with equally lovely tones of damson-purple, is *Angelica tingitana*, which was given to me by a Dutch nurseryman in 1997. It has thus far been an exciting addition to the garden, its somber hues fading to purple-green by midsummer. *Angelica tingitana*, though reported to be a long-lived perennial, has proven to be a monocarpic species in our garden. The flowers of light pink to white are presented on multibranched stems to 10 ft. (3 m) in early summer in broad, flattened umbels to 8 in. (20 cm) across.

Hardiness: By most accounts, the angelicas are good additions for gardens in zones 4–10. Even though many species hail from high elevations, they have proven to be adaptable to warm summer climates.

Cultivation: Foremost, young plants must be protected from slugs, as they are among the favorite fodder of the slimy pests. A moist but well-drained soil in full sun or light shade is ideal for *Angelica*. Staggering the planting of seedlings into the garden over a few years will maintain a population of varying maturity and thus allow for enjoyment of blossoms on a yearly basis.

Propagation: Seed is generously produced by most species, all of which will germinate the following spring. Seedlings often go dormant by midsummer of their first year but reappear the following spring none the worse for wear.

Astrantia

If historically the masterworts (*Astrantia*) were thought to be effective treatment for all maladies, then, at least in a horti-allegorical sense, the name is still appropriate in regard to their use in contemporary gardens. Members of the genus offer up an exceedingly long flowering season, take either full sun or dankish shade in

Angelica taiwaniana 'Vicar's Mead' (Photo by Lynne Harrison)

stride, and require little in the way of primping throughout the season—facts that make their relative obscurity in American gardens all the more difficult to understand. In addition, if I have failed to mention it already, they are simply beautiful.

The inflorescence of an *Astrantia*, a buttonlike umbel, is composed of numerous flowers surrounded by handsome and long-lasting bracts, providing the overall illusion of a single flower. Because the bracts remain attached long after fertilization of the flowers, they provide enormous value to the garden. As with so many genera of plants, the story of *Astrantia* is at once simple and extremely complicated. Though only a few species of *Astrantia* exist, these have been delineated into numerous subspecies that are represented in cultivation under synonymous nomenclature.

Of those in cultivation, *Astrantia major* remains the major player and, in its various forms, has been and will continue to be a respected component of my garden. In my estimation, the one most worthy of seeking out is *A. major* subsp. *involucrata* (referred to by some as subsp. *carninthiaca*) in the cultivar known as 'Shaggy' or 'Margery Fish'. Though this is an outstanding plant in its best forms, the names are somewhat meaningless, as the plant has been propagated by seed rather than division for years, and great variability exists among different clones. I've been told by better gardeners than I that my clone is an outstanding form, presenting a long procession of white-blushed-pink umbels surrounded by a jagged assemblage of ivory, green-tipped bracteoles to 1 in. (2.5 cm) in length. The flowering stems rise to 2 ft. (0.6 m) above mounds of glossy green, palmately lobed foliage from early April to the end of September. *Astrantia major* subsp. *involucrata* is reported to range naturally from northwestern Spain and the Pyrenees through the Alps, though I have never observed this, or any other *Astrantia* for that matter, in the wild.

The flower of *Astrantia major* subsp. *involucrata* 'Shaggy' (Photo by Lynne Harrison)

Overlapping the natural distribution of *Astrantia major* subsp. *involucrata*, the subspecies *major* is reported to extend throughout much of Europe. The shorter bracteoles surrounding the umbels set this subspecies apart, though this shortcoming is compensated for by the fact that there is greater plasticity in regard to color, offering up numerous named forms and strains with pink and red bracts. Like the previous subspecies, *A. major* subsp. *major* is represented most often by seedling-grown strains, and great variation exists. Although true-to-name spec-imens of the cultivar 'Rosensymphonie' may indeed exist and may possess suf-ficient ornament to justify its inclusion in the garden, I have never observed any plants offered under this name in commerce that are worthy of anything outside of the compost pile. The cultivar 'Rubra' is likewise muddled in commerce, rep-resenting seedling-grown plants that may, if you're lucky, possess bracts that are rosy red to muddy pink, though dingy white is an equally likely possibility. The named forms of *A. major* subsp. *major* that represent the best of the lot, if divi-sions are secured, are 'Ruby Wedding' and 'Hadspen Blood'. 'Ruby Wedding' was selected as a superior seedling at the Royal Horticultural Society Gardens at Wisley; it possesses medium-sized heads of sincerely red-purple bracteoles. Equally good is 'Hadspen Blood', selected by Nori Pope of Hadspen House in Castle Cary, England. This cultivar shows the same intensity of hue as 'Ruby Wedding'. I should also mention that a frequently encountered English selec-tion known as 'Claret' simply represents seedling-grown plants of 'Ruby Wed-ding' and will show variation in intensity of bract color. *Astrantia major* 'Canne-man', selected by Piet Oudolf of the Netherlands, offers the largest flowers of the red-flowered forms to date, and it shows affinity to *A. major* subsp. *involucrata*, which is reported to be one of its parents.

Astrantia major subsp. *major* has also provided a handful of clones with varie-gated foliage that are brilliant additions to full-sun or partial-shade garden loca-tions. *Astrantia major* subsp. *major* 'Sunningdale Variegated' has light and glossy green leaves that emerge in spring with creamy white margins and remain effec-tive throughout the summer. The small, blushed-white heads of flowers are not unattractive, but they do not hold muster to the foliage. In my nursery, the ger-minated seed of 'Sunningdale Variegated' produces a uniform but odd group of albino individuals, which are surprisingly effective in the early spring woodland combined with *Omphalodes cappadocica* 'Starry Eyes'. By early June, the leaves transform to light green and store enough energy for their next self-imposed hun-ger strike the following spring. I also grow an unnamed variegated cultivar from John Coke and Marina Christopher of Green Farm Plants in England, and it is a lovely plant with more subtle, but equally charming, lime-margined foliage.

Compared to *Astrantia major*, two additional species, *A. maxima* and *A. mi-nor*, accept a less-prominent position in Western borders, though I find that *A. maxima* offers one of the most peculiar shades of pink to be encountered in the plant kingdom. For a long period in late spring to midsummer, this species pro-duces quantities of umbels surrounded by 1/2-in. (1.25-cm) bracts of flat, gray-ish pink—a color that I profess to liking or loathing depending on the company I'm with, the amount of sleep I had the night before, or the quality of the Pinot

Astrantia major 'Hadspen Blood' (Photo by Lynne Harrison)

Astrantia major 'Hadspen Blood' (Photo by Lynne Harrison)

Astrantia maxima cleverly combined with *Hakonechloa macra* 'Aureola' in the garden of Barbara Flynn in Redmond, Washington (Photo by Lynne Harrison)

Gris I happen to be sipping. *Astrantia maxima* is used brilliantly in the perennial border of the Northwest Perennial Alliance at the Bellevue Botanic Garden, where it is planted in full sun near *Elymus magellanicus* and *Polygonum amplexicaule* 'Fire Tail', though as yet I have lacked the inspiration needed to bring it into better use in my own garden.

Astrantia minor hails from the higher elevations of south-central Europe in the Pyrenees, southwestern Alps, and the northern Apennines. It forms low mounds of palmate, long-petioled foliage above which are produced a long display of white- or pinkish-bracted flowers that are smaller than those of *A. maxima*. This species tends to come into flower much later in the season, which can extend the freshness of flower effects delivered by the genus, though other than this trait, little can be said to recommend *A. minor* over the better-known masterworts.

Hardiness: All *Astrantia* species are quite hardy and adaptable, acceptable for zones 4–10, though they may not be appropriate for arid climates.

Cultivation: I have grown masterworts in both sun and shade, but I find light shade to be preferable for extending their flowering effects. The red-flowered forms in particular tend to fade entirely too soon in hot positions. *Astrantia* is well suited to well-drained but moist, acidic soils that receive supplemental water during the growing season. I do not find it necessary to deadhead the plants in the summer, although deadheading will undoubtedly extend the flowering season even longer, if you have a generous surplus of time on your hands.

Propagation: Freshly sown seed of *Astrantia* will germinate the following season without difficulty. Though the named forms cannot be reliably increased by this method, they do come relatively good, as opposed to true, from seed, if kept in isolation from other clones. The red-flowered forms can be chosen from the seedling flat before flowering by selecting only those with dark red petioles. The masterworts hybridize readily, and I would only assume a species or subspecies to be true if seed was secured from the wild. Division of the named forms can be accomplished easily in early spring as growth resumes.

Hacquetia epipactis

Hacquetia, a monospecific genus in the family Apiaceae, often begins emerging in midwinter—in fact, during one mild winter I observed growth resuming as early as Christmas. Those familiar with the genus *Astrantia* know that the inflorescences are in actuality umbels of many small flowers surrounded by a ring of petal-like bracts. This is precisely the case with *Hacquetia epipactis*, but here the bracts are a most arresting electric green surrounding small clusters of yellowish flowers. The umbels first appear directly at ground level and then rise and expand more fully on stems to 6 in. (15 cm) as the winter continues. In late spring, the flowers are overcome by clumps of leafy foliage, to 1 ft. (0.3 m), that belie the demure habit exhibited during the flowering season. I have always been of the mind that a plant will let the gardener know when a site meets its requirements by offering an overabundance of self-sown seedlings—which in some cases is not necessarily the gift the gardener would hope to receive. I have found that most seedlings from this species appear near the plants that grow on the north side of our home in rather moist soils and bright shade; I can only presume that this is the ideal location, at least for us in the Pacific Northwest. *Hacquetia epipactis* has proven hardy to zones 4 and above.

While visiting the garden of Jack Elliot in the county of Kent, England, I first observed a variegated cultivar known as *Hacquetia epipactis* 'Thor'. Although I don't consider myself to be unflappably lustful with regard to variegated plants (many of my friends might dispute this assertion, however), this was a plant that I simply could not live without. The leaves of this clever selection had creamy white margins, certainly not unlike the effects of the variegated masterwort, *Astrantia major* subsp. *major* 'Sunningdale Variegated'. Yet the effects did not stop

Hacquetia epipactis (Photo by Lynne Harrison)

here, as the bracts surrounding each inflorescence possessed the same clean and even whitish margin. I returned to visit Jack and Jean Elliot two years later, and waiting for me was a generous division of 'Thor' to bring back to my garden. In this division, which I neither asked for nor was promised at the time, it has become very apparent to me that not only is there a prevailing astuteness among gardeners in recognizing the longing in other gardeners' eyes, but also a benevolent and generous spirit that embodies and connects the greater horticultural community.

Hardiness: Zones 4–9, perhaps colder areas with protection.

Cultivation: Well-drained but moist soils in full sun or light shade. The charms of *Hacquetia* in blossom will be lost if sited to accommodate its rather robust summer foliage. The flowers are best observed directly along a garden path and are stunning when combined with black lily turf (*Ophiopogon planiscapus* 'Nigrescens').

Propagation: Seed is freely produced and ripens in early summer. Self-sown seedlings around the parent plant can be lifted and replanted. Division is required for the variegated form, 'Thor', and is appropriate for the type form as well. Division should be performed in early spring after flowering and before the foliage begins to emerge.

Hacquetia epipactis 'Thor' (Photo by Lynne Harrison)

Chaerophyllum, Pimpinella, Selinum, and *Meum*

Countless other members of the Apiaceae are more straightforward in their appearance, though their lack of disguise should not disqualify them from use in our gardens. Indeed, there are very few early blossoming hardy perennials that I am as fond of as the pink-flowered form of the cow parsley, *Chaerophyllum hirsutum* 'Roseum'. The finely dissected, silky haired foliage begins to emerge in late winter, bringing to the mostly dormant perennial borders that patter of activity required by the equally dormant gardener. Shortly afterward, in late April, the low, fretted mounds of green foliage transform to a misty pink, as countless 4-in. (10-cm) frilly umbels open in a long progression atop 15-in. (38-cm) stems. (In the species's natural range throughout most of southern Europe from Spain to Greece, white flowers are the rule.) It is a good match with early blossoming bulbs as well as with the saturated freshly emerging foliage of perennials. This timeless, classic garden plant grows adjacent to *Stachys byzantina* 'Big Ears' in our full-sun borders to what we think, at least, is good effect.

The pink cow parsley, *Chaerophyllum hirsutum* 'Roseum', used in the front of a full-sun perennial border at Heronswood (Photo by Lynne Harrison)

Chaerophyllum hirsutum 'Roseum' (Photo by Lynne Harrison)

Pimpinella major 'Rosea' (Photo by Lynne Harrison)

The effects brought to the garden by another European umbellifer, *Pimpinella major* 'Rosea', are quite similar to those of the *Chaerophyllum*, though it blossoms much later, in June and July. Stems rising to nearly 3 ft. (0.9 m) in height are topped by pretty umbels of soft pink flowers. This is a valuable but short-lived plant for me, and it's probably best cultivated in extremely well-drained soils in full sun.

In eastern Nepal, I collected seed of *Selinum tenuifolium*, a species that has a well-respected reputation but is still rarely encountered. It grows in moist alpine meadows in the Himalayas and does best in similarly rich, moisture-retentive soils in cultivation. Rising to 5 ft. (1.5 m) in height, the fronds of extremely fine-dissected foliage provide the perfect backdrop to the lovely heads of lacy white flowers produced in late spring. *Selinum tenuifolium* is an extremely long-lived perennial species in cultivation, and our wild collections have settled in nicely in our bright woodland.

Meum athamanticum, a monotypic species from Europe, is similar in effect to *Selinum*, but on a much smaller scale and with an exceedingly finer texture. Producing low mounds of soft, filigreed, fennel-like foliage in spring, *M. athamanticum* displays heads of fretted white flowers, opening from pinkish-blushed

Selinum tenuifolium (Photo by Lynne Harrison)

buds, just above the foliage on stems to 15 in. (38 cm). This long-lived perennial grows in our full-sun borders with *Paeonia veitchii* var. *woodwardii*. The two flower together in mid-May and early June, providing a dazzling duet performance.

Meum athamanticum blossoming with *Paeonia veitchii* var. *woodwardii* (Photo by Daniel J. Hinkley)

The genera discussed here represent only a minute fraction of the remarkable species and selections that are served up by the Apiaceae. The longer I garden, the more prominent they become in my borders and woodland, attesting to the effects of their foliage, flower, and overall texture.

Hardiness: Zones 6–10. If provided early season moisture, *Chaerophyllum* and *Pimpinella* will tolerate the arid climates of the Southwest. *Selinum* and *Meum* are more content in cooler summer climates.

Cultivation: Full sun and moist but well-drained soils are ideal. Cut these umbellifers to the ground as the flowers begin to fade to obtain a regrowth of fresh foliage, which provides a finely textured foil for later blossoming border companions.

Propagation: As *Chaerophyllum hirsutum* 'Roseum' increases at a respectable clip, we simply divide clumps on a yearly basis, a chore that we would have to endure even if we were not potting the plants for sale in the nursery. *Chaerophyllum* is apparently self-sterile, and since we grow only one clone, we have never had fertile seed produced. *Selinum*, *Pimpinella*, and *Meum* generally set good seed, which offers the best method of propagation. These germinate in a single season from seed.

CHAPTER 14

Herbaceous Hydrangeas:
Cardiandra, Deinanthe, and *Kirengeshoma*

Although we as simple gardeners or even advanced horticulturists often cannot see those common traits that bind together the like-minded groups of genera known as families, it nonetheless makes for interesting exploration once they have been invited to the family reunion by the more knowledgeable plant taxonomists. The hydrangea family (Hydrangeaceae) is one that includes among its members genera of herbaceous plants that are highly desirable components of the woodland garden.

Cardiandra

I first made my acquaintance with *Cardiandra alternifolia* in its native haunts of Chiba Prefecture in central Honshu in 1993, and since then I have observed the species in Shizuoka Prefecture of Honshu as well as on Shikoku Island. As suggested by the species name, the foliage of *C. alternifolia* is alternately arranged along 18-in. (45-cm) stems, with each ovate leaf growing to 3 in. (7.5 cm) and bearing a serrated margin. Terminal cymes of light pink flowers are produced in late summer and early fall. Each cyme is attended by sterile florets composed of three rather large, pinkish white sepals that later fade to lime-green; in the fashion of a lace-cap hydrangea, these sterile appendages are there for the purpose of attracting insect pollinators. Currently quite rare in cultivation, *C. alternifolia* is a lovely component of the light-shaded garden, and it tolerates temperatures to at least 10°F (−12°C), and perhaps lower. Imagine my excitement when I came across a double-flowered form of this species, *C. alternifolia* 'Flore Pleno', at Gotemba Nursery in Japan in the autumn of 1995. Each sterile floret surrounding the inflorescence has twice the normal number of sepals, presenting a sensational though demure flower effect for a long period in late summer through autumn.

I also cultivate in my woodland both *Cardiandra formosana* and *C. amamioshinensis*. *Cardiandra formosana* was collected in the mountains of Taiwan by my friends Bleddyn and Sue Wynn-Jones of Crûg Farm Plants in northern Wales. This species also has leaves alternately arranged along its 18-in. (45-cm) stems, but its flower heads are of a more richly saturated hue and emerge on somewhat taller stems, to 24 in. (60 cm), than those of its aforementioned Japanese counterpart. It provides a sensational display in my woodland from early September throughout much of October. I have encountered *C. amamioshinensis* only in nurseries in Japan, and it is quite distinct from the other species in general format. The primary difference lies in the glossy, ovate leaves (with a prominent serrated edge), which are held in pairs along the stems rather than being alternately arranged. Terminally borne atop 15-in. (38-cm) stems, the inflorescence is a cyme composed of sterile florets that open very light pink, fading to near white, surrounded by sterile florets possessing expanded and showy sepals. *Cardiandra amamioshinensis* has thus far been a very handsome and distinctive woodland element.

The pink fertile florets of *Cardiandra alternifolia* are surrounded by sterile florets with expanded sepals (Photo by Lynne Harrison)

Hardiness: Little information is available to support hardiness data for *Cardiandra*, but my educated guess says these will be hardy in zones 5–9, perhaps colder.

Cultivation: *Cardiandra alternifolia* prefers light shade and moist, humus-rich soils. Despite what one might suspect after observing *C. alternifolia* in its native haunts and in cultivation, *Cardiandra formosana* and *C. amamioshinensis* do not seem as dependent on shaded conditions. I have successfully grown these in both full sun and light shade, planted in soils of average fertility and with supplemental water.

Propagation: I have successfully propagated *Cardiandra* from softwood cuttings while plants are still in vegetative growth in early summer. Once flower initiation occurs, propagation from cuttings most likely will not be successful. The seed of this genus is extremely tiny and must be sown when relatively fresh before it becomes desiccated. Seed has not yet successfully formed on my plants under cultivation, though the seed from my wild collections germinated readily when sown as per *Hydrangea* seed. We sow the seed directly on top of a $^{1}/_{2}$-in. (1.25-cm) layer of fine gravel covering the seed compost. The seed germinates in the gravel while the roots establish in the compost.

Deinanthe

The similarity to the inflorescence of *Hydrangea* that is exhibited by *Cardiandra* is also seen in a most remarkable genus known as *Deinanthe*. Consisting of only two species, *Deinanthe* is unfortunately obscure in cultivation and generally found in only connoisseurs' collections. *Deinanthe bifida* was the first to enter western cultivation, found and first described in 1863 by the Russian botanist Carl Johann Maximowicz in the southern woodlands of Japan. As its specific epithet implies, the species bears leaves that terminate into two distinct, pointed lobes (that is, they are bifid), and the 8-in. (20-cm) leaves are rich green and leathery in texture. The extraordinary foliage is what first caught my attention when I witnessed the plant being cultivated by a nurseryman near the base of Mount Fuji in the autumn of 1995. The following year it blossomed in my garden, with terminal clusters of nodding, waxy white flowers held by ghostly white pedicels slightly above the foliage on 18-in. (45-cm) stems. Similar to hydrangea inflorescences, some florets along the outside perimeter of the inflorescence are completely sterile and are there simply to attract pollinators to the fertile flowers toward the center.

In the autumn of 1997, I observed vast stands of *Deinanthe bifida* in moist, cool, shaded locations on the Kii Peninsula of Honshu at altitudes of 4500 ft. (1350 m). The species was growing, and had blossomed, with no fewer than eight species of *Hydrangea,* and the scene was quite remarkable, with a plethora of dried heads in the typical fashion of a lacecap hydrangea. Though abundant at this location, *D. bifida* did not seem to be widespread throughout this region of Japan. The individual specimens rose to nearly 3 ft. (0.9 m) in height, putting to shame my meager attempts at cultivating the species in my woodland. Each flower head yielded thousands of tiny seeds (the norm for members of Hydrangeaceae), and the resultant seedlings will eventually be planted in areas of the garden with more moisture than where the plants are currently growing.

The Chinese counterpart, *Deinanthe caerulea,* was first discovered after the turn of the twentieth century by the Irish physician Augustine Henry in Hubei Province. Though the significance of this discovery was diminished by the fact that the plant was at first thought to be simply a continental population of *D. bifida,* later examination separated this collection into its own species. Indeed, this species is, superficially, quite distinct, at least judging by the clones that I have under cultivation. On more than one occasion, however, I have found that taxonomic designations based on observation of limited number of collections often leads to conclusions that are less than accurate. Although most clones of *D. caerulea* do not exhibit the bifid leaf tip of its insular counterpart, the specimens col-

lected by E. H. Wilson, from the same mountains where the species was first collected by Henry, show that some do indeed have notched leaf tips.

Taxonomy aside, *Deinanthe caerulea* is an exquisite woodland plant and a prize often sought by the woodland plant enthusiast. The leaves, rich green and coriaceous, are produced in pairs along 15-in. (38-cm) stems that terminate in lovely clusters of nodding, lilac-suffused flowers, each with a gorgeous assemblage of lavender-gray stamens crowded inside. Reginald Farrer described this flower color as "sad, pale violet," though I do not find sorrow when this species blossoms in my woodland. It demonstrates somewhat the same shyness as a hellebore blossom, requiring that those who

Deinanthe bifida (Photo by Daniel J. Hinkley)

Deinanthe caerulea (Photo by Daniel J. Hinkley)

wish to admire the blossom bend or kneel to truly appreciate it, and I believe that is all the more reason to have it in my garden. We all need more excuses to slow down our frantic pace and capture moments of exquisite beauty that surround us through the seasons.

Hardiness: Both *Deinanthe* species are considered perfectly hardy in zones 4–8.

Cultivation: Successful cultivation requires shaded positions and adequately moist and rich edaphic environments. I have seen *Deinanthe caerulea* cultivated in situations of full sun with the disappointing results of burnt and blemished foliage, even in cool climates.

Propagation: *Deinanthe* is exasperatingly slow to increase in cultivation. Inspection of even small clumps dug in late winter will reveal large numbers of dormant buds that will not break into growth unless removed and planted independently. Because little seed set occurs under cultivation, perhaps due to the paucity of distinct clones being grown in gardens, division is the principal means of propagation. My seed collections of *Deinanthe bifida* have germinated successfully, sown as per *Cardiandra*. The slow-growing seedlings should be left in the seed tray for an entire year before transplanting.

Kirengeshoma

I first encountered *Kirengeshoma palmata* at the Washington Park Arboretum in Seattle in the spring of 1984. The jagged and bold maplelike foliage is what initially inspired me to make its acquaintance, but later in summer, when the plant produced its nodding, lemony bells in terminal clusters, the deal was sealed on our permanent relationship. Long after the novelty of this first encounter had worn off, my association with Gerald Straley of the University of British Columbia Botanical Garden brought me to more intimate associations with a genus that I will never be without in the garden.

Two species of *Kirengeshoma* are currently recognized, and they differ only slightly. *Kirengeshoma palmata* grows naturally, though is rarely encountered, on

Shikoku and Kyushu Islands of Japan. The large, sharply lobed, maplelike leaves are borne in opposite pairs, displaying a handsome silvery pubescence when first emerging in spring, and the foliage provides interest throughout the spring and summer. Atop stems that rise to 6 ft. (1.8 m) on content individuals, cymes of elegant pendulous, pastel-yellow flowers are produced on lax pedicels in late summer, delivering a dazzling late-season gift to the woodland. The nodding floral branches are what distinguish this species from *K. coreana* (also referred to as *Kirengeshoma* Koreana Group), the flowers of which are borne on a stiffly upright inflorescence. With stems reaching nearly 7 ft. (2.1 m) high on robust specimens, *K. coreana* can be somewhat larger than the Japanese counterpart. Some consider this only a form of *K. palmata*, and further study is needed to determine if it is indeed an individual species.

In the early 1990s, the University of British Columbia Botanical Garden successfully crossed the two taxa and lined out numerous individuals for evaluation. None of the progeny, however, showed sufficient improvement over the unalloyed species to justify introduction into cultivation.

Hardiness: Both *Kirengeshoma* forms are equally hardy and will thrive in zones 4–10. Some of the best garden specimens that I have observed were growing in southern Vermont (zone 5).

Kirengeshoma palmata (Photo by Lynne Harrison)

The upright flowering stems of *Kirengeshoma coreana* distinguish it from the more common *K. palmata* (Photo by Lynne Harrison)

Cultivation: Though *Kirengeshoma* will live and blossom in average garden loam, by far the best effects are achieved in rich, moist soils heavily amended with organic matter, where the foliage and stems will show remarkable robustness.

Propagation: Cuttings that are taken in early summer, after the stem tissue has hardened off (become less fleshy) and before flower initiation, can be successfully propagated under mist, though survivability of the resultant plants through the first winter is dependent on firm establishment before dormancy commences. Seed is generously produced and will germinate the following spring if sown fresh, with seedlings blossoming in two or three years. Division of mature plants is certainly possible and should be done in early spring as growth begins.

CHAPTER 15

Singular Saxifrages:
Chrysosplenium, Mukdenia, and *Peltoboykinia*

In confronting any plant family, good horticulturists know when to stay the course and when to run for their lives. If I were faced with the daunting task of picking out the most appropriate members of the Saxifragaceae for discussion in a book—or, heaven forbid, attempt to write about every garden-worthy subject found in its ranks—I'd set a new world record for the 100-meter dash. The family Saxifragaceae is a universe unto itself. Once a massive taxonomic pot filled to the brim with more than 80 genera embracing 1200 species of alpines, herbaceous perennials, shrubs, small trees, and woody climbers in the temperate regions of both hemispheres, the family is gradually becoming manageable, as taxonomists have begun the arduous task of repackaging this gargantuan beast into smaller, more digestible parcels. Even with that task accomplished, however, countless genera of garden-worthy and often-cultivated plants remain within its inventory; of these, I reflect on three genera that await discovery by a larger gardening audience.

Chrysosplenium

Chrysosplenium, an evergreen groundcovering perennial native to both the New and Old World, is mostly unknown in cultivation in the United States, but the numerous species are excellent components for the moist woodland. *Chrysosplenium davidianum* is relatively new on the scene, being introduced to cultivation by the Sino-British Expedition to Yunnan Province in 1980. Prostrate stems, carrying reniform, hairy foliage held in pairs, produce expansive mats in a relatively short period of time. In early spring, clusters of small yellow flowers, attended by rather electric-chartreuse bracts, are formed in the crown of the plant and provide a long and effective showing. Although I had already successfully established the species in my woodland garden (where it thrives in well-amended and moist soils), it was still an exciting moment when I saw *C. davidianum* as the prominent groundcover in a remarkable and rich shaded ravine on Ninety-Nine Dragons, a mountain slightly northwest of Genjuan in Yunnan. Because it was autumn, long after the blossoming sequence was through, I could only imagine the effects produced in early spring, when this one species assuredly lights the entire forest floor with an incredible iridescent glow.

Later during the same visit to China in 1996, I was thrilled to observe the very distinctive *Chrysosplenium macrophyllum* on Emei Shan in Sichuan Province. Certainly not belying its specific epithet, *C. macrophyllum* created sensational rosettes of large, rounded-oval leaves to 6 in. (15 cm), pubescent green above with a slight purplish cast beneath, self-layering to form handsome colonies in moist but sunny areas. Until I noticed its stoloniferous habit, I was ready to proudly proclaim to my traveling companions that I had found a *Bergenia*. In fact, this similarity is what ultimately led me to its proper identity, as Roy Lancaster had had precisely the same reaction when he found *C. macrophyllum* on Wu-

Chrysosplenium davidianum (Photo by Lynne Harrison)

dang Shan in the same province in 1983. The cuttings that I took of this plant failed to survive the trip home and the associated USDA inspections, and so I am left with only an unblossomed memory.

Numerous species of *Chrysosplenium* are found throughout Asia, and many of these should be better known and grown by Western gardeners. In particular, the moist deciduous woods of Korea and Japan play host to several garden-worthy species. *Chrysosplenium japonicum* occurs in both countries, where it inhabits moist, shaded sites alongside streams. Clusters of rather large (to ¼ in. [0.6 m]), yellowish green flowers surrounded by bright yellow bracts are produced at the apex of self-layering stems, which carry pairs of glabrous, ovate to triangular, dentate foliage. Though this species is considered quite common throughout the Japanese Archipelago, I have observed it only on the Kii Peninsula on Honshu, where it grew near a small tumbling brook.

Chrysosplenium macrostemon is also found in both Japan and Korea, occupying a more southerly range. Though the foliage is similar to that of *C. japonicum*, the flowers of *C. macrostemon* possess an understated charm that I find disarming. Small, yellowish green flowers are surrounded by bright green bracts, the collective effect being reminiscent of a mutant form of *Anemone nemorosa* called 'Green Fingers', which I have grown for several years.

My first encounter with a New World species from this genus was with *Chrysosplenium valdivicum*, which I met growing in moist, cool soils beneath the shaded evergreen forests of southern Chile. The rounded leaves, which are held in pairs along stoloniferous stems, grow to 2½ in. (6 cm), decidedly larger than those of the Asian species (except, of course, *C. macrophyllum*). Axillary clusters of brilliant golden flowers are produced in early spring. The few cuttings that I took from along the upper elevations of the Volcano Puyehue managed to hang on to life and are now firmly established in our nursery, though I have not yet established the species in my garden.

Hardiness: The genus *Chrysosplenium* represents a large cache of widely distributed species, with some inappropriate for colder climates and others resentful of summer heat and humidity. For example, the northern European *Chrysosplenium tetrandum* is rated to USDA zone 1, while I suspect *Chrysosplenium valdivicum* is more appropriate for the summer-cool regions of zones 6–9.

Cultivation: Cultivate in moist, shaded sites where plants can be allowed to colonize. At Heronswood, we have planted *Chrysosplenium davidianum* as a low groundcover in association with the black-flowered *Helleborus* ×*hybridus* as well as with the luscious blue flowers of *Pulmonaria* 'Highdown'. In both instances, the remarkable floral effects of the *Chrysosplenium* are enhanced.

Propagation: Easily divided in early spring as growth resumes, though this shallow-rooted perennial is difficult to maintain in nursery pots.

Mukdenia

The plant that most stands out as the turning point in my realization of the importance of observing plants in their native habitat is *Mukdenia rossii*. I had cultivated this species for several years under the moniker *Aceriphyllum rossii*, a generic name that is decidedly more useful for conjuring a mental image of the plant's foliage ("*aceriphyllum*" translates literally as "maple leaf") than the name currently held in favor; in fact, the only image elicited by the term *Mukdenia* is not appropriate for discussion in this book. Knowing only that this plant belonged to the family Saxifragaceae, and armed with the somewhat dangerous notion that I was a knowledgeable plantperson, I grew my specimen in a full-sun location in a mound of pit-run sand (a very coarse rock and sand mixture) that I called my rock garden, and there the plant dwindled. Then, during my first trip to Korea, I observed firsthand the species's circumstance of choice. Having colonized the rock cracks in weathered granite along swiftly moving streams, it

Mukdenia rossii growing on a rock surface on Mount Sorak in South Korea (Photo by Daniel J. Hinkley)

formed a beautiful autumn display, with its network of foliage transformed to orange and red etched in the ancient rock walls. Not only were these plants receiving copious quantities of water during the growing season, but they were surely submerged completely during spring runoff. I returned home and promptly relocated my plant to a more appropriate setting, and in a single year's time, it had grown sufficiently robust to allow for division.

The leaves of *Mukdenia*, at least a content *Mukdenia*, are indeed bold and beautiful, as Gerald Straley, who had a particular liking for this plant, would often say. Deeply lobed blades to 8 in. (20 cm) across create hearty mounds that

Mukdenia rossii (Photo by Lynne Harrison)

spread generously by a creeping rhizome. The degree of lobing is quite variable: the foliage on my collections from Korea is much more deeply divided than that found on the clones most frequently available in North American commerce. In May, cymes of starry, white flowers appear as false umbels above the foliage on 12- to 18-in. (30- to 45-cm) branched stems. If grown in bright conditions, plants develop good autumn tints before slipping into dormancy.

While in Japan in 1995, I found a plant offered for sale as *Mukdenia* sp. "China." In addition to producing a very distinctive specimen—with bronzed foliage more elongated than that of *Mukdenia rossii* and pink flowers produced on 10-in. (25-cm) stems—this species planted a seed of curiosity in my mind regarding other members of the genus. Time will ultimately tell what this species proves to be and what other treasures *Mukdenia* holds for the North American and European gardener alike.

Hardiness: Quite hardy, in zones 4–10. The natural range of *Mukdenia rossii* extends from South Korea to northeastern China, and collections from the more northerly portions of the range certainly may prove even hardier.

Cultivation: As already discussed, moist but well-drained sites in full sun or partial shade are best.

Propagation: I successfully obtained seed of *Mukdenia rossii* from along the rivers of Cheju Island in 1997, and it germinated by the spring of 1998. These collections are from the plant's most southerly locale, and I am eager to compare the resultant individuals to my original collections made nearly 600 miles to the north. Division of plants in early spring is easily accomplished, preferably before growth resumes.

Peltoboykinia

I made my acquaintance with both of the two known species of *Peltoboykinia* in 1989, and I have had a love-hate relationship with them ever since. Initially, I was immensely pleased to witness the new foliage of *Peltoboykinia tellimoides*, a rare species from the mountains of central and northern Honshu in Japan. It emerged in spring in tones of translucent red and then expanded to 10-in. (25-cm) umbrellas of green, sharply lobed, peltate leaves on 18-in. (45-cm) petioles as the season progressed. Later, in early summer, lovely cymes of white flowers are borne atop stems to 2 ft. (0.6 m). This was all the love part; the loathing comes in mid- to late summer. As the temperatures increase and the soil beneath our overstory of Douglas firs begins to dry, the leaf edges of *P. tellimoides* crisp, curl, or generally disengage themselves from the concept of ornament. I begin removing the unsightly leaves by early July and continue throughout the summer, but the rate of departure is somewhat faster than that of arrival, and gaping holes often develop where they are planted in the woodland.

Peltoboykinia watanabei is another rare species in its native habitats of southern Japan on Shikoku and Kyushu. It is very similar to *P. tellimoides*, but *P. watanabei* produces foliage that is much more deeply divided, with 7 to 10 lobes on a somewhat larger scale, growing to 12 in. (30 cm) across atop 15-in. (38-cm) petioles. Cymes of creamy yellow flowers are produced in early summer atop pedicels that also reach 15 in. (38 cm) in height. I have experienced the same cultural difficulties with this plant as with the former—though I believe this is due mostly to my incompetence as a gardener rather than to any genetic flaw in the plants. I have observed both species grown as handsome additions to peaty, moist beds in the cool climates of northern England, where in foliage and flower they shine.

Hardiness: Zones 5–9, if provided a cool, moist site.

Cultivation: Site *Peltoboykinia* in cool, moist, humus-rich situations that are not allowed to dry out during the growing season, in shade, and protected from desiccating winds. Why not just consider building a cool temperate conservatory?

Peltoboykinia tellimoides (Photo by Lynne Harrison)

Propagation: These two species of *Peltoboykinia* will easily hybridize if grown in close proximity, with the offspring possessing intermediate characteristics. The true species (or the hybrids, for that matter) can be maintained by division in early spring.

Flanked at Heronswood by *Primula japonica* on either side and a colony of *Dactylorhiza grandis* in front, *Peltoboykinia watanabei* lends its deeply dissected foliage to this moist border in partial shade (Photo by Lynne Harrison)

CHAPTER 16

Bodacious Bounty:
Rodgersia and *Darmera*

Through film, fiction, and fact, inhabitants of the northern climes have come to associate immensity of leaves with the exotic. The inclusion of large-leaved herbaceous species adds an "out-of-garden" texture to our landscapes, transporting us to places unfamiliar and exciting. I am fond of including many species for this effect, both in full sun as well as in the partial shade of my woodland, and I never tire of the drama they bring to the space. Creating tropically touched gardens with bananas and cannas is one of numerous garden fads that will come and go, but the use of hardy plants with a bold foliage presence will remain a time-honored contribution to our gardens.

Rodgersia

The use of *Rodgersia* in Western gardens has a long history, and there is no apparent evidence of declining interest. The star of the saxifrage family, the genus consists of four to six species, depending on the taxonomist interviewed, and all species are native to Asia. For new spring growth, summer foliage, remarkable flowers, and in some cases, excellent autumn tones, this group of plants demands a space in every garden that can accommodate their size and environmental requirements.

Rodgersia podophylla, the only species native to Japan and Korea, was the first one introduced into cultivation and is the type species. The genus name commemorates Admiral John Rodgers, a U.S. commander who led an expedition to Hokkaido, Japan, where *R. podophylla* was first collected. I have observed this species in its wild state in both countries, where it grows in deeply shaded, cool

A clump of *Rodgersia podophylla* growing in a border at Heronswood. These were raised from seed I collected in Korea in 1993. (Photo by Lynne Harrison)

and moist areas, producing substantial colonies. With regard to textural qualities brought to the garden, the foliage of this species is perhaps the finest. The palmately compound leaves are composed of five to seven leaflets, each to 10 in. (25 cm) in length and possessing a jagged, three- to five-lobed, truncate leaf tip. The foliage color shows remarkable variation in *R. podophylla*, and numerous cultivars have been selected by nurseryfolk over the years. Classics include Ernest Pagels's 'Pagode' and 'Rotlaub', both of which possess bronzed new growth that fades to deep green during the summer, and 'Smaragd', with deep emerald leaves. Numerous unnamed forms were selected by Eric Smith at the Hobhouse estate known as Hadspen House in Somerset, England, and they remain intact and valued by Nori and Sandra Pope, who now tend these gardens. These unnamed selections were shared with us in the spring of 1998, and I look forward to observing and comparing them with the other clones we cultivate. Perhaps the best that I have seen is an unnamed seedling that was selected by the University of British Columbia Botanical Garden and distributed to keen gardeners in the area by Gerald Straley. The foliage emerges in early spring with an impressive dark purple gloss, fading later in the season to purple-bronze. The inflorescence of this selection emerges in midsummer as erect and narrow, 5-ft. (1.5-m) panicles of white, apetalous flowers. After fertilization, the sepals and ripening seed capsules take on pleasing tones of red.

This exceptional bronze-foliaged clone of *Rodgersia podophylla* was raised from seed at the Botanical Garden of the University of British Columbia in Vancouver (Photo by Lynne Harrison)

North of Lichang in Yunnan Province, I observed expanses of *Rodgersia pinnata* throughout the grassy and rather dry scrub, growing amidst dense hummocks of *Quercus monimotricha*, *Paris yunnanensis*, *Gentianopsis grandis*, and *Arisaema consanguineum*. The pinnately compound foliage of *R. pinnata* grows to 2 ft. (0.6 m) in length and is among the largest in the genus. The leaves are composed of six to nine individual rugose leaflets to 8 in. (20 cm) borne in a compressed fashion along the petiole; in fact, they often appear more palmate than pinnate. (Gerald Straley would often say that this *Rodgersia* species might have been better called "*pseudopinnata*" or "*pseudopalmata*.") When apparent, the leaf rachis often reveals itself as a small segment between the three terminal leaflets and the three to six basal leaflets. Because of this apparent discrepancy between name and form, as well as the fact that the species will eagerly interbreed in cultivation, *R. pinnata* is often misidentified in commerce. Flowering panicles arise in early summer, creating stiff, tiered stems to 3 ft. (0.9 m) carrying small apetalous flowers of variable color, from white and creamy yellow to rose-pink. The often-encountered, as well as often-disappointing, cultivar *R. pinnata* 'Superba' is reported to have rich pinkish red flowers, though more often than not the seedling-grown plants to which this name has been applied range in floral color from muddy white to the slightest hint of pink. The best form of *R. pinnata* that I have obtained to date came from the superb garden of Helen Dillon in Ireland. Known as *R. pinnata* 'Elegans', it possesses dense, graceful panicles of rosy red that grow to 3 ft. (0.9 m). Numerous references consider this selection to be of hybrid origin, while others place it under the dubious species name of *R. henrici*. *Rodgersia pinnata* 'Alba' has white flowers, although some of the best pink forms that I have grown were brought in under this name.

During the same trip to China that I observed *Rodgersia pinnata* in its native haunts, I was excited to observe plants of *R. aesculifolia* in the Wenchuan Wolong Nature Reserve of Sichuan Province. This species can be superficially similar to *R. pinnata*. The palmate leaves are generally seven parted with each individual leaflet overlapping at the base and strongly suggesting the shape of its namesake's foliage—the horse chestnut, genus *Aesculus*. The leaf petiole, the leaf veins, and the undersurface of the marginal teeth are covered with a ruddy, shaggy pubescence that provides an easy method of identifying this species in the field or garden. *Rodgersia aesculifolia* blossoms in early summer to produce loosely branched panicles of petal-less flowers rising to over 3 ft. (0.9 m) in height. Depending on the interpretation, this species is either closely allied to or representative of plants that have made their way into gardens and literature as *R. henrici*. Differences between the species become clear when one examines the sepals and the degree of leaf pubescence: on *R. aesculifolia*, the sepals enlarge after

Rodgersia pinnata 'Alba' (Photo by Lynne Harrison)

A good example of *Rodgersia pinnata* 'Elegans', displaying soft rose-pink flowers (Photo by Daniel J. Hinkley)

fertilization (that is, they are accrescent), and a pubescence is evident on both the leaf veins and on the teeth below; by contrast, *R. henrici* bears sepals that are nonaccrescent after fertilization and has pubescence only on the veins of the leaf. In addition, the range of *R. aesculifolia* is much further to the north, in Sichuan, Gansu, and Hubei Provinces, while *R. henrici* occurs in Yunnan and Burma. Adding to the confusion, many taxonomists list *R. aesculifolia* as a synonym of *R. pinnata*, so where it fits into the puzzle of life, if indeed it is an individual piece at all, must still be determined. Plants grown under the name *R. aesculifolia* in our garden have an accentuated drip tip to the leaf apex, and they emerge in spring in tones of bright reddish bronze. Among the selected cultivars of this rodgersia, *R. aesculifolia* 'Irish Bronze' takes top marks, creating highly textural, glossy bronzed mounds of foliage in spring.

When I returned to Yunnan in the autumn of 1998, I paid particularly close attention to the *Rodgersia* that grew here. On the western slope of the Cang Shan grew what appeared to be two species, along with a bewildering variety of intermediates between them. The two species were identified by our botanists as *R. pinnata* and *R. henrici*. Isolated specimens of *R. henrici* possessed large leaflets, to 10 in. (30 cm) or more, emanating from a common point on the petiole, which rose to 2 ft. (0.6 m) or taller. Where the two species grew together, which was the norm rather than the exception, individual plants demonstrated a vast spectrum of affinity to one parent or the other. This made it immediately apparent that simply seeking wild-collected seed of this genus will not be sufficient in preventing misnamed plants in commerce. We collected seed of *R. henrici* from plants that were isolated from *R. pinnata*, and we hope this will provide undiluted plants for subsequent study in cultivation.

Another thrill from my 1996 expedition was to observe *Rodgersia sambucifolia* growing in the wild along the eastern flank of the Cang Shan. Unlike the other species, *R. sambucifolia* consistently offers up pinnate foliage that looks remarkably like that of its namesake, in this case the elderberries of genus *Sambucus*. *Rodgersia sambucifolia* is also the smallest of the species and considered to be the least hardy. In nature, this species extends throughout most of western China, in particular Sichuan and Yunnan Provinces, where the apetalous flowers can vary in color from white to light pink, rising in midsummer in panicles to 4 ft. (1.2 m). Numerous selections have been made based on the degree of bronzing in the foliage; one of the best is 'Rothaub', a selection by a German nurseryman named Goetz. 'Rothaub' offers vigorous growth and reddish bronze foliage that is most intense in early summer.

I have had several brief encounters with a plant known as *Rodgersia* 'Purdomii'—brief in that I have managed to kill my plants by one unintentional method or another long before I could determine exactly what this species might be. It is believed to be closely allied to *R. pinnata*, though its leaflets are much narrower, do not overlap at the base, and often are saturated with bronze-purple. The flowers are white, I am told, and produced atop 3-ft. (0.9-m) panicles in midsummer. Because of the substantial amount of variation that occurs from seedling-grown plants, it is highly likely that *Rodgersia* 'Purdomii' is indeed of hybrid origin.

Astilboides tabularis was once considered part of the genus *Rodgersia*, and it is still referenced as *Rodgersia tabularis* in the occasional book or catalog. It is an extremely hardy species hailing from North Korea and eastern China, where it is reported to reach enormous sizes with rounded, umbrella-like leaf blades to 3 ft. (0.9 m) across supported by a $2^1/2$- to 3-ft. (0.8- to 0.9-m) petiole attached to the center of the leaf. The distinctive leaf type, compared to that of the true *Rodgersia* species, is certainly one reason why this plant has been packaged under a different name. Furthermore, the flower structure, which consists of plumy panicles of creamy white flowers, *with petals*, produced atop 3- to 4-ft. (0.9- to 1.2-m) stems in early to midsummer, itself provides sufficient justification for separating this species from *Rodgersia*. The clone that I grow in my garden does not reach the spectacular proportions of those in the natural habitat, yet it still creates imposing colonies with handsome leaves to 18 in. (45 cm) in diameter. Like the rodgersias, *A. tabularis* is best suited to rich, moisture-retentive soils.

Hardiness: All species of *Rodgersia* are hardy in the upper reaches of zones 4 to zone 9, though they will not tolerate the dry climates of the Southwest.

Cultivation: Moist, humus-rich soils in semishade will foster the most handsome specimens as well as sizable stands in a relatively short period of time. Reduction of the colonies as they spread rhizomatously will be required. Rodgersias are effectively combined with the upright spears of variegated *Acorus cala-*

Astilboides tabularis (Photo by Lynne Harrison)

mus, Aruncus dioicus, Meconopsis, Primula japonica, Ourisia coccinea, and *Dactylorhiza.* Leaf scalding will occur if plants are allowed to dry out during the growing season.

Propagation: Propagation by seed is quite easy for all species if sown fresh, although one should not assume that seed will come true if collected from gardens where more than one species is planted. Named forms grown from seed should not be offered under their cultivar names, as great variation among seedlings will undoubtedly occur. Division of species and named forms can take place throughout the season, although I am partial to performing the task in early spring as growth resumes.

Darmera

In early spring, lovely heads of pink flowers emerge naked from the ground and rise to over 2 ft. (0.6 m) on one of our loveliest and certainly most underused natives, *Darmera peltata*. The plant was formerly known as *Peltiphyllum peltatum*, but the taxonomic rules have restored the name under which it was first described. Regardless of the confusion that still exists in the trade, this is a top-notch hardy perennial with magnificent foliage and deserves to be more widely grown throughout much of North America.

While the flowers of *Darmera peltata* provide early sustenance for the frustrated gardener, the large umbrella-shaped leaves emerge shortly after flowering to add high drama to the garden for the remainder of the season. Vigorously growing clumps may produce leaves to 15 in. (38 cm) across, with a pebbly texture and glossy green color that transforms to remarkable tones of reds, oranges, and corals as the leaves die off in autumn; this is especially intense on plants grown in full sun. The thick, rhizomatous stems are slowly creeping and can be easily controlled if the colony becomes too large for the space. In smaller gardens, *Darmera peltata* 'Nana' should be considered. This form is approximately one-half the standard size in all regards and possesses flowers of very light pink to near white.

Hardiness: *Darmera* is successfully grown in the lower reaches of zone 5 in New England and will probably take colder temperatures if provided with some mulching in late autumn.

Cultivation: Though I have observed *Darmera peltata* (with *Aralia californica*) growing in standing water in its native habitat of the Siskiyou Mountains in southern Oregon, it will easily tolerate average garden loam if provided adequate

Darmera peltata (Photo by Lynne Harrison)

The late Gerald Straley pictured with native stands of *Darmera peltata* in the Siskiyou Mountains of southern Oregon (Photo by Daniel J. Hinkley)

supplemental water throughout summer. I grow this species in full sun as well as in my woodland, and the texture provided is unparalleled in both spaces, although the autumn color is better in full-sun sites.

Propagation: Abundant seed is produced after flowering, but be aware that it is often expelled from the capsules by late May and must be gathered at that time and sown fresh. Germination often occurs that autumn or the following spring. If kept isolated, the dwarf form of the species comes perfectly true from seed. Division is easily accomplished by simply slicing the rhizomes with a sharp knife in early spring into 3- to 4-in. (7.5- to 10-cm) segments. Dormant buds along the rhizomes will quickly break into growth.

CHAPTER 17

The Prickly Rhubarbs:
Gunnera

If there is one genus that possesses the ability to excite the nongardening public while endearing itself to a more sophisticated audience, it is *Gunnera*. Worldwide, nearly 50 species of *Gunnera* exist, running the full spectrum of sizes and dimensions, from demure groundcovering species to those of gargantuan proportions. The mammoth *Gunnera masafuerae*, from Chile's Juan Fernández Islands, with foliage to 10 ft. (3 m) across, represents one of the largest-foliaged plants on earth. Though the majority of the species are from the Southern Hemisphere, a few can be found north of the equator throughout Central America and Mexico. The genus as a whole is either dioecious or monoecious, producing apetalous, imperfect flowers along curious spikes in mid- to late summer.

Gunnera tinctoria is found naturally throughout the southern Andean range, geographically centered in the Lakes District of Chile. In cultivation, if provided a rich edaphic environment and supplemental water, the foliage of *G. tinctoria* can develop to tremendous dimensions, ranging from 2 to 5 ft. (0.6 to 1.5 m) across. The rounded leaves, with sharply pointed lobes, are borne on spiny petioles to 3 ft. (0.9 m) in length. The otherworldly inflorescence is an erect cone to 2 ft. (0.6 m) consisting of numerous short branches to 4 in. (10 cm) in length. The small individual flowers result in greenish or reddish colored fruit.

I have observed *Gunnera tinctoria* in a remarkable diversity of microclimates in its natural range: stunted but viable on the dry, cindered slopes surrounding Volcano Osorno north of Puerto Montt; stabilizing coastal dunes to tideline on Chiloé Island; and forming lush, surreal stands of immense foliage in the temperate rain forests of the Alercé. The common overriding theme of these three sites is subsurface water, though this is not to say that *G. tinctoria* will fail in normal garden loam; as long as they are provided with supplemental water through-

Gunnera tinctoria, pictured with *Cortaderia selloana*, at the base of Volcano Osorno in Chile (Photo by Daniel J. Hinkley)

Gunnera tinctoria (Photo by Lynne Harrison)

out the growing season, plants can attain healthy proportions. In colder climates, the crowns should be protected by piles of sawdust or bracken fern in late autumn. The species has escaped from cultivation in Ireland, and with its native brethren *Fuchsia magellanica*, it has claimed wide reaches of the island and generally made a rather robust nuisance of itself. Nomenclaturally, *G. tinctoria* is fairly muddled in the trade and is often offered under its synonym *G. chilensis*.

The more widely encountered *Gunnera manicata* is frequently confused with *G. tinctoria*, from which it differs in the size of the inflorescence as well as the foliage. *Gunnera manicata* is the more stately one and, in fact, represents the largest of the hardy *Gunnera* species. References to its nativity are inconsistent; British publications give Brazil as the homeland for *G. manicata*, whereas the U.S.-published *Hortus Third* assigns it to the mountains of Colombia. Regardless of its true natural environs, the species is perfectly at home in mild temperate climates of North America, and it provides an effect quite unlike any other plant. The immense, rough-textured foliage ranges from 6 to 8 ft. (1.8 to 2.4 m) across—though it can take on even larger proportions in richer sites—and is formed by many sharply pointed lobes. A cone-shaped panicle of minute flowers is produced in late summer and can extend to nearly 7 ft. (2.1 m) in length; the inflorescence's fleshy, pointed branches grow to 6 in. (15 cm) in length and each is dotted by numerous seeds barely covered by flesh.

Gunnera manicata (Photo by Lynne Harrison)

Occurring with *Gunnera tinctoria* in south-central Chile, though extending much farther south, *G. magellanica* forms robust, dioecious colonies of rounded leaves, each from 2 to 5 in. (5 to 12.5 cm) in diameter, on 5-in. (12.5-cm) petioles. I observed this species growing as a groundcover in dry, shaded sites around Volcano Puyehue, where it was more clumping and decidedly less vigorous. *Gunnera magellanica* will grow in perpetually moist sites in sun as well as in well-drained garden loam in shade. Though I have long cultivated this species in my bog garden, where it has formed strapping colonies in short order, it was not until I observed the plant in the wild that I realized how effective the short racemes of female flowers are when they carry the resultant richly red berries. Unfortunately, male plants are more frequently encountered in cultivation than the females. I look forward to providing my colony with a mate of the female persuasion as seedlings of my collections mature.

Gunnera prorepens is the most widely grown of the diminutive species and perhaps the most handsome in the genus for fruit effects. The small purplish-blushed foliage, to 2 in. (5 cm), forms dense rosettes, and vigorously stolonifer-

Gunnera magellanica, with the striking black leaves of *Colocasia esculenta* 'Black Magic' poking through (Photo by Lynne Harrison)

ous colonies of this species have thrived in a small, artificial bog garden outside of my office for nearly ten years. In late summer, the bright red fruit ripens on 4-in. (10-cm) spikes—this can often be the first and only indication that flowers were indeed produced. The show is carried long into autumn and early winter, offering memorable scenes of rich red in startling contrast with the occasional early, pre-Thanksgiving snow. Unlike several *Gunnera* species, *G. prorepens* is self fertile and can produce fruit with a single clone.

I have only recently begun growing a New Zealand species known as *Gunnera flavida*. It superficially resembles *G. prorepens* and is considered by some botanists to be simply a variety of that species. The bronze-colored leaves of *G. flavida* are broadly ovate to 2 in. (5 cm) and form low rosettes of foliage, spreading vigorously by stolons in moist situations. The 4-in. (10-cm) spikes of apetalous flowers are produced in early summer and result in handsome yellowish fruit in autumn.

Growing in the same bog with *Gunnera prorepens*, a small colony of *G. hamiltonii* has proven unable to compete, and it will soon be moved to a less-hostile environment. In appearance it is quite distinctive, forming near-prostrate, starry rosettes of coppery green. In its native New Zealand, this dioecious species is considered endangered, and only one of two colonies that have ever been discovered still exists along the coastal dunes of Stewart Island. Curiously, the two original colonies represented homogeneous stands of separate sexes, with the extant population being totally male. Fortunately, plants from the lost female population are in cultivation.

By contrast, *Gunnera monoica*, as its name implies, is a monoecious species, with male and female flowers formed on the same plant. This species lies on the opposite end of the size spectrum from the gargantuan tropical species. *Gunnera monoica* creates charming, quickly spreading colonies of minute, rounded leaves less than $1/2$ in. (1.25 cm) in length and width. Tiny flowers are produced on short racemes and are followed by globular, white fruit, though I admit that my rather sizable colony has never set seed, for reasons that I do not understand.

Perhaps the hardiest member of the genus is the little-known and infrequently cultivated *Gunnera cordifolia* from Tasmania. It is vigorously stoloniferous, form-

Gunnera prorepens (Photo by Daniel J. Hinkley)

ing expansive mats of prostrate rosettes of ovate foliage, each leaf growing to 1½ in. (3.8 cm) in length. The foliage is glabrous above and pubescent beneath. Small spikes of densely arranged apetalous flowers are produced in midsummer and result in scarlet, ovoid fruit.

Because *Gunnera dentata* has such a wide natural range in its homeland on both islands of New Zealand, from coastal dunes to high alpine meadows, it is considered quite hardy, depending on the provenance of the cultivated material. *Gunnera dentata* has survived temperatures as low as 5°F (−15°C) without mulching, and it would manage much lower temperatures with careful siting and protection. Handsome rosettes of ovate leaves to 1 in. (2.5 cm) in length are held by pubescent petioles. The leaf blades themselves are irregularly dentate or sometimes lobed, while the squat racemes of flowers result in rich orange-red fruit.

Hardiness: The species of *Gunnera* listed here are hardy through the lower reaches of zone 7, though they hail from cooler climates and will certainly melt in heat and humidity faster than a Sumatran glacier. The crowns of the large species are best mulched during the winter with sawdust or piles of bracken fern. In colder climates, the rhizomes of the smaller species can be potted in autumn and protected in a cool, bright environment until winter has passed. These are vigorous growers and will easily recolonize any moist, fertile ground in a single season.

Cultivation: The operative word in regard to the cultivation of any *Gunnera* species is moisture. The large-foliaged species can be encouraged to establish more quickly and maximize their foliage size if planted in soils heavily amended with manure and given supplemental feed and water during the summer. Conversely, the spreading capabilities of the stoloniferous species will be subdued if given a leaner diet. Full sun or very light shade is recommended for all species. In situations of too low light, the weighty foliage of *Gunnera manicata* and *G. tinctoria* cannot be supported by the petioles.

Propagation: The diminutive stoloniferous species are easily produced by division at nearly any time of the year, though I find that doing it in early spring after growth resumes offers the best chances of survival. The larger species lend themselves to division as well, but with great difficulty. Fortunately, copious seed is produced on *Gunnera manicata* and *G. tinctoria*, both of which form male and female flowers on the same plant. The seed ripens to a tawny brown, at which time it can be harvested and, if sown fresh, will germinate immediately. The mammoth inflorescences of these species offer the horticulturist not only an enormous quantity of seed but also a curious substance that is nearly impossible to wash off hands and will permanently stain clothing a rather unsightly brown.

CHAPTER 18

The Lesser *Lathyrus*

I have pondered many different phenomena during my lifelong calling in horticulture, but the one that has been most intriguing, and one that I have alluded to with regard to a variety of different plants, is the circuitous evolution of our botanical interests and garden fashions. Past horticultural acquaintances that were formerly dismissed as unworthy or vulgar perpetually resurface, with seemingly more appeal than ever before.

Such it has been with my own once-soured relationship with the genus *Lathyrus*, the perennial and annual sweet peas. *Lathyrus latifolius*, the perennial pea, is a coarse-foliaged vine that has naturalized throughout much of the United States. Since my emigration from northern Michigan in the early 1970s, this species has colonized vast areas of disturbed soils along the highways and country roads of my youth. Now my parents speak of it enthusiastically, stopping to gather seed in autumn and coaxing it to colonize the rocky, sandy soil in which I struggled as a beginning gardener. They don't remember that this plant once grew there, and that I abandoned my efforts after witnessing its yellowed, ratty-tattered foliage from midsummer onward. Even along the interstates in my adopted homeland, the Pacific Northwest, the folial failings of the perennial pea cannot be seen when you are zipping by at 65 miles an hour, especially if you're wearing polarized sunglasses and the magenta-pink clusters of flowers are electrified to a sensational, show-stopping burnished vermilion.

This is not to say that *Lathyrus latifolius* has not had its share of admirers, including the Princess Royal of perennial gardening herself, Gertrude Jekyll, who to my knowledge never wore sunglasses, polarized or otherwised. She would plant the selected white form of the perennial pea in midborder to smother the withering stems of early perennials. The pea vines would then serve as scaffolding for later-flowering *Clematis*, which in turn would shroud the pea's derelict foliage. Obviously, the divine Ms. J. embraced the creative process in her garden more passionately than that simple-minded lad from northern Michigan who disdained this plant so readily.

Other than a short and sentimental affair with the annual sweet pea (*Lathyrus odoratus*) in the early 1980s, I flippantly dumped the genus and moved on to "more important" plants. Don't bother me—sweet peas, indeed!!! I desired gutsy sorts of plants, plants with a future, like hellebores, snowdrops, smilacinas, and polygonatums.

The proverbial return of this prodigal gardener occurred in the late winter of 1987, when those first jewel-like blossoms of the spring vetchling, *Lathyrus vernus*, emerged from a still-mostly-dormant woodland landscape. The plant had arrived in a box of treasures sent by our friend J. C. Raulston, from North Carolina State University. In those last days of February, I marveled at the magenta-rose flowers, each aging to greenish peacock-blue, crowning a tight, 15-in. (38-cm) clump of ferny, pinnate foliage. The enchantment continued well into May, outperforming weeks of blossom from snowdrops, pulmonarias, trilliums, erythroniums, and other constituents of the woodland.

Lathyrus vernus (Photo by Lynne Harrison)

The following spring, *Lathyrus vernus* reappeared on schedule, the clump having gained in girth only slightly—this is a trait that I have come to perceive as an admirable quality in all plants, rather than a deficiency. Beware of any plant that you can consider dividing for a friend within three years. Good friends can wait, but rampant perennials can swamp our borders like there's no tomorrow.

I now tend my collection of lathyroids with an enthusiasm easily recognized by those familiar with addictive behavior. Forays to England, Japan, Korea, Chile, and China have led to additional cultivars and species of perennial sweet peas, as well as of the closely related genus *Vicia*.

The species that receives credit for this personal renaissance, *Lathyrus vernus*, hails from the mountains of central and eastern Europe, extending into the Caucasus and northern Turkey. It is found naturally in light wooded areas growing on limestone, though as is the case with hellebores (with which the spring vetchling associates well in the garden), this affinity for alkalinity does not translate to necessity in the garden. While adhering to the species's undemanding demeanor as well as its drought tolerance, several color forms of *L. vernus* are available, all of which expand the utility of and interest in this perennial. *Lathyrus vernus* 'Alboroseus', sometimes seen as 'Variegatus', softens the early spring performance with bicolored flowers of pink and white, whereas the pure white *L. vernus* 'Albiflorus' offers an extraordinarily brilliant and long blossoming component to the semishaded garden. Perhaps the most lovely selection, *L. vernus* 'Caeruleus' produces flowers of light lavender-blue, sans the magenta overtones found in the species type. Planted among early blossoming, pastel-yellow selections of *Primula veris*, 'Caeruleus' provides a most memorable early spring vignette in my garden. A very distinctive narrow-foliaged form, *L. vernus* 'Flaccidus', makes a handsome and textural addition while possessing the same magenta-toned flowers of the type species. All forms of the spring vetchling are hardy to zone 5, or perhaps colder regions, and they thrive in shade or semishade in any well-drained soils. Supplemental water during the summer months will extend their season in foliage; if allowed to dry out, however, they will be just as content slipping below ground level by midsummer, none the worse for wear the following spring. Mature clumps will set copious quantities of seed, but it generally will not come true even if the color types are sufficiently isolated, although I have had decent consistency with 'Alboroseus' seed. Division can be accomplished in early spring from selected forms just as growth commences; 'Alboroseus' and 'Caeruleus', however, offer very few divisions on a yearly basis, which explains their relative obscurity in commerce.

The last flowers of *Lathyrus vernus* in mid-May welcome the first flowers of a closely related species known as *Lathyrus venetus*. Often mistaken for the for-

This near-white-flowered seedling of *Lathyrus vernus* 'Alboroseus' at Heronswood was raised by Marina Christopher and John Coke of Green Farm Plants in England (Photo by Lynne Harrison)

Lathyrus vernus 'Caeruleus' (Photo by Lynne Harrison)

mer, *L. venetus* is native to roughly the same area of southern Europe, eastward to Turkey and central Russia, and it grows in a similar habitat of light-shaded woods. Flowers of lavender-pink, in tightly packed upright racemes, are produced in great abundance during May and June; at Heronswood they rise through plants of *Corydalis flexuosa* 'Purple Leaf', which blossom concurrently. They thrive in semishade under a canopy of tall Douglas firs in well-drained soil that receives supplemental summer irrigation. *Lathyrus venetus* sets quantities of seed, which germinate readily when gathered and sown, though oddly I have never observed a self-sown seedling in the garden.

The tall yet surprisingly sturdy stems of *Lathyrus davidii*, rising to 6 ft. (1.8 m) or more, present a distinctive and textural effect to the full-sun or partially shaded garden. The long-lasting display of exceptional nodding clusters of yellowish orange flowers with orange-brown overtones emerges in midsummer. My original plant came from Christopher Lloyd at Great Dixter, though I also collected seed of this species in the wilds of South Korea in the autumn of 1993. Exploring an open, moist meadow with dense stands of *Patrinia scabiosifolia*, *Lysimachia clethroides*, and *Staphylea bumalda*, I came upon a single plant of *Lathyrus davidii*, easily recognized by its upright stems cloaked in its signature foliage

Lathyrus davidii (Photo by Lynne Harrison)

and long and narrow brown legumes. It is a highly valued plant in our sunny, well-drained borders for folial effects as well as for its flowers. The many unfurling stems display spring-green foliage in superb complement to the early blossoming perennials in the garden. Despite its fairly sturdy stems, *L. davidii* benefits from staking or being allowed to grow through a shrub or small tree.

With flowers of a hue very similar to that of *Lathyrus davidii*, but in a much smaller format, *L. aureus* is a most useful and unusual addition for a frontal position in the full-sun perennial border or semishaded garden alike. In truth, the taxa comprises an assemblage of several similar, rather anomalous species from southeastern Europe, with *L. laevigatus* being the better known. Nonetheless, *L. aureus* is the form that represents this muddled lot in my garden. It is found naturally in the mountains of Romania, northern Turkey, and southwestern Russia, growing in light shade and open scrub at elevations around 7000 ft. (2100 m). The intriguing flowers of lovely light orange-brown are produced on 12-in. (30-cm), non-twining stems from late spring into summer from erect and leafy clumps of pinnate foliage. This species responds well both combined with the bright yellow daisies of *Anthemis tinctoria* 'E.C. Buxton' in our full-sun perennial borders and refurbishing a stand of *Helleborus* and *Trillium* in the bright woodland. *Lathyrus aureus* prefers well-drained soils and is quite drought tolerant once fully established. Though exciting to everyone who encounters it in flower, it remains an uncommon species in cultivation.

Having been born again, so to speak, to this genus, I thought it would be a bit unfair to ignore the vining *Lathyrus* species that I had so ruthlessly abandoned two decades earlier. At the base of a small deciduous elm (*Ulmus* ×*hollandica* 'Jacqueline Hillier') in my small scree garden, I have planted the tuberous-rooted *Lathyrus grandiflorus*, which is known in the vernacular as the everlasting pea. Unfortunately, this common name has also been applied to *L. latifolius*—that weedy species that my parents are still trying to establish in their garden—which discourages many from giving *L. grandiflorus* a try in gardens of zone 6 and above that will accommodate it. The handsome blue-green leaves of this species scramble over the densely sculpted elm, and rich pink-red or purple-red bicolored flowers, in three-flowered clusters, are presented for weeks from midsummer onward. *Lathyrus grandiflorus* possesses a frisky demeanor, emerging here and there, and while it takes several years to exhibit this personality trait, its true colors will ultimately show through, so siting must be carefully considered.

Lathyrus rotundifolius is another perennial vining species with striking floral effects. In my garden, the brick-red flowers blossom concurrently with the pristine white and equally drought-tolerant mockorange (*Philadelphus lewisii*) through which it twines. It makes a magnificent pairing. Although *L. rotundifolius*

Lathyrus aureus (Photo by Lynne Harrison)

Lathyrus grandiflorus, the everlasting pea (Photo by Lynne Harrison)

is probably only hardy in zones 6 and above, greater hardiness can be achieved by providing the sharpest drainage possible.

Worthy of note is an annual vining species, *Lathyrus sativus*, from which I collect a small handful of seed in late summer to insure its continuation in the garden. Its short, lax stems trail about the border, bearing rich *Meconopsis*-blue flowers throughout early summer. Though this species is grown as a common forage crop in Europe, I find it to be a top-notch species and worthy of much greater attention by those seeking a distinctive annual addition to the garden or garden pot. Sow early for successful germination and treat as one would any sweet pea.

Acquaint yourselves with at least one member of this treasured genus, and it will lead you to more of its kin—all ready to delight the gardener. There is a remarkable life beyond the trellis of sweet peas.

Hardiness: The nonvining species generally show greater hardiness than the twining contingent and will thrive in zones 5–9. The vining species must be taken on a case-by-case basis; there is little reference to their hardiness outside of the gardens of Europe, where they are more commonly grown.

Cultivation: Full sun or light shade is ideal for the majority of the species, with well-drained, average to poor soils.

Propagation: Even if isolated, the seed of color forms of *Lathyrus vernus* does not come true and division of the clumps in early spring is the only viable means of increasing the plants. *Lathyrus vernus* and its cultivars possess a rather woody rootstock, and some do not offer much material. Seed production by the species is generally sufficient enough to be a useful method of propagation, although the seed can be quite susceptible to fungus infection if stored for any length of time before sowing. To minimize chances of infection, either sow seed fresh or dust with a mild fungicide.

CHAPTER 19

Far and Away from 'Johnson's Blue':
The Hardy Geraniums

Selecting a hardy geranium from a vast and evolving mass of species, cultivars, and hybrids is somewhat like trying to purchase a computer: the next generation awaits to ambush carefully weighed decisions, making one's choice obsolete or inferior in the face of the "new and improved." As with any such dilemma in a fast-paced enterprise, one can simply defer the decision and do nothing, or one can take the plunge and accept whatever enjoyment or benefit can be achieved for the moment. My intention here is to remove the fear from decision, to distill from this daunting inventory of possibilities those *Geranium* species, cultivars, and hybrids that possess timeless qualities.

Those who already include hardy geraniums in their gardens—even those who have grown only *Geranium* 'Johnson's Blue', that garden stalwart embraced by mainstream horticulture—are certainly familiar with the utility these plants offer. With a durable demeanor, handsome foliage, and delicate but substantial blossoms, hardy geraniums are among the workhorses of the American border. Though most possess more than one attribute that makes them desirable components of our gardens, for ease of digestion my nominees are lumped together under the headings of geraniums for groundcover, those for effects of foliage, and those that shine in blossom.

My appreciation of hardy geraniums has come primarily from my association with friends in England, where a tidal surge of new hybrids and renewed use of uncommon species is a decade or more ahead of a similar frenzy across the Atlantic. On numerous occasions I have had the opportunity to observe the species as they exist in the wild. Though I am loath to admit it, the breeder's hand has greatly enhanced the overall beauty and durability of this genus for garden use without diminishing the refinement they already possessed.

Geraniums for Groundcover

If drought is a misfortune to gardeners, then shade devoid of moisture is certainly their bane. Many plants, once discovered, will triumph over this annoyance, but several species of *Geranium* certainly reign supreme in this regard. *Geranium macrorrhizum* rises above the lot, with a large number of superb selections. This species, which hails from southeastern Europe, produces robust clumps of thick, fleshy stems and large-lobed, somewhat felted foliage that are distinctively pine scented, a fragrance that will continue to serve as the best identifying characteristic of this species. Early, profuse blossoms of white to rich cerise add to the desirability of *G. macrorrhizum*.

Several selections of *Geranium macrorrhizum* are well known, but they are often misrepresented in the trade and under cultivation, namely 'Bevan's Variety', 'Spessart', and 'Ingwersen's Variety'. This has more to do with the propensity of the geraniums to self sow directly into the clump that is ultimately to be divided during propagation than with questionable nursery ethics. The hardy geraniums are star performers of such underhanded trickery, though a vast number of herbaceous perennial species follow suit. In controlled circumstances (meaning in nurseries that do not allow plants in their propagation blocks to set seed), this problem has been brought under control—yet the older cultivars of this species, as far as I am concerned, are quite extinct. I should probably digress at this point to say that even if the cultivar name represents a dubious assortment of variants, the plants offered under these names likely will not disappoint.

Fortunately, the newer selections of *Geranium macrorrhizum* provide sufficient inducement for bypassing the older cultivars. *Geranium macrorrhizum* 'Czakor' produces sizable mounds of odoriferous foliage and an early display of highly charged magenta blossoms. This might aptly be described as a more intensely saturated form of *G. macrorrhizum* 'Bevan's Variety', though the origins of 'Czakor' are quite original, having been extracted directly from the wild. The same is true of *G. macrorrhizum* 'Pindus', which is found in the wilds of Greece and bears similarly hued flowers to 'Czakor' but in a much smaller format, creating dense 8-in. (20-cm) mounds of foliage

The cultivar name of *Geranium macrorrhizum* 'Album' implies that the flowers are pure white, but this has not been true in my observation. In fact, I have had much purer white-flowered forms occur spontaneously in my garden. The flowers blush with the faintest pink, amplified by an association of the pink calyces and stamens attending each flower

Search long and hard enough, and you will find a variegated version of any plant that you have in mind. *Geranium macrorrhizum* does not deviate from this principle, with a selection offering creamy marbled, somewhat pinkish-stained foliage that slowly produces a handsome clump—slowly, in this case, is to be well noted, since *G. macrorrhizum* 'Variegatum' is exasperatingly nonvigorous, and this selection must receive extra cultural attention initially in the form of moisture and fertilizer. The rich rose flowers are infrequently produced, though the superb foliage provided is compensation enough.

Geranium macrorrhizum and its many selections bring to the garden a freshness in spring that is hard to achieve through any other plant. Bright green foliage emerges as verdant foil to the early narcissus and crocus, while giving way shortly thereafter to a long display of blossoms that successfully marks the transition of the garden from late winter to spring.

If you have grown *Geranium procurrens*, you have no doubts whatsoever as to the meaning of its specific epithet. This plant procures every patch of soil in its path, running and romping over, through, and across the dry, shaded garden, occasionally sending its long stems upward into small shrubs and trees to reach even the upper atmosphere of its surroundings. Interestingly, I observed *G. procurrens* only once while trekking in its native haunts of eastern Nepal, and here it demurely trailed over a steep bank in cool, shaded soils, more intent on commingling than conquering. The bright magenta, dark-eyed flowers of this species are produced in early to midsummer and are a welcome sight, even while you are pondering how to thwart its forward advance through the garden. All of us, however, have areas in our garden where few desirable things will grow, and this untamed geranium species should be considered as an ideal colonist for those uninhabitable wastelands.

Geranium procurrens has been tamed through matrimony to other species, however, and the resultant hybrid progeny are exceptional garden-worthy plants. Perhaps best-known of the bunch is *Geranium* 'Ann Folkard', which resulted from a union of *G. procurrens* to *G. psilostemon*. Chartreuse foliage on stems to 6 ft. (1.8 m) explore the surrounding areas of the garden but retreat yearly to their point of origin. Throughout the summer, 'Ann Folkard' provides a nonstop display of large, purple-toned magenta flowers with black eyes. Because it is a sterile hybrid, it was until recently a hard-to-find plant in commerce, spreading slowly across the continent from one top-notch garden to another; now in tissue culture, its rarity has diminished without affecting its desirability. A sister seedling from the same cross, 'Anne Thomson', possesses nearly identical flowers and foliage but in a much more clumping format, rising to only 15 in. (38 cm). Both hybrid cultivars are extremely useful in combination with purple-foliaged shrubs and herbaceous perennials. I have used them to good effect with the rich purple ferny clumps of *Anthriscus sylvestris* 'Ravenswing' in the full-sun border,

Geranium 'Ann Folkard' growing alongside *Aster* 'Chequers' (Photo by Lynne Harrison)

Geranium 'Anne Thomson' combining nicely with the dark foliage and small, pinkish flowers of *Aster lateriflorus* 'Prince' at Heronswood (Photo by Lynne Harrison)

as well as nearby *Aster lateriflorus* 'Prince', the black-purple foliage of which is prevalent throughout summer and into autumn.

Geranium procurrens paired with *G. lambertii*—a species bearing large and lovely rose flowers richly veined in pink—has given rise to a spectacular cultivar that, like the above hybrids, possesses yellow foliage that remains quite intense throughout the season. In *Geranium* 'Salome', flowers of deep rose are veined with a purple that becomes more prevalent in the center. Produced throughout the late summer and autumn, the flowers are extraordinary, especially when carried with the pastel-yellow foliage. 'Salome' planted alongside the unfurling, dark violet bracts and steely blue leaves of *Cerinthe major* 'Purpurascens' in full sun makes for a superlative combination. 'Salome' is a sterile hybrid and must be propagated vegetatively.

If the trait of yellow foliage is beginning to seem a bit redundant, then it is perhaps appropriate to finally come clean regarding this foliage trait: in the case of geraniums, yellow foliage is a strong indication that you are dealing with a sterile hybrid. Whereas I speculate that physiologically this variegated foliage simply represents insufficient chlorophyll production due to an inappropriate pairing of DNA, it is a particularly useful tool to the nurseryperson in locating possible new garden-worthy selections from seedling trays or while weeding the garden itself, since nearly all hybrid geraniums germinate with yellow foliage. I lift these aberrant seedlings and grow them on in pots to evaluate their performance before discarding. This foliage trait may be retained, as in 'Ann Folkard' and 'Anne Thomson', or may disappear with age.

I grow *Geranium* 'Dilys' as much for the name as for the plant itself; it commemorates author and superb plantswoman, and personal friend, Dilys Davies, who gardens in the Lake District of northern England. This hybrid is the last in a long series of relationships pursued by the promiscuous *Geranium procurrens*, in this case with the well-known bloody cranesbill, *G. sanguineum*. The overall growth habit and appearance of 'Dilys' keeps true to the latter parent, though the late-summer and long-produced rich pink flowers, suffused with and veined in purple, are solely the influence of *G. procurrens*. The two distinct colors on the flowers of a single plant provides a remarkable effect. Geranium breeding, though quite actively pursued by several English nurserypeople, is still in its infancy, and I suspect that we have not heard the last of the siring exploits of *G. procurrens*.

A species that has a somewhat similar but more restrained demeanor in regard to growth, but with a nonstop presentation of light pink or near white stars, is known as *Geranium asphodeloides*. It is exceptional for interplanting with roses or similarly sized, short-blossoming shrubs, in full sun and well-drained soils.

Wiry branches carry the long progression of blossoms and very pretty dissected foliage into the limbs of the shrubs, creating interest in the otherwise quiet bones of the garden. No self-sown seedlings have appeared from the two cultivars of this species that I grow, which are 'Prince Regent', with pink flowers that are richer than what is thought to be typical, and 'Starlight', with flowers of white blushed lightly with rose.

Hardy Geraniums for Foliage Effect

Certainly well suited to be groundcovers, especially in areas of dry shade, *Geranium phaeum* and its many cultivars are also superbly put to use as singular specimens for effects of foliage and flower in the mixed border. Known commonly as mourning widow for its somber, bruise-colored flowers with strongly flaring petals, the species provides additional interest by the blackish purple markings on its dark green, rounded foliage. A superior seedling, found in the wilds of Croatia by Elizabeth Strangman of Washfield Nursery, has foliage with a broad purplish

banding, resembling that of a zonal pelargonium (that is, the hybrid group *Pelargonium* ×*hortorum*, the foliage of which is marked with a semicircular zone). Named for the village where it was found, 'Samobor' is one of the most striking new foliage plants to come to gardeners for some time. It combines remarkably well with the glaring golden foliage of *Philadelphus coronarius* 'Aureus' or the similarly colored *Filipendula ulmaria* 'Aurea' and *Hosta* 'Sun Power'.

The three white-variegated forms of *Geranium phaeum* are exceptional components of my woodland, enlivening plantings of ferns, arisaemas, and hostas. In the dappled shade, where their lightening quality is most appreciated, 'Variegatum' and 'Taff's Jester' put on a good show throughout the summer months. 'Variegatum', which made the rounds for many years under the misnomer of *G.* ×*monacense* 'Muldoon', possesses irregularly blotched white and green foliage with random coral and

Geranium phaeum 'Samobor' (Photo by Lynne Harrison)

plum streaking. It appears quite as if rays of sunlight, broken by the limbs of Douglas firs through which it streams, were captured on the foliage of this geranium. The leaves of 'Taff's Jester', on the other hand, begin the season suffused with whitish gold and then fade to frosted green. New to the scene, but certain to become a wildly popular cultivar over time, *G. phaeum* 'Margaret Wilson' has foliage that emerges in tones of white-yellow in early spring and remains astoundingly effective throughout the season. It has proven to be perfectly robust despite obviously lacking its full share of chlorophyll.

Geranium phaeum has shown extreme plasticity in flower as well as foliage, much to the gardener's benefit. 'Joan Baker' presents copious quantities of reflexed, grayish lavender blossoms on 15-in. (38-cm) stems above luscious clumps of green foliage. The distinctive and refined color is wonderfully combined with the platinum filigree of artemisias or in a container with the superb if not tender, subshrubby, silver-foliaged morning glory (*Convolvulus cneorum*). *Geranium phaeum* 'Album' remains one of my favorite geraniums that I cultivate in the woodland, with pure white flowers held above mounds of bright green foliage. In late April, the flowers of this selection commingle with the still-intact dark purple sepals of a selected *Helleborus ×hybridus* in our woodland—and the composition forms an enchanting bridge between the winter and summer garden. A third cultivar of *G. phaeum*, 'Lily Lovell', represents the richest color achieved to date from this species; rich grape-purple flowers are held on upright stems above wholly green foliage.

Relying nearly on foliage alone for its continued invitation to gardens, *Geranium renardii* is among the loveliest of all geraniums for folial interest. Forming

The remarkable foliage of *Geranium phaeum* 'Variegatum' (Photo by Lynne Harrison)

ever-expanding handsome clumps of pewtered, felted foliage, this species would be welcome even if it never blossomed at all. The flowers are whitish lavender, but the sound of that shade is more desirable than the delivered effect, as the hue is weakened to a dirty white in combination with foliage of such presence. Enter, however, *G. platypetalum*. This robust, violet-flowered species, which perhaps is best known for parenting, with *G. ibericum*, the hybrid *G. ×magnificum*, has paired with *G. renardii*. How exciting when the superb traits of two different plants—in

The lovely foliage of *Geranium renardii* is accentuated by the dark, upright spears of *Phormium tenax* 'Amazing Red'. (Photo by Lynne Harrison)

this case the flowers of *G. platypetalum* and the foliage of *G. renardii*—are brought together in one superior individual. *Geranium* 'Phillippe Vapelle' possesses the same folial desirability of *G. renardii* with the added bonus of flowers in deep shades of lavender that carry sufficient presence to compete with the exquisite foliage. It is interesting to note (while providing a convenient transition to our discussion of floral effects) that a cross of *G. renardii* with a Turkish species known as *G. gracile* gave rise to the handsome *Geranium* 'Chantilly'. The felted, bright green, and lobed foliage of this hybrid appears midway between that of the two parent species. Perhaps the influence of *G. gracile*, the best garden performance of which is seen in sites with more-than-adequate moisture, has flawed the performance of 'Chantilly' in full sun and hot positions, where its foliage will often burn. In rich, moist soils, or under light-shaded positions, the handsome foliage is a superb backdrop to a long display of pinkish lavender flowers produced in abundance.

Hardy Geraniums for Flower Effect

The flowers are indeed what most of us seek initially in the process of discovering the utility and breadth of ornament offered by the genus *Geranium*. Supreme in this regard are the double- or semidouble-flowered species, which have considerably extended blossoming times, since energy is not expended in producing seed. *Geranium himalayense* 'Plenum', often seen as 'Birch Double', is the best-known of this lot. Indeed, the low mounds of this antique cultivar, with finely cut foliage and multipetaled lavender roses on 1-ft. (0.3-m) stems, are a wonderful addition to the front of the border in full sun. It successfully combines with the fluid lemon blades of *Hakonechloa macra* 'Aureola' or flanking the upright, white-striped fans of the variegated gladwyn iris, *Iris foetidissima* 'Variegata'.

Many double-flowered hardy geraniums that are less commonly encountered are also worth seeking, though I can attest that the search itself can be a challenge. *Geranium pratense* is common in meadows throughout northern Europe, and it has offered from among its ranks three outstanding, if too infrequently found in commerce, double-flowered forms: 'Plenum Album', 'Plenum Caeruleum', and 'Plenum Violaceum'. *Geranium pratense* 'Plenum Album' is perhaps the rarest of the three. Along with double white flowers produced in moderate abundance, it possesses a weak demeanor that must be coaxed with increased fertility during the growing season. 'Plenum Violaceum' is hardly deep enough in hue to deserve its name, but the effect of rich lavender double flowers atop mounds of deeply dissected foliage rising to 18 in. (45 cm) is a lovely sight when the plant blossoms in early June. Of the three, I am most partial to *G. pratense* 'Plenum Caeruleum'. In early summer, a long display of large, lavender, sterile double flowers suffused with light blue are held on stems rising to 2 ft. (0.6 m). It forms a robust clump after time and will benefit from division on a regular basis. This cultivar is superbly paired with the pewter, filigreed foliage of *Artemisia* 'Powis Castle' in full sun.

It is not simply the double-flowered forms of *Geranium pratense*, however, that offer clever additions to the early summer garden. Various color forms of this species make fine components of the precisely planted herbaceous border as well as in more freely designed informal settings. *Geranium pratense* 'Mrs. Kendall Clark' is a lovely form that comes true from seed, possessing flowers of a most intriguing silvery lavender and veined with a deeper hue. Coming reasonably true from seed, but better if divided, *G. pratense* 'Silver Queen' sports shimmering pink flowers with darker veins from robust clumps more suited to the midborder. Flowers of both pure white and lavender-blue, as well as flowers streaked and spotted in both colors, are produced on a single plant of *G. pratense* 'Striatum'. This curious but lovely "3-in-1" hardy geranium comes nearly true from seed and can be sorted in seedling stage by discarding any that show pinkish coloration to the leaf petioles.

Though the subject of folial effects has already been dealt with (and I may risk undermining my deliberate attempt to ease the process of exploring the

Geranium pratense 'Plenum Caeruleum' (Photo by Lynne Harrison)

shining members of this genus), I must digress momentarily from the matter at hand to discuss the colored-leaf forms of *Geranium pratense*. There are currently only two, both of which are variations on a theme of plum wine. *Geranium pratense* 'Victor Reiter' occurred spontaneously in the San Francisco garden of the nurseryman of that name in the early 1970s, and subsequently a seedling strain of this superb foliage plant was distributed under the name Victor Reiter Group. The finely dissected, forest-green leaves of this strain emerge in early spring with a deep violet suffusion. As the foliage matures, the rich tints are diluted, and the overall color intensity is diminished, but throughout early summer, as rich lavender-blue flowers are presented in a near-nonstop performance, there remains clear evidence of a continued purplish blush to the foliage. When grown in isolation, or with controlled selfing of the flowers, the *G. pratense* Victor Reiter Group exhibits the classic principles of Mendelian genetics in the resultant seedlings. One quarter of the progeny revert to the standard green form of the species, one half continue in the traditions of their parent, and one quarter emerge with extremely dark purple foliage that does not fade. The latter strain, which is currently available under the name Midnight Reiter Group, produces the most striking specimens. The finely fretted foliage of these seedlings remains as dark as a midsummer Midwestern thundercloud through the entire season and provides a superlative foil to purple-blue flowers produced in early summer. The only failing of this plant is its relative slowness to establish and make sizable clumps, which considering its lack of chlorophyll, is understandable. I have used the *G. pratense* Midnight Reiter Group to good effect in full sun, interplanted with the upright, jagged, white and green spears of *Sisyrinchium striatum* 'Aunt May' and the rich pink, spurred flowers of *Diascia* 'Wendy'. With the availability of the extraordinary darker leaved strain increasing, not only in the U.S. but abroad as well, it will only be a matter of time before new crosses are made that carry the superb foil of this plant to new heights.

All the forms of *Geranium pratense* mentioned may suffer from a midsummer infection of powdery mildew, which can be remedied by a quick and painless crew cut immediately after blossoming. The renewed foliage growth not only will be resistant to infection but will bring fresh and verdant foil to the summer garden, adding strength to the garden long after its flowering season is finished.

Geranium 'Spinners' is a (suspected) child of *Geranium pratense*, with the other parent not yet claiming responsibility. The history of 'Spinners' is rooted in my beloved Seattle and is associated with my late friend Marvin Black, who was city arborist before his death in 1987. Marvin sent seed of *G. pratense* to Spinners Garden, a superb specialty nursery located slightly southwest of Southampton, England. There the proprietor, Peter Chappell, germinated the lot of

The *Geranium pratense* Midnight Reiter Group forms a superb combination with *Sedum cauticola*, *Diascia* 'Wendy', and *Sisyrinchium striatum* 'Aunt May' at Heronswood (Photo by Lynne Harrison)

seed and selected from the ranks a seedling that displayed superb deeply dissected foliage and apparent vigor. Unlike the more diminutive *Geranium* 'Nimbus', which tends to falter in blossom by midsummer, *Geranium* 'Spinners' continues unabated, presenting large, bluish lavender cups in remarkable quantity from mounds of foliage rising to 4 ft. (1.2 m) by summer's end. Though its strong and continued floral presence allows for ease of union with many summer-blossoming stalwarts, its most favorable reviews have come from its combination with a simple garden bench that fronts its position in a sunny island border at Heronswood. By late summer, the explorative strands of flower and leaf have journeyed above and through the bench's bleached wooden slats, making it nearly impossible to sit, but it is well worth it to simply stand and enjoy this remarkable geranium.

    Geranium 'Nimbus' is destined for greatness on the merit of both foliage and flower. Parented by *G. collinum* and *G. clarkei* 'Kashmir Purple', it bears handsome, finely dissected, medium green leaves that by themselves are reason

A simple garden bench at Heronswood is enveloped by the virtually nonstop floral display of *Geranium* 'Spinners' (Photo by Lynne Harrison)

enough to grow this hybrid. An extremely long progression of rich lavender-blue, white-eyed flowers are produced from early June through the end of July along delicate stems, which will reach 4 ft. (1.2 m) by summer's end. Paired with *Iris sibirica*, the geranium will clamber through the upright thrusts of iris foliage, the two joining in a duet of blossom; later, 'Nimbus' provides superb textural relief to the stark vertical columns of foliage.

I have already made passing mention of *Geranium psilostemon* in discussing the intriguingly beautiful hybrid cultivars *Geranium* 'Ann Folkard' and *Geranium* 'Anne Thomson', but this species is worthy of inclusion in the garden in its own right for its striking blossoms of rich magenta-cerise, centered by a dark purplish black eye. The species is quite robust, producing mounds of deeply cut foliage to 2 ft. (0.6 m) or slightly more, and it puts on a sizzling display of flowers from mid-June onward. I have grown a selected form known as *G. psilostemon* 'Bressingham Flair', but I have not found it sufficiently different to recommend it over the species. Being a bit too punchy in color, this species is a challenge to integrate into the border. I have used it to some degree of success with the dark blue-

Geranium 'Nimbus' (Photo by Lynne Harrison)

velvet blossoms of *Salvia guaranitica* and flanking a small specimen of *Cornus mas* 'Aurea', which offers bright golden foliage throughout summer.

Geranium sylvaticum is native to Europe, where it is known as the wood's cranebill, and it is another superb and hardy species for floral effect in our gardens. Atop distinctive broad, lobed leaves, the flowers open and turn upward in long progression from crowded clusters of nodding buds, which possess enough voice to aid in identifying the plant in the garden or field. A chance seedling of *G. sylvaticum* occurred in our garden not far from where we had buried our cocker spaniel, and time and again knowledgeable visitors to the garden would stop to admire its blossoms, which consist of rounded, deep lavender petals that lighten to near white at their base. Comparisons of this plant to the more widely known *G. sylvaticum* 'Mayflower' showed that it was indeed distinct and superior, and we subsequently named it 'Nikita' in honor of our dog's memory.

Geranium sylvaticum 'Amy Doncaster' is undoubtedly the form that takes top billing in this species and, in fact, in nearly any category of geranium that might be conjured. Is it the plant or the memories that I find so superb? As with so many other fond memories associated with my garden and plants, I will probably never know for certain. Though I met Ms. Doncaster shortly before her death, in a nursing home in the south of England, I did not know her well. As we talked, however, plant names brought forth in her mind images of her once-superb and meritorious garden, and her eyes would light up with the pure joy that only true gardeners can know. The geranium 'Amy Doncaster' speaks to the same joy that I saw in her eyes that day. Deep blue flowers, without even a hint of lavender and eyed with pure white, are produced atop 15-in. (38-cm), bright green mounds of foliage in early summer. In my garden, the lovely upturned blossoms are produced on plants at the base of a weeping larch, mingling with the bright spring-green needles on the tree's lowest branches. It is a combination of which even this perspicacious plantswoman would have approved.

I will not linger on *Geranium traversii* var. *elegans* for long, as it is a tender species with limited scope for even the least jaded gardeners of the maritime West. Yet I wish to dwell here momentarily for two reasons. First, this is a geranium that is native to the Chatham Islands, to the east of New Zealand. Having, in my own limited travels, observed hardy geraniums in eastern and western North America (including Alaska), Mexico, Japan, Korea, and China, I find it of great interest that the genus has also done well for itself in the Southern Hemisphere—in fact, on every continent save Antarctica. Though I have come to appreciate the short but sweet encounter with *G. traversii* var. *elegans* in my own garden, where

Geranium sylvaticum 'Amy Doncaster' (Photo by Lynne Harrison)

it produces low mats of small, silvery foliage and precious marbled pink-and-white flowers, it is mostly for its hardier and long-lived hybrid progeny that my true appreciation is born. Which brings us to the second reason for mentioning this not-so-hardy geranium here. Coupled with the sturdier *G. endressii* (whose own child, 'Wargrave Pink', has graced the pages of more than one catalog centerfold in the past decade), *G. traversii* created the sterile seedling progeny that have been given the rather uneuphonious collective moniker of *G. ×riversleaianum*. The original hybrid, *G. ×riversleaianum* 'Russel Pritchard', is still among the best, with a seemingly unending display of rich rosy red flowers produced along low, spreading carpets of foliage. At season's end, and after such a massive display, one can hardly reconcile the small clumping crown that remains after first frost. I have used this selection in concert with *Diascia* 'Blackthorn Apricot' in a small island bed in full sun to create a superb flower show for weeks on end, from early to late summer. *Geranium ×riversleaianum* 'Mavis Simpson' is much more restrained in habit and possesses more affinity to its New Zealand parent with regard to its lovely pewtered, pubescent foliage and quantities of silvery pink flowers—but the hardiness of *G. endressii* comes through in the end. A more recent introduction, *G. ×riversleaianum* 'Little Gem', is more like 'Russel Pritchard' in floral color but more restrained in growth. It is reportedly the hardiest of the kin, although I cannot support that finding, having lost it in my garden during a relatively mild winter.

The progeny resulting from the hybridizing of *Geranium versicolor* and *G. endressii* are perhaps the most commonly grown hardy geraniums in gardens and are responsible for popularizing the genus as a whole. Unfortunately, these hybrids are not sterile; in fact, they are exceedingly fecund, and hours will be spent removing seedlings that self sow throughout the garden. For this reason alone, many named forms of *G. ×oxonianum* exist, with a large number possessing little more than a different name to distinguish it from the next.

Of the numerous cultivars of the hybrid *Geranium ×oxonianum* that I cultivate, the double and semidouble forms are the most worthy of inclusion in the garden. *Geranium ×oxonianum* 'Thurstonianum' bears quantities of rich rose flowers with very narrow straplike petals. The star-shaped flowers are produced throughout the summer on long, explorative strands that climb into the branches of *Rosa glauca* in our perennial border. Long after the rose has finished blossoming, the flowers of this geranium continue to provide a nearly identical color and shape. In similar form and hue, *G. ×oxonianum* 'Southcombe Double' carries the effect even further by adding an extra complement of petals to the center of each flower, making for double or nearly double flowers throughout summer and early autumn. I have them resting among the upright, variegated spikes of *Iris foetidissima* 'Variegata'.

Geranium ×oxonianum 'Walter's Gift' provides additional folial interest by adding a dash of bronze in the zonal banding across the leaf blade, which is most intense in full-sun situations. This cultivar will self sow with abandon, while its progeny further express the banding trait in similar or more intensely toned variations. The flowers are light silvery pink and lovely, though I have included the plant in my garden mostly for its remarkable departure in form. I have paired a particularly fine seedling from 'Walter's Gift' that occurred in our garden with *Persicaria filiformis*, which itself carries an intense purplish brown chevron across its narrow-ovate leaves. Nearby, a dwarf German iris blossoms in early spring in tones of bronze, effectively pulling together the color spectrum shared with the geranium and the *Persicaria*, which remain effective throughout the summer.

Of those garden classics that seemingly never fade but only create more demand as the years proceed, none can be more lovely than *Geranium wallichianum* 'Buxton's Variety', selected by E. C. Buxton nearly 100 years ago. Spode-blue, white-eyed flowers are produced throughout summer from low, spreading

Geranium ×riversleaianum 'Mavis Simpson' (Photo by Lynne Harrison)

mounds of small, handsome foliage. Though some seedlings from this plant do come true, decades of including inferior seedlings under this cultivar name has diminished the desirability of much of the stock seen in cultivation.

Hardiness: Hardy geraniums are simply that; the greater part of the genus hails from the Northern Hemisphere and thus offers an enormous breadth of species and hybrids to the gardener in zones 4–9. Many forms will, unfortunately, resent the heat and humidity of the Southeast, though trials indicate that this problem is not as great as once perceived.

Cultivation: Although each species exhibits a personality of its own, they share an adaptive quality that allows their enjoyment in a wide range of garden conditions. Most prefer well-drained soils; *Geranium ×magnificum* and *G. maculatum* will take very moist soils in stride. As discussed, several species will tolerate dry shade, although they are a bit more cheery if planted in somewhat moister soils in full sun. Cutting plants to the ground after flowering is vital for preventing the plethora of self-sown seedlings that will certainly appear from the fertile species and hybrids, as well as for providing a fresh growth of foliage to be enjoyed throughout the season.

Propagation: Division in early spring is the best method of propagation for the named cultivars and hybrids. *Geranium macrorrhizum* is best suited to propagation by cuttings, which is easily done under mist in midsummer. Seed is my preferred method for the species; the seed is dispersed over a long period, however, and care must be taken to procure the seed regularly as it ripens. Hybrid seedlings are easily recognizable in the flats, as their foliage generally shows a yellowing or variegation. I encourage gardeners to isolate these seedlings and grow them on to evaluate their potential as garden-worthy plants.

CHAPTER 20

Shrieking Solanoids:
Mandragora and *Scopolia*

Ethnobotanically speaking, few plant families, outside of grasses, have had a greater impact on our human condition than the Solanaceae. From tobacco to deadly nightshade, brugmansias to potatoes, members of this rather immense jumble of medicinal, edible, and poisonous plants have been both held in high regard and steeped in myth and mystery for centuries. Even the ubiquitous tomato was, for some time, thought to be poisonous and its vitamin-rich fruits were religiously avoided. *Lycium chinense*, used as a culinary spice in Asia, was worth its weight in gold in early Rome. The plant was imported from the "barbarians," and the name barbarian berry, and later barberry, was applied to the shrubs erroneously believed to be the source of this curative fruit.

Hidden from an enormous congregation of ornamental or oddly attractive genera are two that have brought a great deal of fascination as well as intrigue to my garden and travels: *Mandragora* and *Scopolia*.

Mandragora

I encountered my first mandrake in Rosemary Verey's garden at Barnsley House in Gloucestershire. Near the front of her July borders were several "piles" of large, greenish yellow fruit held near the ground on short pedicels, looking more like an entry by the esteemed British environmental artist Andy Goldsworthy in a vegetable art fair than a living plant. I was immediately intrigued and questioned my host as to its identity, only to learn that it was quite common and rather good. It was demanded that I give it a try, so I accepted a plant for myself and one for our mutual friend Steve Lorton in Seattle. Within five minutes' time,

I was not only introduced to a new genus by the First Lady of English Gardening, but was entangled in its international trafficking.

Reginald Farrer was not as kind to *Mandragora officinarum* as was Ms. Verey. In his characteristic volley of light artillery, Farrer opens fire by referring to a "dingy innocent plant of awful reputation." The reputation he refers to is the claim that the branched, anthropomorphic roots will shriek when pulled from the ground. Furthermore, this primal scream had the potential to drive one insane, and dogs were traditionally employed to do the dirty work. (Whether Mad Dog disease was as notorious as its modern-day bovine counterpart is unknown.)

Mandragora officinarum is native to only northern Italy and western Yugoslavia, where it grows naturally in slightly shaded, rocky sites. In late winter, rosettes of dark, pubescent leaves with an accentuated undulating leaf margin emerge from the ground, while rather handsome lavender-blue, solitary flowers are produced on short pedicels. The flowers result in rounded, yellowish green fruit the size of small tomatoes; although the fruit offer a note of interest for the midsummer garden, they are poisonous. *Mandragora autumnalis*, from coastal sites throughout the Mediterranean, is similar in effect but with less-hairy foliage than the former, although it may be prickly, and with more elongated fruit of yellow or orange.

The large, greenish yellow fruit of *Mandragora officinarum* (Photo by Daniel J. Hinkley)

In 1995, while in an open meadow surrounding a sacred lake known as Gola Pokari at an elevation of 13,000 ft. (3900 m) in eastern Nepal, I observed the rarest species of mandrake growing among barberry hummocks. As suggested by its specific epithet, *Mandragora caulescens* is a stemmed (caulescent) species, the only one of its kind in the genus, and it is certainly the most showy of the trio in blossom. In early spring, as the foliage emerges, numerous outward-facing bells—each composed of a dark, sinister purple corolla mostly concealed by a greenish purple calyx—are produced on 5-in. (12.5-cm) stems, superficially resembling a purplish hellebore from a distance. The leafy stems grow to nearly 2 ft. (0.6 m) carrying wavy-margined foliage coated in fine pubescence. Though we were unsuccessful in locating seed of this species at Gola Pokari, a year later members of our expedition to Yunnan Province in China found *M. caulescens* in fruit near Tianchi Lake at 12,500 ft. (3750 m). I have germinated the seed and currently wait for the plants to gain in stature and blossom in my garden.

Hardiness: The European species of *Mandragora* are hardy in zones 6–9, probably lower if heavily mulched in winter. The sole Asiatic counterpart, *Mandragora caulescens*, has such limited distribution in cultivation that an abysmal lack of data is available regarding its hardiness. Because of its natural occurrence at such high elevations, it will certainly resent any summer heat and humidity. *Mandragora caulescens* grew in concert with *Meconopsis* and *Primula*, and these may be used as a standard for appropriateness in one's climate.

Cultivation: Ideally suited to well-drained soils with adequate winter moisture. The Asian species will perhaps tolerate more summer moisture but will depend on cool temperatures in summer. I have lost the mandrakes in my garden from too much winter wetness; water-logged soils must be avoided. Site in bright, shaded areas with a tall overstory.

Propagation: Quite easily propagated by seed sown fresh in autumn. The rootstocks are deep-rooted and woody and so do not lend themselves to division— with or without the squealing.

Scopolia

The genus *Scopolia* is neatly bundled within the Solanaceae, keeping good company with other ornamental members of the family, including the aforementioned *Mandragora* as well as *Atropa*, *Jaborosa*, *Physochlaina*, *Rehmannia*, and *Solanum*, among others. *Scopolia* most closely resembles *Atropa* in flower, though the general format is tidier and it is less invasive, less poisonous, and earlier to blossom. *Scopolia carniolica* is found growing naturally in eastern Europe, from Austria to the Baltic Sea and the Caucasus, and is a cherished member of the spring woodland chorus at Heronswood. It breaks from dormancy in early spring, pushing forth in leafy growth as its showy bell-shaped flowers are presented. This species is represented by a very soft yellow form, which is the showier but less common one, as well as by a metallic-chocolate-purple form. The pendulous cups have a large, green calyx and are composed of five fused lobes. Bright yellow fruit follow in midsummer to provide a second season of interest. The flowers and subsequent fruit are borne in the axils of the ovate, sometimes lobed foliage along stems to 2 ft. (0.6 m). The leaves, to 5 in. (12.5 cm), are often borne in false pairs, one large and one half sized, which offers a good identifying trait for the genus in the field.

The yellow-flowered form of *Scopolia carniolica* is rarely encountered in commerce, but its pendulous bells illuminate the early spring garden (Photo by Lynne Harrison)

The more common form of *Scopolia carniolica* offers blossoms of deep purple (Photo by Lynne Harrison)

This leaf arrangement aided in identifying two species in South Korea, which grew throughout the peninsula in moist, shaded sites under *Quercus aliena*. *Scopolia parviflora* rises to 18 in. (45 cm), and its bells of rich, sheeny burgundy are produced in similar fashion to those of its European counterpart, though somewhat larger in size—to 1 1/4 in. (3 cm)—and fewer in number along the stems. This species has great affinity to *S. japonica*, which occurs throughout the mountains of Honshu, Kyushu, and Shikoku in Japan. The leafy stems of *S. japonica* rise to 2 ft. (0.6 m), brandishing yellow-suffused purple flowers in March and April. *Scopolia lutescens*, with pure yellow flowers, is a recognized taxa by Korean botanists, though it may simply be a color form of *S. parviflora*. I collected fruit of several *Scopolia* specimens in Korea in 1993, but they have yet to blossom so I have not been afforded the opportunity to examine their color and other floral characteristics.

In high elevations of Nepal, *Scopolia stramonifolia* is collected and dried for yak fodder in winter, though the leaves are poisonous when fresh. Bleddyn Wynn-Jones and I observed this species growing in the wooded sites below Topke Gola at 11,500 ft. (3450 m), where its characteristic whitish down coated the undersurface of each leaf. Unfortunately, we were too late for seed, and consequently *S. stramonifolia* exists only in my garden of memories—a landscape that seldom needs weeding and watering but where the flowers become larger and more intensely colored, and the recognizable specimens become fewer in number as the river rolls on.

Hardiness: *Scopolia carniolica*, the most commonly encountered species, is hardy to zones 5–9, perhaps colder areas if mulched. Little data exists for the other species, which are virtually absent in cultivation.

Cultivation: *Scopolia* will thrive in a well-drained, humus-rich soil in the open woodland, though it seems to tolerate of a wide range of soil types. It makes for a superb component early in the season, combining nicely with *Pulmonaria*, *Primula*, *Corydalis*, and *Epimedium*. Those species that I have cultivated are not aggressively stoloniferous and will behave quite politely. The fruit and foliage may show evidence of toxicity to humans, pets, and livestock and should be sited accordingly. I have not seen self-sown seedlings occur.

Propagation: Though somewhat berrylike in appearance, the fruit is technically a capsule, each containing many seeds. These germinate in a single season and establish quickly, although the yellow-flowered form of *Scopolia carniolica* does not consistently come true. Division in early spring is readily accomplished after full establishment in the garden.

CHAPTER 21

Starry Charms:
Omphalodes and *Myosotidium*

Attesting to their seemingly inherent ornamental qualities, a large assemblage from the family Boraginaceae are already present in our gardens, whether we are aware of it or not. The forget-me-not family is represented in the woodland and full-sun borders at Heronswood by no fewer than 17 genera of herbaceous plants, in addition to one robust, large-leaved tree, known as *Ehretia acuminata*. Beyond the woody anomaly to the family, our early spring garden is blessed with expansive colonies of more recognizable genera: *Brunnera, Lithodora, Mertensia, Moltkia, Pentaglottis, Pulmonaria,* and *Symphytum,* to name just a few. Though encompassing a broad range of flower colors and sizes, the family as a whole becomes easily understood when one learns to recognize the coiled inflorescence common to nearly all taxa held within. Often referred to as a scorpioid cyme, it unfurls and straightens as the flowers open—like a graceful and colorful (never menacing) curled tail of a scorpion.

Two genera within the Boraginaceae rank supreme in ornamental merit. Though they can hardly be touted as unknown by keen collectors across North America and Europe, *Omphalodes* and *Myosotidium* are, without a doubt, in need of greater attention by the swelling ranks of professional and amateur horticulturists alike.

Omphalodes

I encountered the genus *Omphalodes* early on in my gardening education, and I can recall repeating the awkward name over and over until it rolled easily off my tongue—though over time it took on a decidedly inappropriate Italian accent, as

264

if I were ordering an exotic form of Sicilian foccacia. Many years later, my first and only garden offers a home to a wide range of these plants, which I have come to consider charm personified.

A member of the family Boraginaceae, *Omphalodes* is a completely Old World and primarily eastern European genus, though the 25 assorted species in its ranks extend through Asia Minor into China. *Omphalodes verna* is perhaps the best-known and among the hardiest species in the genus. Its stems snake along at ground level, sporting oval, bright green leaves in early spring. The foliage emerges as its first bright blue, forget-me-not-like flowers appear. *Omphalodes verna* can be somewhat aggressive and difficult to remove once fully established, though the plant's ornamental offerings, especially early in spring, far outweigh this problem, and I would never be without it in my garden. It is especially good planted under early *Forsythia giraldiana* or the emerging golden-yellow foliage of selected forms of elderberry (*Sambucus*). *Omphalodes verna* 'Grandiflora' possesses flowers that are nearly twice as large as those of the clones of the species currently in cultivation, and this selection is preferable to the type. A new European selection with sky-blue flowers, known as *O. verna* 'Elfenauge', is still under evaluation in our garden. The white-flowered *O. verna* 'Alba' creates a charming carpet in early spring, as multitudes of white stars emerge on the low, snaking stems. It is especially treasured at Heronswood, where it enlivens a planting of dark-flowered hellebores.

Omphalodes verna 'Grandiflora' (Photo by Lynne Harrison)

Omphalodes verna 'Alba' (Photo by Lynne Harrison)

Omphalodes cappadocica, from the western Caucasus, embraces a more clump-ing growth habit than *O. verna*, producing matte-green mounds of lanceolate, long petioled, semi-evergreen foliage. Loose racemes of blue-lavender to mauve flowers appear in midspring. This species has proven to be less hardy than *O. verna* and will benefit from overhead protection from late frosts. *Omphalodes cap-padocica* 'Cherry Ingram' is a good, rich blue form with larger flowers than the type and should be sought out; it commemorates the late, great British gardener Captain Collingwood "Cherry" Ingram. We also propagate Alan Bloom's selec-tion, *O. cappadocica* 'Anthea Bloom', which is similar to 'Cherry Ingram' except for the more upright carriage of its flowers. Most endearing of all is *O. cappadocica* 'Starry Eyes', which was found as a spontaneous mutation in an Irish garden and introduced into cultivation by Helen Dillon of Dublin. Masses of mauve buds open to blue flowers rimmed with a band of mauve-white that fades to pure white. Few plants are more striking in the early April garden. *Omphalodes cappadocica* 'Lilac Mist' arose from attempts to produce 'Starry Eyes' by tissue culture. With flowers that reverted to a rather sleepy mauve without a picotee edge, this selec-tion perhaps deserves the proposed tongue-in-cheek name of "Blurry Eyes."

Omphalodes cappadocica 'Cherry Ingram' (Photo by Lynne Harrison)

Omphalodes cappadocica 'Starry Eyes' grows beside the golden foliage of *Filipendula ulmaria* 'Aurea' at Heronswood (Photo by Lynne Harrison)

On countless occasions, I have attempted to procure *Omphalodes luciliae*, which is native to Greece and Asia Minor. Time and again the plants turned out to be *O. cappadocica*. In 1997, success came in the form of seed received from the Gothenburg Botanical Garden in Sweden, and the seed has germinated true. The leaves of *O. luciliae* are decidedly more gray-green and certainly shorter than those of other species. The foliage forms dense tufts to 3 in. (7.5 cm) from which short racemes of sky-blue flowers arise in April and May. Though equally ornamental as the species already discussed, *O. luciliae* must be sited a bit more carefully; it requires sharply draining soils that receive adequate water during the growing season in light shade.

I have grown *Omphalodes nitida* for several years, and though the blue flowers are indeed lovely in midspring, arising on airy 1-ft. (0.3-m) stems from evergreen mounds of narrow, 6- to 8-in. (15- to 20-cm) long leaves, I have found this species to be too aggressive with regard to self sowing to recommend it. However, it would be an ideal component of a meadow garden in a cool, somewhat shaded situation. *Omphalodes nitida* naturally occurs in the mountains of Spain and Portugal.

If you will permit me to stray from hardy perennials for just a moment, I would like to briefly mention a charming annual that comes from the same natural haunts as *Omphalodes nitida*. A handsome self-sowing addition for the full-sun garden, *O. linifolia* rises to 1 ft. (0.3 m) in height and offers glaucous foliage and a long-lasting display of white flowers in early to midsummer. I would never be without this charmer, and it has never been overly exuberant in spreading through the garden.

Hardiness: *Omphalodes verna* is the hardiest of the lot, tolerating zones 5–9. *Omphalodes cappadocica* will probably not tolerate extended periods below temperatures of 10°F (−12°C). *Omphalodes luciliae* and *O. nitida* are hardy in zone 7, while *O. linifolia* is an annual in zones 5–9.

Cultivation: All species of *Omphalodes* do best in humus-rich, well-drained soils in bright but sheltered positions. To prevent self sowing in clumps of the named forms, shear to the ground after flowering. Shearing should also be performed before growth resumes in midwinter to tidy the semi-evergreen species, *Omphalodes cappadocica* and *O. luciliae*.

Propagation: Division of the perennial species is best performed in early spring. Taking stem cuttings of the named cultivars in mid- to late summer and rooting them under mist is also a quite successful method. The named forms, in particular 'Starry Eyes', are not stable in tissue culture.

Myosotidium

The Chatham Island forget-me-not (*Myosotidium hortensia*) is undoubtedly one of the most striking foliage plants that I currently have in my garden, where it holds a position at the northern front of its hardiness limit. Unlike specimens grown in gardens with a kinder and gentler disposition, where large, glistening, emerald-green, and deeply ribbed foliage creates a sensational presence in the winter and summer garden alike, my garden plants of *M. hortensia* sputter in the first freezes of late autumn, bravely holding the fort until the reinforcements arrive with the coming of spring temperatures, though by then they wear a ravenous, war-weary look. None the matter, for the magnificent foliage rises phoenix-like to add a reflective substratum to the dense cymes of rich lavender-blue flowers in early summer. Each flower results in four rather large, greenish, winged nutlets. I recently received seed of a white-flowered form of the species, but I have not witnessed it in blossom.

Myosotidium hortensia is endemic to New Zealand's Chatham Islands, where it is nearly extinct, growing near tide line among beach grasses in the well-drained, albeit salty, sand. To this and countless other species with such a limited range that have deliberately and intricately evolved to fight for a tooth-hold on this spinning planet, I raise my glass—may they forever share our world with us.

Myosotidium hortensia, the Chatham Island forget-me-not (Photo by Lynne Harrison)

The lavender-blue flowers of *Myosotidium hortensia* (Photo by Lynne Harrison)

Hardiness: *Myosotidium hortensia* is hardy only in summer-cool areas in zones 7–10, though it is an excellent candidate for container culture.

Cultivation: Plants will succeed in bright areas with some overhead protection during the winter, in well-drained, acidic soils, though I have seen *Myosotidium hortensia* forming beautiful evergreen colonies in a well-protected garden on the shaded, north side of a home. In the cool, mild maritime areas of southern Oregon and northern California, this New Zealand native can be grown in full-sun situations without fear of damage from light frosts. *Myosotidium* is exceptionally forgiving to pot culture and thus a superb candidate for the deck or patio container in cool climates that cannot guarantee a temperate winter.

Propagation: *Myosotidium hortensia* is self fertile and will set copious quantities of seed. The nutlets should be harvested when fully ripened and sown immediately. Some sources recommend that the seed pots be watered in once with sea water. We have followed this advice religiously, dipping them in water from Puget Sound, and have obtained extremely good germination results, but other reliable sources have told us that they achieve equally good germination without this added procedure. If for nothing but a new tradition and an interesting anecdote, we will continue to approach our seed sowing in this fashion.

CHAPTER 22

Comely Composites:
Syneilesis and *Ainsliaea*

During my first trip to South Korea, in 1993, I became acquainted with two genera that were previously unknown to me. It was an initial glimpse into a fascinating cache of woodland composites that are remarkable not only for their extraordinary foliage but also for the fact that they do not produce heads of yellow flowers. (The profound nature of this fact will not be lost on anyone who has tried to sort out a plethora of genera possessing the vulgar floral format of yellow daisies!) Upon returning home, equipped with the arrogance of having, I thought, exclusivity of knowledge, and viable seed to boot, I was surprised (OK, devastated) to find that both genera were already growing exuberantly at the Botanical Garden of the University of British Columbia in Vancouver. The rewards of plant hunting are many, but the humbling moments equally severe.

Syneilesis

Syneilesis palmata is frequently encountered colonizing the understory of deciduous oak forests throughout the Korean Peninsula. It produces deeply divided, peltate foliage, coated in white pubescence when young, that pushes through the ground in early spring. Later, the leaf blades expand to 10 in. (25 cm) or more across, on petioles to 1 ft. (0.3 m) in height, and take on a mien of glossy green. The demure flower heads, borne in midsummer atop 3-ft. (0.9-m) pedicels, possess a purplish pink cast, and though hardly showy, they carry enough interest to justify letting them remain. Over time, *S. palmata* will create sizable colonies by rhizomes, but I have not felt the slightest tinge of annoyance with it in this regard.

271

Airy sprays of purple-blushed flowers tower above the foliage on *Syneilesis palmata*
(Photo by Lynne Harrison)

The boldly textured foliage of *Syneilesis palmata* (Photo by Lynne Harrison)

When it first emerges in spring, with frosty white foliage thrusting through the woodland litter, *Syneilesis aconitifolia* appears nearly identical to *S. palmata.* Later, however, the foliage expands to finely fretted mounds of grayish green, surpassing in ornament even the finest foliage forms brought to the garden by hellebores or peonies. *Syneilesis aconitifolia* is restricted to the southerly areas of the Korean Peninsula and extends into the Japanese Archipelago. In 1997, I collected this species in a remarkable, highly weathered crater on the island of Cheju-do south of South Korea. It too will slowly colonize a somewhat moist woodland soil, though *S. aconitifolia* is proving to be an exceptionally drought-tolerant plant once fully established. Unlike those of the previous species, the flowers of *S. aconitifolia* warrant nothing more than a few minutes with a pair of pruning scissors; they distract from the overall effect without lending any interest. Nevertheless, with its superlative textural quality, *S. aconitifolia* is gaining momentum in popularity across North America.

Though I have not observed *Syneilesis intermedia* in the wild, I do have an expanding colony of it established in my garden, which I obtained from seed originally collected by Bleddyn and Sue Wynn-Jones in Taiwan in 1993. So far, it is

The new foliage of *Syneilesis aconitifolia* is covered with white hairs (Photo by Lynne Harrison)

more diminutive in cultivation than the other species, arising to a mere 8 in. (20 cm) in height, while providing the overall textural qualities of *S. palmata*.

Hardiness: *Syneilesis intermedia* is not currently in general cultivation, but I suspect that it will join the other two in providing choice durable and distinctive herbaceous plants for the shaded garden in zones 4–10. Initial reports are encouraging from the hot and humid areas of the Southeast and deep South.

Cultivation: All three species are quite adaptable; although they will particularly shine in shaded areas with rich, somewhat moist, humus-rich soils, they will colonize, albeit more slowly, in well-drained, rather droughty soils in light shade.

Propagation: Because I have never successfully germinated seed from my garden plants, which are represented by a single clone, I suspect that *Syneilesis* may be self-infertile. Fresh seed collected from native stands is quite easy to germinate and will do so immediately upon sowing, without cold stratification. For commercial needs, division of the colonies in early spring is the easiest method and certainly presents few challenges.

Ainsliaea

A genus within the family Asteraceae (Compositae) that also hails from East Asia and often grows there side by side with its *Syneilesis* relatives, *Ainsliaea* has long been absent from Western horticulture. Most frequently encountered in the northern part of the Korean Peninsula, *Ainsliaea acerifolia* provides exceptionally handsome foliage effects to the garden, with broad, deeply lobed, maple-like leaves to 8 in. (20 cm) across. Panicles of small white composites rise to 18 in. (45 cm) and lend an airy if not somewhat transparent quality to the late-summer woodland. A much more diminutive species, *Ainsliaea apiculata* creates rosettes of foliage to 3 in. (7.5 cm) and sprays of white flowers rising to a mere 6 in. (15 cm). It thrives in areas with higher moisture and offers a distinctive addition for the streamside garden. I found this to be a lovely plant in the moist woodlands of South Korea, although I have not yet established it in my woodland garden.

Though I initially came to know the genus *Ainsliaea* as primarily an assortment of plants notable for the effects of foliage, I was surprised to find during my first trip to China that many species possess an element of floral charm as well. Late-summer flowers of many-petaled pink composites were encountered in both Yunnan and Sichuan Provinces, although in the end, attempts to provide these with species names proved hopeless. Nonetheless, the experience provided me with the remarkable opportunity to once again build upon prior knowledge and offer a clearer picture of the whole that confronts me on a daily basis in this world of plants.

Hardiness: This genus is thoroughly untested, though I suspect it will be hardy in zones 5–9, with some overstory protection in colder areas.

Cultivation: Best in light shade and humus-rich soils. *Ainsliaea apiculata* should be planted in soils with more moisture.

Propagation: Seed freshly sown will germinate in short order without cold stratification. Resultant seedlings establish quickly and will blossom within a year from germination.

CHAPTER 23

Birthworts and Wild Gingers:
Asarum and *Saruma*

The Aristolochiaceae are a relatively small clan as plant families go, encompassing only five genera, represented in temperate and tropical areas of both the Old and New World. Of these, two are widely known in horticultural circles: the woody vines of the genus *Aristolochia*, with their odd but charming "pipes," and the handsome groundcovers in the genus *Asarum*. A growing cache of remarkable species of *Asarum* are becoming increasingly available to the North American gardener. In addition, a little-known genus by the name of *Saruma* is deserving of wider recognition.

Asarum

The genus *Asarum* presents a conundrum to my gardening soul. It is a genus that I have never approached with great gusto, nor have I grown it extensively or known it intimately. But with each plant-gathering trip, international or domestic, I seem to come home with more species for my garden, a better understanding of their distribution and cultivation, and a greater reverence for their mind-boggling diversity. For those of you who are already *Asarum* aficionados (the number of which doubles on a yearly basis), I may shed but little light on your beloved genus. If you are like me, however, and are simply curious about the lot, then I welcome you to join me in getting our feet wet. More often than not, it takes only one pleasurable acquaintance with any species of wild ginger before you are welcoming the entire family into your garden.

Before we start, one caveat: asarums are primarily foliage plants. Though you may be momentarily dazed by a close-up photo of the intriguing flowers of one species or another, you must realize that these are generally cleverly hidden beneath the handsome rounded or hastate foliage—often, in fact, buried in forest litter. The standard floral fare for all asarums are short-pediceled, three-sepaled, apetalous flowers, generally in tones of purple or brown. As they are pollinated by flies, they have no need to strut their stuff for successful transfer of pollen.

Taxonomically, the genus *Asarum* renders its own version of a Nightmare on Elm Street. In a temporary frenzy, ravenous botanists ravaged the genus, ripping it apart into numerous small tidbits: *Heterotropa*, *Hexastylis*, *Japonasarum*, *Asiasarum*. One by one, these fragmented taxa have been reassimilated into a cohesive and understandable whole, only to be shattered once again by well-intentioned but overzealous taxonomists. Native to both the New and Old World, *Asarum* includes more than 100 species worldwide. Undoubtedly, as familiarity with the genus grows and with an increasing number of new discoveries in China, these estimates will change as rapidly as the Dow Jones in a bear market.

The wild gingers occur on both coasts of North America, with 4 species native to western North America and 11 species hailing from the East Coast. *Asarum caudatum* is the species most common in the Pacific Northwest, and I first encountered it while working at the Bloedel Reserve on Bainbridge Island, Washington. This handsome, semi-evergreen to evergreen species exists throughout the Reserve's natural areas, and it also is tended as a superlative, expansive groundcover in light shade below second-growth Douglas firs. It forms a low sea of green, heart-shaped foliage, with an ethereal metallic sheen throughout much of the growing season, arising from rhizomatous stems. In early spring, ruddy flowers composed of three long, caudate sepals are formed from the ground and, as with all asarums, are mostly hidden by the foliage. This species does not show the folial diversity exhibited by many others in this genus. I am, however, currently growing an interesting white-flowered form—interesting, that is, if you take the time to get down on your hands and knees, peel away the foliage, and take a gander. This often represents the finest moments in gardening.

I have observed another western species, *Asarum hartwegii*, growing in dry, exposed sites throughout the Siskiyou Mountains of southern Oregon and into northern California. The deciduous foliage of this species is smaller, to $1\frac{1}{2}$ to 2 in. (3.8 to 5 cm) in length, than that of the previous species discussed, but it is handsomely veined in white and marbled by pewters and silvers in variable patterns. With the ever-increasing popularity of the Asiatic species known for their superb folial presence, I am surprised that this native species has not garnered a more celebrated status in the United States, though it is considered difficult for the summer-warm areas of the country. The reddish brown flowers, composed of three hairy sepals, are produced in early spring.

Asarum lemmonii, found naturally in moist, shaded sites in northern California, possesses handsome semi-evergreen, heart-shaped foliage, to 3 in. (7.5 cm) in length, that reportedly is lemon scented. I have had no garden experience with this or the remaining western species, *A. wagneri*, and am incapable of commenting on their overall garden worthiness.

The members of the genus *Asarum* that occur on the eastern half of North America—having survived an earlier hostile takeover attempt by taxonomists wishing to split the genus into two taxa—are once again facing a messy divorce. The argument for separation is based on the composition of the styles: whether the flower's six styles are fused into a single column (genus *Asarum*) or carried distinct from one another (genus *Hexastylis*). This thinking seems logical as long as only American species are brought before the judge. If Asian species are allowed to testify, it becomes obvious that the differences do not sufficiently warrant the creation of a new genus. In following with popular opinion, I have lumped all in the genus *Asarum*.

Found naturally occurring in flood plains from Nova Scotia to North Carolina and west to Missouri, and too infrequently seen in cultivation, *Asarum canadense* is a handsome, drought- and alkaline-tolerant, and completely deciduous species that will tolerate extremely cold temperatures as well as extremely moist sites. The attractive heart-shaped foliage is pubescent on both sides, while the 1-in. (2.5-cm) wide, purple flowers, produced in spring, are hidden beneath. The species is completely hardy across the entire northern tier of the United States, as well as along the southern boundaries of Canada, though it is seldom offered for sale in this country.

Asarum virginicum was sent to me by my friend Richard Schock from the mountains of western North Carolina, and it has proven to be remarkably adaptive to the cool maritime climate of the Northwest. Native from Virginia to South Carolina and Tennessee, *A. virginicum* has evergreen foliage that is handsomely marbled in white, superficially resembling the West Coast *A. hartwegii*. The dark purple flowers are produced in late spring and into early summer. *Asarum virginicum* is extremely close in appearance to *A. minor*, which is a more widely distributed species, differing only in the wider, more opened flowers of the former.

I observed the distinctive and variable species known as *Asarum arifolium* growing in the deciduous woodlots in and around Raleigh, North Carolina, and I was overwhelmed by the striking beauty and variability of its arrow-shaped foliage, which grew to 6 in. (15 cm) in length. In contrast, my puny garden specimens of this species have made it crystal clear that they are not appreciative of the chilly summers offered by the Pacific Northwest. The flowers, rather bizarre purplish orbs that only partially open, are more inspirational to writers of science fiction than to gardeners.

Asarum shuttleworthii is somewhat more tolerant of our climate, and I have grown only the vigorously stoloniferous form *A. shuttleworthii* var. *harperi* 'Calloway'. It makes a handsome specimen, with pewter-mottled evergreen foliage on long petioles. The tubular flowers of black-purple are quite striking, rivaling the fantastical floral creations brought on by many of the Asiatic species.

These and other species from the East Coast of North America are often overlooked in gardens in deference to the sole European member of the genus, *Asarum europaeum*. This evergreen species, with sheeny, heart-shaped leaves and spring blossoms of purple-green, creates exceedingly handsome, weed-suppressing colonies. The best use of the species that I have seen was in the remarkable garden of Morris West and Nicholas Klise in southeastern Pennsylvania; any farther to the south, however, and it is reportedly difficult to grow under the oppressive heat and humidity. Should it perform so well in my own garden, I too would be tempted to shirk our West Coast species in lieu of this plant.

Nearly one-third of the 100-plus species of *Asarum* recognized by taxonomists occur in Japan, and of these I am currently cultivating an ever-increasing inventory myself. I have observed *Asarum sieboldii* throughout the rich deciduous forests of its natural range in the northern reaches of South Korea and northern Honshu in Japan. Superficially resembling *A. canadense*, *A. sieboldii* is a deciduous species that, in my experience, exhibits little of the folial variation found in other species. Nonetheless, the matte-green foliage is quite handsome, with an undulating leaf edge as well as overlapping basal lobes. Flaring purple flowers are produced at ground level in spring.

Asarum takaoi boasts a long history of cultivation in Japan, with near-religious subtleties surrounding the methods of growing and displaying it. More than a hundred classical cultivars of this species remain in commerce, as well as numerous contemporary introductions. There are entire nurseries devoted exclusively to this species and its many forms, and encountering securely displayed cultivars offered for sale for thousands of dollars is not an uncommon experience. In nature, the small, rounded leaves of *A. takaoi* present a diverse medley of colorful patterns. Its overall hardiness and slowly spreading habit, similar to that of *A. shuttleworthii* var. *harperi* 'Calloway', make for a superlative and easy-to-grow groundcover for the woodland.

Asarum caulescens, hailing from the mountains of Honshu, Shikoku, and Kyushu, is a deciduous species that has performed quite well in the cool maritime climate of the Northwest. As its name implies, this species is caulescent, with the 3-in. (7.5-cm), orbicular leaves carried above ground level on stems rising to 2 to 4 in. (5 to 10 cm). The foliage is glossy green and decidedly puckered, while possessing a silky white pubescence on the upper surface of the leaf blade. The squat, white or pale purple flowers are produced in early spring.

Perhaps the most striking Japanese species for foliage alone is *Asarum savatieri*, which occurs on Honshu. The small, rounded, evergreen foliage grows to 3 in. by 2 in. (7.5 cm by 5 cm) and is marbled by a spectacular if not irresistible blending of silvers, grays, plums, and greens. The relatively large flowers, to 1 in. (2.5 cm) across, are produced in midsummer. I have had limited experience with this species in my garden, and the jury is still out as to whether it will prove adaptable to the Pacific Northwest.

Nearly identical to *Asarum savatieri*, except for its late-autumn or winter blossoming season, is *A. nipponicum*, a species I encountered while in Japan in the autumn of 1997. Such variation in foliage from a single taxon I have never seen, with a bewildering array of marked, marbled, and streaked evergreen foliage, each plant bearing a somewhat different shape and size than the next. These grew in rather dryish shade throughout Chiba Prefecture and elsewhere in central Honshu. Later, I encountered fantastic forms of *A. nipponicum* in nurseries devoted to the genus, attesting to the long Japanese tradition of looking for variation among the native flora.

Asarum blumei occurs in the same area as *A. nipponicum*. It is a handsome evergreen species of deep green with a variable degree of silver mottling. The solitary, hastate leaves, to 3 in. (7.5 cm), are held on long petioles to 5 in. (12.5 cm) and possess a rather unapparent pubescence on both sides of the leaf, evident only along the margins and leaf veins. The short, purple flowers are produced at ground level in midspring.

Yet, to those in the country most keen on the genus, still better species are to be found for folial drama. Barry Yinger, currently the foremost proponent of the genus in North America, recommends *Asarum kumagianum* from the Japanese island of Yaku Shima for its extremely glossy foliage and remarkable variation in mottled effects. Another that receives high marks for folial supremacy is *A. hexalobum*, which is currently blossoming in my greenhouses from stunning specimens obtained in the mountains of central Honshu in 1997. The foliage is brightly marked with white and silver, while the distinctive flowers provide ample opportunity to safely diagnose the species, as the floral tube is deeply constricted near the tip.

I have observed *Asarum maculatum* only in South Korea, where it occupies the southern regions and is quite common in the wooded hills surrounding

Asarum caulescens (Photo by Lynne Harrison)

Asarum savatieri (Photo by Lynne Harrison)

Wando. The foliage of this evergreen species is quite striking and variable, with regular splotches of silver and pewter throughout the leaf, although the plant has not yet produced such lusty clumps in my nursery as other Asiatic species have. Nodding somber bells are produced below the foliage in early spring.

Numerous Japanese species do provide a remarkable flowering effect; so much so, in fact, that I must momentarily backpedal from my dogmatic recommendation of using this genus exclusively for folial effects. *Asarum minamitanianum* produces immense black-purple flowers, with spidery sepal tips, extending to 6 in. (15 cm) or more beneath the handsome marbled foliage. It is thought to be extinct in the wild, although it can be found commercially in the Unites States through Plant Delights Nursery in Raleigh, North Carolina. From Yaku Shima and Kyushu, *Asarum hirsutisepalum* offers enormous quantities of purple flowers with yellowish white marbled sepals nestled among dark, glossy green foliage.

The Chinese species of *Asarum* probably represent a larger and certainly more complex inventory than is currently imagined, but even now they represent a full third of the known species. Most are found in the warm, humid areas of southern China, concentrated between the Chang (Yangtze) River and Vietnam.

Asarum splendens is an evergreen species that I have grown for several years, having received my first plants from J. C. Raulston, who was instrumental in distributing this species for greater use across the United States. It is a splendid foliage plant, and perhaps the single species most responsible for stirring a national interest in the genus as a whole. It bears 8-in. (20-cm) spears artfully blended in patterns of aluminum and a bevy of variations of green on green. The large, blackish purple, white-throated flowers to $1\frac{1}{2}$ in. (3.8 cm) across are produced in spring. Sadly, this species is resentful of the coolness that pervades my summer garden and so is unlikely to become a staple in my woodland, though it performs admirably as a container subject in greenhouses and in the summer-warm areas of the East Coast. *Asarum splendens* has been wrongly distributed in this country under the name of *A. magnificum*, a species to which it is indeed superficially similar in foliage.

Properly identified, *Asarum magnificum* is also exceedingly striking in foliage. With various clones currently growing in my garden, this evergreen species shows the most marked diversity of foliage, in addition to one of the most remarkable flowers in the genus. The velvety black-purple flowers, produced in early spring, possess a textural white center.

The blossoms of *Asarum maximum* are perhaps the most stunning of the genus, with 2-in. (5-cm) white flowers rimmed by a broad band of black-velvet produced in spring. The striking and variable evergreen foliage of this species is glossy green with variable pewter markings and marblings along the interior of

Asarum magnificum (Photo by Lynne Harrison)

Asarum maximum (Photo by Lynne Harrison)

the blade. It currently is extremely rare in cultivation and demands a high price wherever available.

I have limited experience with *Asarum campaniforme*, but I find the flowers of this species to be the most intriguing, if not the most comical, of any of the wild gingers that I cultivate. In early spring, curiously long tubular flowers to nearly 2 in. (5 cm) in length lie flat on the ground, greenish white on the outside and with a broad, purple-black band on the inner edge of the sepal. The thin-textured, narrow-hastate, deciduous leaves to 6 in. (15 cm) in length are glossy green or handsomely mottled in mercurial patterns.

I first observed *Asarum chinense* in Sichuan Province in 1996, where it grew in a narrow, densely shaded canyon with *Disporum bodinieri*, *Disporopsis perneyi*, and *Epimedium acuminatum*. This is a rather easy species to identify when in flower: the globose, purple flowers with short reflexed sepal lobes are densely coated with white hairs, as are the petioles and upper surfaces of the leaf blades. The foliage color is light green with or without a variable blending of pewter and silver mottles and streaks. Thus far, it has translated well to cultivation in the Pacific Northwest.

Also in Sichuan Province, *Asarum himalaicum* was a common component of the deciduous woods above Wolong at elevations of 10,000 ft. (3000 m). I was excited to find this deciduous species, which is quite rare in cultivation, simply because its cool and moist native habitat would seemingly allow it to transfer well to the climate of the greater Puget Sound. Unfortunately, it has been disappointing in its performance, emerging countless times during the year only to falter and slip again into dormancy. *Asarum himalaicum* is the only species native throughout the Himalayas.

Bleddyn and Sue Wynn-Jones collected several handsome *Asarum* species in the mountains of Taiwan, and many are currently growing in the woodland at Heronswood, though they have yet to be exposed to a normal, rigorous winter. I have seen the same species in large colonies at the Wynn-Jones's garden in northern Wales, and the stunning foliage effects brought from this group of plants are nothing shy of unadulterated magnificence.

Asarum caudigerum carries medium-sized, arrow-shaped foliage on 5-in. (12.5-cm), densely haired petioles. The upper and lower leaf blades are also coated with hairs, though the upper blade shines with the most remarkable glaze imaginable from a living plant. The tubular, hairy flowers are produced in spring and do not hold significant interest.

With 5-in. (12.5-cm), arrow-shaped, dark green leaves possessing an irresistible satiny sheen and irregular silver and white blotching, *Asarum macranthum* is among the most beautiful wild gingers that I have observed. It increases along creeping rhizomes and will quickly form expansive colonies of cyclamen-like foliage. The flowers are dark purple and produced in April.

Asarum infrapurpureum is another of Bleddyn and Sue's collections, and it bears very pretty heart-shaped foliage to 3 in. (7.5 cm) in length, spotted with white above but completely dark purple on the lower leaf blade. Because the leaf margin is somewhat undulated, this ruddy undercoating is observable from above and provides a striking contrast in color. Small, purple-red flowers are produced at ground level in spring.

Hardiness: The deciduous species of *Asarum*, such as *Asarum canadense* and *A. sieboldii*, are more than likely the hardiest of the clan, tolerating temperatures offered in zones 5–9, though providing a bit of protection with a heavy mulch in late autumn is certainly advisable in cooler areas. Gardeners in colder climates across the country (including the Pacific Northwest) have found these plants to be good candidates for container use. Some of the most spectacular specimens of *A. splendens* that I have observed were growing in a hanging basket! The summer-warm regions of the eastern seaboard are ideal for growing these remarkable plants. Nearly all the Japanese species will thrive in zones 7–8, and several, including *A. nipponicum* and *A. takaoi*, are hardy to upper zone 5.

Cultivation: The majority of the species, if not all, will respond best to humus-rich soils in partially shaded sites with adequate summer moisture. They are especially prone to damage by slugs in early spring, and protection should be provided.

Propagation: Division of individual clones in early spring provides an easy method of replicating colorful-foliaged variants. Small pieces of rooted rhizome with leaves or buds may be potted or placed directly in the garden, though humidity should be increased for a short period to allow for proper establishment. *Asarum* seed is quite easy to germinate if collected and sown fresh; the fruit ripens early in the season (of spring-blossoming species) and attention must be paid to collect it in a timely manner. Tissue culture has also proven successful.

Saruma

Closely related to *Asarum*, in name as well as in form, the monotypic genus *Saruma* has a short but splendid history in cultivation. It was first described by Daniel Oliver in 1889 from herbarium pressings collected by Augustine Henry, whose name is commemorated in the specific epithet of the genus's solitary member, *Saruma henryi*. The generic name was created by simply removing the "A" from *Asarum* and assigning it to the end of the queue. Both Henry and, later, E. H. Wilson observed *Saruma* growing in shady, mesic locations in Hubei, Guizhou, and Yunnan Provinces of China, but little lore or scientific inquiry surrounds this plant. The Japanese plant explorer Mikinori Ogisu has reported that the roots of *S. henryi* are used medicinally for stomach ailments and that newly emerged shoots are collected for boiled greens by the peoples inhabiting its native range.

My first introduction to *Saruma henryi* came in 1990, when I received a plant from Lawrence Lee, then-curator of the Asian Collection at the U.S. National Arboretum in Washington, D.C. Lee had successfully established the species in the deciduous woodland there, but I was initially skeptical of its chances of thriving in the cool maritime climate of the Pacific Northwest. My concerns were soon put to rest, however, as the plant at once settled into place. I have been charmed by its consistent and polished performance ever since, and I recently planted a substantial colony that will serve as a top-notch groundcover during the growing season. The flowers and foliage of *S. henryi* nicely complement the finely textured, purple-laced foliage of *Cimicifuga simplex* var. *simplex* 'Brunette', which occupies the same garden habitat.

The stems of *Saruma henryi* emerge from the ground in early spring, ultimately rising to 18 in. (45 cm) and carrying heart-shaped, felted leaves that have a purplish bronze tint that fades to medium green by midsummer. A nonstop progression of $^3\!/_4$-in. (1.9-cm), three-petaled, pastel-yellow flowers are produced from the leaf axils from early April until late October. In fact, the presence of these petals is precisely what sets this genus apart from *Asarum*, the petals of which are absent or vestigial within their cuplike calyx. The flowering season of *S. henryi* may be more compressed, albeit more dazzling, in warmer climates.

Hardiness: *Saruma henryi* has proven hardy in gardens of Massachusetts (zones 5–6) and is reportedly tolerant of the heat and humidity of the southeastern United States.

Cultivation: Due to this genus's rare status in gardens, information about its ideal cultural requirements is equally hard to come by. It has thrived in my garden in a bright, shaded spot in well-drained, acidic, sandy loam that receives some supplemental irrigation in summer. I have read reports of *Saruma* growing successfully in a cool, shaded site in south-central England, where it is said to match well with *Corydalis flexuosa*.

Propagation: The seed of *Saruma* ripens throughout the summer, and a good dose of discipline is required to harvest the seed before it is discharged and lost. If sown fresh, it will generally germinate the following spring; germination may take two years if the seed is allowed to dry out before sowing. Though I have

Saruma henryi (Photo by Lynne Harrison)

successfully rooted cuttings of the plants in early spring, the window of opportunity is quite small and the results inconsistent. Division in early spring is certainly a possibility, but it takes several years to achieve a plant of enough girth to
produce viable quantities by this means.

CHAPTER 24

Enchanting Jacks:
Arisaema and *Pinellia*

The genus *Arisaema* includes a vast number of species, to 150 or more, mostly from the temperate areas of the Northern Hemisphere, with the highest concentration of species found in the Himalayas, China, and Japan. Anyone who ventures into the woodlands of the East Coast of North America, especially when the trilliums and morel mushrooms are at their finest, will certainly be familiar with at least one of the two species of *Arisaema* native to North America. Known in the vernacular as jack-in-the-pulpit, *Arisaema triphyllum* is common from Nova Scotia to Georgia and east to Missouri. Its curious chocolate-striped spathe (the pulpit, in this case) encloses a short, upright spadix (the jack). These two appendages are found on the inflorescence of every member of the Araceae, the plant family to which this genus belongs, and they are basic to understanding the lingo in the descriptions of the species encountered in the literature. Even though the foliage, stems, and ripening fruit are reason enough to grow these plants, it is generally for these blossoms—which can, depending on the species, appear quite sinister or simply elegant—that this genus is increasing in popularity among the gardening community worldwide. At the base of the spadix, which may be only inches in length as in the case of *A. triphyllum* or nearly 2 ft. (0.6 m) in length in several other species, are the individual flowers; the female flowers are always in clusters at the bottom, while the pollen-bearing male flowers will be found slightly above. Perhaps the most intriguing aspect of this rather lengthy floral description is the fact that the sexuality of each inflorescence can change from year to year. Generally, the premier blossoming of young plants will almost always be exclusively male, with larger, more-established plants presenting either female flowers or both male and female (depending on the individual species). This scenario makes total sense when one considers the energy differential between simple pollen production and that of seed production. It has been noted that on years following severe drought or other environmental stresses, established female plants will revert back to being solely male. In the descriptions of the species that follow, I may refer to the inflorescence as a "flower," taking this literary license for the ease of reading—be aware, however, that in this instance the term refers to the entire flowering structure, and not to each individual male or female flower.

Also essential to correctly interpreting the descriptive verse on these engaging plants is understanding exactly what is considered a typical leaf. A basic *Arisaema* plant is composed of an underground tuber from which one or two leaves ascend on sturdy leaf stems or petioles. Atop the petiole, generally one of four types of leaf arrangements is found: trifoliate, digitate, pedate, or whorled (meaning, respectively, three leaved, many leaves arranged radiating in the same basic direction as in fingers on a hand, palmately lobed with the two outer side lobes again divided, and many leaves arranged evenly as in the spokes of a wheel). The inflorescence may be borne on an independent flowering stem from the tuber itself, or it may emanate from the side of the leaf stem; the point of attachment is one good method for identifying each species. I have tried to be consistent in the use of descriptive terms in regard to each species.

There is currently no published work that deals with the collective systematics of *Arisaema*, though there undoubtedly will be in the near future. Currently, the taxonomy is overwrought with synonymy, especially for those taxa that have a wide distribution, that is, the China-Himalayan complex. Add to this difficulty the greater accessibility to the flora of China, which has resulted in a tremendous influx of newly described species (or those previously unavailable for study), and our rather narrow perceptions of what this genus can offer the gardener will be further challenged. In 1997, my frequent traveling companions Bleddyn and Sue Wynn-Jones mounted a two-week reconnaissance trip to northern Thailand, where they collected several species that have not been previously described; this in addition to their having obtained numerous and obscure species from collections in the mountains of Taiwan and the Philippines. In 1994, I collected seed of a species from Mexico in the mountains above Monterrey, which partially confirms reports that two additional New World species will ultimately be named. With this bombardment of so many new species, subspecies, varieties, and forms, it will take years to sift through and diagnose the results. Thus (and fortunately) the intention of this chapter is to provide more of a personal commentary on those plants that I have cultivated or have observed in their native habitats. Hopefully, it will offer a point of departure for those wishing to explore this remarkable genus in greater depth. I will also touch upon a fellow member of the aroid family, the genus *Pinellia*, which deserves greater recognition among gardeners.

Arisaema amurense is a common species in shaded, moist areas in Korea and eastern Russia. The single leaf rises to a mere 10 in. (25 cm) and is composed of five, often serrate, leaflets, while the inflorescence emerges on an independent peduncle to approximately the same height as the leaf. The spathe is green or green with white stripes and is sufficiently short to expose a stubby green spadix within. I have collected seed of *A. amurense* (under the then-accepted name of *A. robustum*) in South Korea, most notably on Mount Kaibang on the northeast coast, where the species grew beneath immense trees of *Acer mandschuricum* and *Kalopanax pictus* while associating with *Trillium tschonoskii* at ground level.

Arisaema angustatum var. *peninsulae* is a handsome plant that is common throughout the Korean Peninsula, as well as in Japan, and I have collected it both in the northeastern corner of South Korea near the Demilitarized Zone as well as far to the south on the island of Cheju-do. The large, digitate, dark green leaves to 1 ft. (0.3 m) in width unfold in early spring atop very beautiful pinkish petioles to 3 ft. (0.9 m). The inflorescences are not particularly showy, being relatively small in comparison to the foliage itself. Flowering stems, which can rise to 4 ft. (1.2 m) or more if provided a diet of humus-rich soil and sufficient moisture, are borne near the apex of the petiole. The short, light-colored spadix does not extend beyond the greenish yellow spathe. The resultant large, erect clusters of red, many-seeded fruit are immensely showy. On the island of Ullung-do in the Sea of Japan, the type form occurs in equal numbers with an extremely striking silver-mottled form, *A. angustatum* var. *peninsulae* f. *variegata*, with remarkable variation in intensity of variegation from one individual to the next. I was surprised to find the plants growing not only in very mucky soils but, in some cases, in standing water along small streams. *Arisaema angustatum* var. *peninsulae* is of easy cultivation in any soil that is provided supplemental water during the growing season. It is hardy through the colder reaches of zone 5.

The species that is perhaps the queen of the genus is found naturally throughout the mountainous regions of western and southwestern China. *Arisaema candidissimum* has enormous trifoliate foliage, with each leaflet to nearly 12 in. (30 cm) in length and more than 10 in. (25 cm) in width. The very distinctive inflorescence possesses a spathe of precious light pink and white striping; the white spadix does not extend beyond the lip of the spathe. In cultivation, this is a notorious late riser, often not showing itself until after the first of June and then blossoming shortly thereafter. The 8-in. (20-cm) fruiting stems recurve down toward the soil as the fruit begins to ripen in early autumn. A prodigious multiplier, *A. candidissimum* forms numerous offshoots on the mother tuber each year, and

Arisaema angustatum var. *peninsulae* (Photo by Lynne Harrison)

Arisaema angustatum var. *peninsulae* f. *variegata* (Photo by Lynne
Harrison)

these can be removed in early spring, or they can be left undisturbed in the garden and large colonies will ultimately develop. When I observed this species in its native habitat of Sichuan Province during the autumn of 1996, I was surprised to find the tubers nearly resting on the soil surface in parched, dry soils in full sun and partial shade on rocky, south-facing slopes. Though *A. candidissimum* is not dependably hardy in areas colder than zone 7, gardening friends in colder climates successfully cultivate this species and others in containers that are protected in cool but nonfreezing locations during the winter months.

Arisaema consanguineum is an elegant species that has a widespread distribution throughout southwestern China. Atop statuesque 4-ft. (1.2-m) stems are borne an elegant whorl of many narrow leaflets, which can vary in number from as few as seven to twenty or more, with each leaflet ending in a rather long, wiry drip-tip. The inflorescences arise from the petiole just under the foliage. The lovely greenish spathe, like the leaflets, has an extremely long and fine acuminate and pendulous tip, and the 6-in. (15-cm) green spadix emerges and rises upward. Later, the fruiting stems recurve downward as the berries ripen to scarlet and orange. I was surprised to find this plant so common throughout southwestern China in such varying habitats and altitudes, from parched and highly degraded south-facing hills, where it grew with naturalized stands of prickly pear cactus (*Opuntia*), to pristine moist and darkened ravines. Equally surprising was

Combining beauty with intrigue, *Arisaema candidissimum* will long reign supreme among the choicest "Jacks" for the garden (Photo by Lynne Harrison)

the variability exhibited among the individual plants: the degree of silver mottling on the foliage; the number of leaflets, with some plants bearing twice the normal complement of leaflets; and the width of the leaflets, including some extremely narrow, less than ¼ in. (0.6 cm). The seed collected from these plants will undoubtedly result in a similarly vast array of variation, offering quite handsome additions to the woodland gardens of North America.

In some Chinese floras, *Arisaema consanguineum* has been usurped by *A. erubescens*, which is an unfortunate error by the Chinese taxonomists. Though superficially resembling *A. consanguineum*, *A. erubescens* is a distinctive, stoloniferous species, which I grew from seed that I collected in eastern Nepal in 1995 under the designation HWJCM 045. Further confusion has arisen in commerce with regard to another similar stoloniferous species, *A. concinnum*, which is absent from Yunnan and Sichuan Provinces but is known to exist in Nepal and Sikkim.

Arisaema costatum is a charming low-growing species similar in appearance to *A. speciosum* and closely related to *A. intermedium*. A single trifoliate leaf with heavily veined individual leaflets rises to 15 in. (38 cm), while the inflorescence, borne on a peduncle to 8 in. (20 cm), is composed of a black-and-white-striped spathe and a narrow, threadlike spadix that tumbles earthward. Making the effort to look up into the spathe of this species provides a dazzling sight, as the white stripes shine like a stained-glass window. If I could cultivate only one plant to introduce young children to the marvels of the natural world, it would be *A. costatum*. It is endemic to central and eastern Nepal.

Very rare in cultivation, the handsome *Arisaema elephas* has bold trifoliate leaves and quite large, white-striped hoods of blackish purple from which extends a thick, black spadix to 10 in. (25 cm). The flowers sit upon low, 4-in. (10-cm) stems that arise directly from the bulb rather than from the leaf petiole. Native to western China, *A. elephas* is remarkably common along the shaded shores of Tianchi Lake in northwestern Yunnan Province at an elevation of nearly 13,000 ft. (3900 m), where the fruit heads turn the moss-covered surface of the forest floor a brilliant red.

Arisaema consanguineum (Photo by Lynne Harrison)

Arisaema exappendiculatum is native to northern India and extending west through the Himalayas. It is notoriously stoloniferous and will quickly spread to form large colonies even in cultivation. The whorled foliage rises to 2 ft. (0.6 m) atop handsome purple-gray petioles, and the purple-striped, greenish spathe surrounds a spadix that extends to 6 in. (15 cm) in length and gracefully droops downward from the flower.

I collected seed of *Arisaema fargesii* near the small village of Tiger Leaping Gorge in Yunnan Province, mistaking it at the time for *A. franchetianum*. This trifoliate species possesses a long, nodding spathe tip striped in purple and white enclosing a white or purple, club-shaped spadix. Interestingly, *A. fargesii* grew on a parched hillside with the tubers at ground surface, in some instances exposed above the soil level.

Atop flowering stems that grow to 15 in. (38 cm), the yellow and yellow-brown flowering heads of *Arisaema flavum* subsp. *abbreviatum* take on the rather beguiling appearance of small and wise owls sitting silently and contentedly on their perch. This charming perennial from the western Himalayas flowers and fruits at a very young age; in fact, I have had seedlings flower and subsequently set viable seed six months after germination. For this reason, the plant may tend to colonize the garden if it finds the habitat to its liking, though I can't imagine it making itself a terrible nuisance.

Very similar to *Arisaema candidissimum* in foliage stature and appearance, *A. franchetianum* possesses dramatic white-and-purple-striped spathes that terminate in long, pendulous drip tips atop 10-in. (25-cm) stems cloaked in a handsome mottled sheath. The spadix does not extend beyond the spathe opening. The trifoliate leaves are very large, to 12 in. by 10 in. (30 cm by 25 cm), making the plant nearly impossible to distinguish from *A. candidissimum* when not in flower. *Arisaema franchetianum* is common in northwestern Yunnan Province, where I collected its large, distinctive seed heads from stems that had recurved toward the ground. Cultivation of this native of western China is as described for *A. candidissimum*.

A most remarkable trifoliate species exists in eastern and central Nepal, Bhutan, and the Indian state of Sikkim. *Arisaema griffithii* possesses if not the most striking then certainly the most bizarre of all *Arisaema* inflorescences. The greenish yellow spathe of this species is veined with deeper tones of black-purple and bears a fluted edge. The spathe bends forward to conceal its inner workings, extending out and then back toward the base to form two large earlike appendages (auricles, as they are called by the botanists). The entire inflorescence is produced on very short stems, nearly at ground level. The trifoliate leaves are extremely heavily veined and textured and sit atop handsome mottled petioles to 15 in. (38 cm). *Arisaema griffithii* is common in eastern Nepal, where I observed it in 1995, always at relatively lower elevations of 7000–10,000 ft. (2100–3000 m). This species is easily cultivated, though is not dependably hardy in zones 7 or lower.

Though I have traveled in its native realm of Korea, Japan, and western China, I have unfortunately never observed *Arisaema heterophyllum* in its wild state. It is indeed a handsome species, hailing from perpetually moist lowland situations throughout eastern Asia. The solitary digitate leaf is composed of 13 to 19 leaflets and rises to 3 ft. (0.9 m) in height. The peduncle emerges from the petiole slightly above the foliage, and a matte-green spathe tumbles forward while a spadix rises stiffly upward. The effect is quite unlike that of any other species and readily distinguishes this jack-in-the-pulpit from the others. I have interplanted this late-emerging species with a colony of *Geranium phaeum* 'Samobor' near the back of our deck; here it provides a stunning and dependable contrast to the geranium, rising above and adding a distinctive floral contribution.

Another species that I collected in eastern Nepal is *Arisaema intermedium*. A rather plain greenish spathe atop 10-in. (25-cm) stems sends forth a most amazing spadix that curls, zigs, and zags to a length of nearly 2 ft. (0.6 m), ultimately coming to rest on the forest floor. The 12-in. (30-cm) long leaves are trifoliate and rest on petioles to 15 in. (38 cm) high. This species is native to much of the Himalayas.

I have had limited experience growing *Arisaema iyoanum*, which is endemic to the Japanese island of Shikoku, but it has proven to be an exceptional species in our garden. The single pedate leaf, with 11 to 13 lobes, rises to 2 ft. (0.6 m) on handsomely purple-mottled petioles. The inflorescence is borne on an extremely short peduncle, with the dark purple or purple-striped, green spathe held just below the foliage.

Arisaema jacquemontii is a very distinctive species that hails from the Himalayas, and I observed and collected seed of this plant in eastern Nepal. Petioles rising to 2 ft. (0.6 m) bear digitate leaves, and green spathes cloak an upright spadix in June. Some people find

The menacing, cobralike inflorescence of *Arisaema griffithii* may never be considered charming, but it remains a favorite of visitors to Heronswood (Photo by Lynne Harrison)

this species to be very prolific in a garden setting, as it is somewhat stoloniferous and quickly forms sizable colonies, though I still use seed as the primary source of propagules. It is hardy to zone 6.

Arisaema japonicum is one of three species (along with *A. ringens* and *A. sikokianum*) that is extremely common on Shikoku as well as on the Kii Peninsula of Honshu, where I observed it in the autumn of 1997. This species possesses pedate foliage on stems to 3 ft. (0.9 m) and a very pretty dark purple spathe, the hood of which is held flat and perpendicular to the short, upright spadix. *Arisaema japonicum* is certainly not common in cultivation, which is interesting considering its seeming abundance throughout its native habitats in Japan.

A stunning species native to Japan, *Arisaema kiushianum* offers one of the most charming, if somewhat comical-looking, flowers of the entire genus. Short, richly toned spathes of purple with white stripes are produced at ground level in early summer. Interestingly, this species sets copious quantities of seed after flowering, but the seed heads are partially or fully buried below the ground surface before they ripen. *Arisaema kiushianum* bears pedate foliage on petioles to 1 ft. (0.3 m). Hardiness will certainly depend on siting, though it is unlikely to be hardy in areas colder than zone 6. It is a reliable and easy species under cultivation.

Arisaema kiushianum (Photo by Lynne Harrison)

In 1995, I collected *Arisaema limbatum* in the Chiba Prefecture of Japan, where this species is common. Since that time, I have found this to be among the earliest of all the *Arisaema* species to flower, often emerging from the ground in early February, long before the sloth of winter has been defeated. *Arisaema limbatum* is a handsome species in foliage, possessing two digitate leaves atop a stem to 2½ ft. (0.8 m), with five to nine leaflets colorfully marbled in white, reminiscent of *A. sikokianum*. The inflorescence, which rises slightly above the foliage to 3 ft. (0.9 m), has a quiet demeanor, with a light green spathe and short green-white spadix. Unfortunately, this species is somewhat difficult in cultivation, as I have lost the majority of my original collections to voles, moles, or rot—since the first two seem more arbitrary and less likely to suggest improper horticulture, I will thus place the weight of blame on these. I returned to Chiba in the autumn of 1997 to once again observe this species; it was plentiful and the only *Arisaema* species present in the area. I suspect this plant has a limited distribution in cultivation, but because of its extremely early blossoming, it deserves greater recognition in climates that can accommodate it.

The handsome and robust *Arisaema negishii* ascends to over 3 ft. (0.9 m) in height, with two large, pedate leaves divided into 9 to 15 leaflets. Peduncles rise slightly above the foliage from the juncture of the two leaves. They are topped by a glossy green spathe striped with bronze and a short, knobby, green spadix. This species occurs only on Honshu and the small Japanese islands of Hachijo and Miyake, and it has settled in quite nicely in my garden, where it produces abundant seed.

Even though I already cultivated *Arisaema nepenthoides* successfully in my woodland, I collected seed of this species in 1995 in its native Nepal in the Himalayas. It is a striking species with tall, beautifully mottled petioles rising to nearly 5 ft. (1.5 m) in height. The early, dark purple and white inflorescence is presented from the apex of the petiole before the large, digitate foliage unfurls. Truly spectacular in flower and foliage, *A. nepenthoides* deserves more recognition in gardens in zones 6–10.

Arisaema limbatum (Photo by Lynne Harrison)   *Arisaema nepenthoides* (Photo by Lynne Harrison)

Other than *Arisaema dracontium* and *A. triphyllum*, *A. ringens* was the first species that I encountered in cultivation and the first that I included in my new woodland garden. For years before the current *Arisaema* frenzy began sweeping the country, Baldassare Mineo of Siskiyou Rare Plant Nursery in Medford, Oregon, readily supplied *A. ringens* to gardeners across the United States, and this supremely lovely plant opened another immense chapter of great garden plants to explore in detail. Among the numerous species that I grow, *A. ringens* is most distinctive and easily recognized. Its two leaves, borne quite low to the ground, are composed of three glossy green leaflets that can reach 1 ft. (0.3 m) or more in length. The flowering stem rises to 8 in. (20 cm) or slightly more, with a green or purple-green spathe that tightly encloses the spadix within while offering two apparent and whimsical auricles on each side. I have observed this species in South Korea, mostly on the southern islands of Taehuksan and Cheju-do, as well as on Shikoku Island of southern Japan; it also grows in China and Taiwan. On Shikoku, the individuals took on dimensions that I had not previously seen from this species, with leaflets extending to nearly 2 or 3 ft. (0.6 or 0.9 m). The large heads of green fruit do not ripen until very late in the season, which presents difficulties in collecting seed from the wild without the benefit of an extended stay in the host country.

Arisaema ringens inflorescence (Photo by Lynne Harrison)

Arisaema sazensoo has a somewhat confused history in cultivation, as it has been mistakenly referred to as *A. sikokianum* in literature and commerce for some time. It possesses a solitary pedate leaf of five to seven lobes and rising to 10 in. (25 cm). The 8-in. (20-cm) flowering stem, which arises separately from the tuber below the ground, is capped by a long, dark purple to purple, green-striped spathe that completely conceals a short, stubby spadix. *Arisaema sazensoo* is a handsome species that can possess both variegated as well as entirely green leaflets. It is native to Japan.

Superficially resembling a more robust form of *Arisaema angustatum* var. *peninsulae*, *A. serratum* grows in masses on the northern end of Honshu in the mountains surrounding Lake Towada, where I observed the species in 1997 growing in dark shade and abundant moisture, often in association with *Epimedium grandiflo-*

rum subsp. *koreanum*. Some specimens rose to over 6 ft. (1.8 m) in height, with enormous tubers that sat nearly on the soil surface. I did not witness any variation in this species with regard to leaf mottling, although variation was certainly to be found in the degree of leaf serration; a few individuals had not only deeply serrated leaf margins but also an overaccentuated undulating leaf edge that provided a remarkable ruffling effect. The two digitate leaves are borne from the main stem and carry a handsome white stem sheath. The inflorescence emerges from the leaf juncture, rising above the leaf; it consists of a white-striped, green spathe and a short, yellow or green spadix. Some taxonomists no longer make a distinction among *A. angustatum* var. *peninsulae*, *A. japonicum*, and *A. serratum*, lumping them together as variations under *A. serratum*; for our purposes here, I will retain each in its own taxa, with the knowledge that a unification has been recommended and may very well take place.

For many years *Arisaema sikokianum* was the most highly sought-after species within the genus, and though many outstanding new species have become commercially available to the collector, there is no question that the desirability of this species remains intact. Each leaf is composed of either three or five leaflets and often, but not always, possesses a striking silver mottling. I observed *A. sikokianum* in its native haunts of Shikoku in 1997, and all the numerous individuals that I came across bore this mottled foliage. The flowers produced in

The seedlings of *Arisaema sikokianum* at Heronswood include both variegated and pure green foliage forms (Photo by Lynne Harrison)

early spring are striking indeed, with a dark purple spadix surrounding a rather startling white, knobby spadix held within.

Several years ago Don Jacobs of Decatur, Georgia, sent me seed that had formed on his garden plants of *Arisaema takedae*. The inflorescences on Jacobs's plants were exclusively female while the nearby specimens of *A. sikokianum* were male, and the hybrid seedlings raised from this cross show characteristics intermediate between the two species. My garden specimens of this hybrid are remarkably robust plants rising to 4 ft. (1.2 m); some have the characteristic silver mottling in the center of each leaflet. The petioles are clasped to the base by a striking, loosely fit, pink fleshy sheath, which looks quite like baggy wool socks. The flowers have affinity to *A. takedae*, bearing a small, dark purple spathe that surrounds the characteristic knobby white spadix of *A. sikokianum*. I am currently raising second-generation seedlings of these plants (fruit bearing fertile seed has been infrequently produced), and I anxiously await their premier flowering to witness the variation that occurs within the population.

A spectacular hybrid of *Arisaema sikokianum* and *A. takedae* (Photo by Lynne Harrison)

A spectacular species, but one that has proven difficult for us in cultivation, *Arisaema speciosum* most likely depends on rich but extremely well-drained sites for successful growth. Each leaf consists of three enormous, heavily veined leaflets. The handsomely mottled petiole, which grows to 2 ft. (0.6 m), is adjoined by the 8-in. (20-cm) pedicel below ground level. The pedicel is capped by a blackish purple, white-striped spathe and an extremely long, thread-like spadix that extends to 2 ft. (0.6 m) or more. In foliage and flower, *A. speciosum* provides pure drama to the garden. It is native to the Himalayas.

We received our original tuber of *Arisaema taiwanense* (though under the name *A. kelung-insularis*) from Bleddyn and Sue Wynn-Jones in 1993 after their first successful collecting trip to Taiwan. I was not prepared for what would emerge the following spring: a magnificent purple-mottled petiole grew to 3½ ft. (1.1 m) carrying a whorl of 15 leaflets, each to 1 ft. (0.3 m) in length and terminating in extremely long, threadlike drip tips. The enormous, sinister-looking flower of black-purple is produced on its own stem, which rises from the tuber to a height of 8 in. (20 cm), and is followed by incredibly large, scarlet fruit that can attain the size of a small pineapple. Plants of *A. taiwanense* exhibit a great deal of variation in foliage, with some displaying a striking silvery pewter cast. These come relatively true from seed if sufficiently isolated in the garden. This species has proven to be remarkably hardy throughout the U.S., with encouraging reports from friends as far north as southern Vermont, which is surprising considering the species's southerly and low-altitude provenance. Because of the enormity of the fruit, the plant's vigor is significantly reduced for two years after fruiting, and it is prudent to prevent *A. taiwanense* from fruiting

Arisaema speciosum (Photo by Lynne Harrison)

unless one needs seed for more plants. Copious quantities of offsets are produced, and these can be harvested without lifting the mother bulb, although there may be a delay of growth from the offsets for up to one year after replanting.

I have cultivated *Arisaema ternatipartitum* as a small colony in my woodland for several years, and I continually mistake it for *A. amurense*, as it is quite similar in its superficial detail as well as its demeanor. The two trifoliate leaves arise from the leaf stem at near ground level, with the flowering stem continuing to 10 in. (25 cm) from the juncture and terminating in a dark purple-striped, green spathe and short spadix. I have under cultivation several specimens with silver-mottled leaflets. *Arisaema ternatipartitum* is native to Japan.

Arisaema thunbergii var. *urashima* is widespread throughout the woodlands of Japan, and it is one of the most curious-flowered arisaemas in our collection. This variety represents the most southerly populations of *A. thunbergii*, and according to the literature it differs only slightly from the species type (which I have never witnessed in flower). Glossy, digitate foliage is held on 1-ft. (0.3-m) petioles. The deep purple spathes emerge atop 10-in. (25-cm) stems, and from the spathes, a long, threadlike spadix rises to an additional 8 to 12 in. (20 to 30 cm) above and then tumbles nearly to the ground. *Arisaema thunbergii* var. *ura-*

Arisaema taiwanense in fruit (Photo by Lynne Harrison)

shima produces a large number of offshoots from the mother bulb on a yearly basis, and these should be removed to encourage growth, which is inhibited if they remain attached. It is notorious for its early dormancy, which disallowed my observation as well as collection of seed during my autumn trips to Japan. I cultivate numerous clones bearing lovely silver-mottled foliage.

Arisaema thunbergii var. *urashima* (Photo by Lynne Harrison)

Arisaema tortuosum is certainly a most spectacular species, and it represents the tallest member of the genus, with mature individuals rising to 8 ft. (2.4 m) or more on dazzling, python-skinned petioles. Two digitate leaves of 5 to 17 leaflets are borne near the top of the stem; slightly higher on the stem, the inflorescence is composed of a stiffly upright spathe from which arises a narrow, erect spadix tip. There seems to be considerable variation in stem and spathe color within the species, and I currently grow a spectacular clone that has ebony-colored stems and spadix; by far, however, the majority of my wild collections of this species have resulted in pure green or bronze-mottled stems. *Arisaema tortuosum* is one of the most commonly encountered species at lower elevations in the Himalayas, near the 7000- to 8000-ft. (2100- to 2400-m) level.

I collected *Arisaema yamatense* var. *sugimotoi* in the botanically rich mountains of central Honshu slightly north of Osaka in the autumn of 1997. This plant has a bold presence, with tall leaf stems to 5 ft. (1.5 m) bearing enormous pedate foliage. The flowers arise from the petioles, and the large fruit that follow grow to 5 in. (12.5 cm) long and 3 in. (7.5 cm) across and are held intact long after ripening to a startling orange-red. I had been told that this *Arisaema* offers up large numbers of silver-mottled plants, though I found only one such individual from among hundreds of plants observed during a week in this area of Japan.

The distinct inflorescence of *Arisaema tortuosum* provides an easy method of identification (Photo by Lynne Harrison)

Arisaema yunnanense is a rather unremarkable species, except for its specific epithet, which always sets my mind racing no matter what genus it is associated with. This is a trifoliate species with stems to 18 in. (45 cm) and small, green- and white-striped spathes surrounding short spadices. It is common throughout Yunnan Province, though not as widespread as *A. consanguineum*.

Hardiness: There are too many individual species to assign a general hardiness rating, but it is safe to assume that most are hardy in zones 6–10. In more extreme climates, consider a heavy mulching of the planting site in late autumn, though this definitely has its limits. When the tubers slip into dormancy, most if not all arisaemas will tolerate digging for storing in a cool, moist medium until spring. If a greenhouse is available, establishing the plants early before putting them out to the garden will be advantageous.

Cultivation: It is an oversimplification to assume that all *Arisaema* species are shade-loving plants. Whereas all that I have planted in my light woodland seem to thrive under these conditions, I have seen numerous species growing under less-than-luxuriant, exposed conditions. The distribution of *Arisaema consanguineum* in Yunnan Province is remarkable, from dry, baking sites associated with naturalized *Opuntia* to rather dank, moist sites in full shade. Until further studies are carried out and requirements of individual species fine tuned, it should be presumed that arisaemas are best planted in moist but well-drained sites in slightly acidic, humus-rich soils. In colder climates, the tubers are best planted at relatively shallow depths and then heavily mulched for the winter. The tubers will ultimately adjust their depth; I have observed species with tubers at ground level as well as nearly 2 ft. (0.6 m) deep. Let each individual species teach you its preferences. If you do not require seed for propagation, consider removing the inflorescence shortly after flowering, as the tremendous energy put into seed production will tax the overall vigor of your garden specimens.

Propagation: Propagation by seed is certainly the most efficient, though it does have its difficulties. Often the inflorescence contains exclusively male or exclusively female flowers. At Heronswood, we have simply inserted the inflorescence of the male specimen (if available at the time) into the spathe of the female specimen. On those occasions when we have the luxury of more time, we will place the male inflorescence in a blender with one-eighth teaspoon of detergent and a small amount of water. The detergent acts to reduce water tension, and the pollen grains adhere easily to the stigmatic surfaces of the female flowers; we have achieved close to 100% seed set using this method. The seed should be cleaned thoroughly from the pulp and sown fresh. Perform this task with great care, as the pulp contains irritants that will affect the skin and mucous membranes. In the field, I have lost all sensation in the tips of my fingers for several weeks as a result of cleaning the fruit without protection. The seed germinates easily without a cold period. Although species such as *Arisaema elephas* germinate during the first growing season, forming a subterranean tuber, they require a second growing season before producing a first true leaf. Several species will blossom within a year from germination, while many others are much more slumberous in this regard. Patience is paramount.

Separation of tuber offsets seems straightforward, but it too can present challenges. The offsets, even when quite large and seemingly vigorous, will not begin growth for a season or two. Often a simple exposure to light for a few hours is all that is needed to overcome this dormancy.

Pinellia

Other than the widely known mouse plant (*Arisarum proboscideum*)—whose mounds of arrow-shaped leaves hide the curious long-tailed spathes of chocolate-purple, appearing quite like a retreating rodent—*Pinellia* represents the only additional genus of woodland aroids sufficiently available to be worthy of exploration. Six species of *Pinellia* exist, all of which are Asiatic in origin and all of which possess flowers superficially reminiscent of those of *Arisaema*. The flowers of *Pinellia* differ primarily by the fact that the flowering stems arise directly from the tuber, independent of the leaf stem, and the spathe overlaps to form a tube within which the male and female portions of the spadix are delineated by a membrane. As a whole, the genus has been dismissed as offering little ornamental merit, but I find several of the species supremely deserving of greater use in our woodlands.

Pinellia cordata is among the best, with heart-shaped foliage that is glossy, dark green above and dark purple underneath, etched in white along the veins. (Though, with that said, I currently have seedlings of this species growing in my nursery with totally green leaves.) Elegant, albeit diminutive, purple-spathed flowers rise slightly higher, on stems to 1 ft. (0.3 m). *Pinellia tripartita* is well integrated into the shaded border, offering a lime-green inflorescence atop 15-in. (38-cm) stems and tripartite foliage. I am also cultivating a striking purple-flowered form that is exceptionally worthy. *Pinellia pedatisecta* is equally worthwhile, with a long, extended spadix that snakes well beyond the spathe. I have not en-

Pinellia cordata (Photo by Lynne Harrison)

countered *P. integrifolia*, which is also said to possess a curiously long spadix and may be worthy of inclusion in the woodland. *Pinellia ternata* should be avoided; it produces a surplus of tubercles at the leaf axils and spreads quickly and dangerously through the garden.

Hardiness: Zones 5–10. I have seen remarkable specimens of *Pinellia cordata* on the East Coast, where this species appreciates the heat and humidity.

Cultivation: As noted for *Arisaema*.

Propagation: Tuber offsets can be divided from the parent bulb, as can the stem tubercles present on some species, particularly *Pinellia cordata* and *P. ternata*. Seed is produced under cultivation and can be treated as per *Arisaema*; it will germinate in a single season if sown fresh

CHAPTER 25

The Wooded Lilies:
Fairy Bells and Solomon's Seals

Bleddyn and Sue Wynn-Jones hold the U.K. National Collection of *Polygonatum* and related members of the Liliaceae, and it is through my association and friendship with these Welsh plantspeople that I have developed my appreciation and fondness for the numerous genera held within the lily family. The richness that is brought to the woodland garden by this grand assemblage of plants cannot be provided by any other. In this appreciation I am not alone, as a hearty contingent of keen plantspeople in North America, Europe, and Japan have begun in earnest to explore and collect members of this remarkably diverse group of plants. For those who are already tuned in to the woodland lilies and are desperately seeking the secret code that will decipher its confused nomenclature, what I can offer here is probably insufficient; but perhaps my observations can help lift the overall confusion surrounding these plants to a somewhat higher plane.

The first six genera discussed in this chapter (*Polygonatum, Disporum, Smilacina, Streptopus, Disporopsis,* and *Uvularia*) have been extracted from the massive family Liliaceae by some taxonomists and lumped together as Convallariaceae. The last genus, *Croomia,* is often delegated to the ranks of the closely related Stemonaceae.

Polygonatum

One could not dispute the assertion that the genus of true solomon's seal, *Polygonatum,* has well been put to use in gardens across North America. Robust stands of elegant arching stems of *Polygonatum* ×*hybridum* carrying deep green foliage and pretty axillary clusters of creamy white flowers, growing amidst ferns and other denizens of shade, has become a signature sight in well-appointed woodland gardens. But as is generally the case in the vast world of plants, an enormous number of remarkable *Polygonatum* species remain largely unknown and underused.

With only one species occurring in the eastern half of the United States, there is a downright paucity of *Polygonatum* species native to the North American continent. Truth be told, until recently there were two recognized species: *Polygonatum biflorum*, previously known as *P. canaliculatum*, and *P. commutatum*, which initially made its horticultural rounds under the alias of *P. giganteum*. The rather exasperating fact that much of the material previously sold in commerce as *P. canaliculatum* was in fact *P. commutatum* is now a moot point, as the whole mess has been neatly repackaged under a single taxon, *P. biflorum*. Plants in my garden grown as *P. biflorum* rise to slightly more than 3 ft. (0.9 m), with arching stems carrying alternately arranged oval and deeply veined leaves to 4 in. (10 cm) and pendulous, axillary pairs of whitish green flowers. Quite gargantuan in contrast, those plants that I have grown under the name *P. commutatum* produce arching stems to 7 ft. (2.1 m), with leaves to 6 in. (15 cm) and many-flowered, axillary clusters of white flowers. The reason for the merging of the two taxa is based somewhat subjectively on the fact that the more robust form of the species is a polyploid of the smaller form, containing twice the normal allotment of chromosomes. As the two are now essentially isolated from one another in their inability to crossbreed, and as they have developed extremely different phenotypic expression and exploitation of habitat, considerable argument in ivorine halls may still be required before the debate is finally settled. (Within other genera, polyploidy has been considered an acceptable justification in the recognition of a distinct species.)

Before I venture onto the Eurasian taxa, which represent an enormous collection of exciting garden-worthy species, I must first digress. When considering the number of North American species in a given genera, horticultural writers too often commit the offense of chauvinistically amputating large portions of any genus that exist south of our national borders. *Polygonatum* is a case in point. This genus has a secondary area of distribution, in the high mountains of Panama and Guatemala, that shows spectacular diversity. Here grows *Polygonatum paniculatum*, which utilizes the low limbs of shrubs and trees to support its 25-ft. (7.5-m) stems cloaked with foliage, flower, and fruit. Obviously, few people will sleep any better tonight by virtue of the simple realization that this and countless other species exist in the mountains of Mexico as well as Central and South America. However, approaching this world of plants in a more all-inclusive and unifying manner will lead not only to a greater understanding of the system of life as a whole, but also to additional respect for life and its associated mysteries.

Venturing on to the more obscure and perhaps most exciting species of solomon's seals, one must linger momentarily in Europe to explore two species as well as a hybrid between them, the latter being perhaps the best-known *Polygonatum* under cultivation. *Polygonatum odoratum* extends from Europe into Asia, and it is best recognized by its low, arching, and decidedly angled stems that grow to 2½ ft. (0.8 m) and carry 4-in. (10-cm), ovate, parallel-veined leaves held stiffly upright. Reginald Farrer, with purpled prose, put it best in describing this species: "Its solid, pale green leaflets, folded back in pairs, like the wings of so many butterflies, seem to be settling on a stem strained backward almost to the point of breaking its spine." In striking textural contrast to this distinctive folial carriage are the pendulous, axillary pairs of lily-scented, green-rimmed white bells that hang beneath. The effect is superb, indeed amplified, if combined with upright and architectural plants, such as *Paris yunnanensis* or *Astilbe chinensis* var. *davidii*. A charming double-flowered form, *Polygonatum odoratum* 'Flore Pleno', should be sought out, especially if you love sticking your face in the soil to fully appreciate the beauty of a plant. I have planted 'Flore Pleno' near the edge of a 4-ft. (1.2-m) rock retaining wall in partial shade to make my own appreciation of this selection less awkward if not more sanitary. With a somewhat more Asiatic accent, but still with close familial ties, *P. odoratum* var. *pluriflorum* hails from Japan and Korea. In my woodland, this variety has formed a lush colony of nodding, angled stems to 3 ft. (0.9 m) with extremely handsome four-flowered axillary clusters of tubular, white flowers to 1 in. (2.5 cm) that are followed by blue fruit. A very lovely variegated selection, *P. odoratum* var. *pluriflorum* 'Variegatum', offers creamy white margined leaves with a carriage identical to that of the species. It is often and incorrectly sold under the name, *P. falcatum* 'Variegatum'. Several other variegated forms of this species, with neatly white-margined leaves, are worth growing for the superb foliage effect.

The detectably angled stems of *Polygonatum odoratum* help distinguish it from *P. multiflorum*, the other species that occurs in Europe. *Polygonatum multiflorum* grows naturally in alkaline habitats from England to Turkey and onward to Siberia, China, Korea, and Japan. This species doesn't hold much over *P. odoratum* as far as ornamental value, though I admire the resolve and fortitude that any taxa must demonstrate in making the climb and promotion to full-blown species rank. It also has rounded stems, which for some people perhaps is more acceptable.

Polygonatum odoratum var. *pluriflorum* (Photo by Lynne Harrison)

Polygonatum odoratum var. *pluriflorum* 'Variegatum' (Photo by Lynne Harrison)

The hybrid between the two European species, *Polygonatum ×hybridum*, is, as hybrids go, quite variable, with many individual clones in cultivation, some good and others not so much so. Seek forms that produce vigorously spreading colonies of upright stems gracefully nodding toward the apex and bear four-flowered clusters of clean, white, green-tipped bells. This hybrid includes a double-flowered form ('Flore Pleno') as well as a variegated form ('Striatum'). I have never had the pleasure of meeting 'Flore Pleno', but the variegated counterpart grows happily, if somewhat sparingly, in my woodland. For me, *P. ×hybridum* 'Striatum' does not make as vigorous stands as *P. odoratum* var. *pluriflorum* 'Variegatum', though it is quite dramatic rising here and there through the garden's green mounding carpets of early spring foliage.

The two European species extend naturally east toward the hotbed of *Polygonatum*-dom in China, Japan, Korea, and the Himalayas. Of the 40 recognized East Asian species, 22 are found in southwestern China, while a secondary center of distribution in the area of Japan, Korea, and northeastern China embraces 11 recognized species. The Asian species, as remarkable as they are, are poorly understood due to their general absence in cultivation and a lack of knowledge regarding their natural distribution. Greater accessibility to the flora of China will ultimately allow for a fine tuning of our familiarity with this incredible group of plants.

Polygonatum ×hybridum (Photo by Lynne Harrison)

Polygonatum hirtum hails from Japan as well as China, and though it shows some affinity to *P. odoratum*, this species possesses far more lustrous and immense foliage, growing to 8 in. (20 cm) long by 4 in. (10 cm) wide. The arching stems rise to 2.5 ft. (0.8 m) from a rather robust colony of spreading rhizomes in the moist, sheltered woodland at Heronswood, producing elegant large, pendulous, white axillary bells in midspring. As excited as I am with the numerous species of *Polygonatum* that I now cultivate, I take great pleasure in witnessing how many visitors to my garden inquire about the identity of this species as they come upon it in its moments of glory. It is through outspoken species such as *P. hirtum* that countless quieter kin will ultimately be introduced to the ever-more-inquisitive gardening community of North America and Europe.

Polygonatum humile forms handsome and dwarf suckering colonies of stems to 6 in. (15 cm) with leaves to 1 in. (2.5 cm). Axillary, pendulous, white flowers grow to less than ¹/₂ in. (1.25 cm) in length, either solitary or, occasionally, in pairs. The species is known to occur in Japan, Korea, China, and in adjacent areas of far eastern Russia, though I have never encountered it in the wild. In my light woodland, *P. humile* thrives and is exceptionally useful, especially if given adequate space to form expansive carpets of its lovely foliage. I observed numerous forms of this species under cultivation in Japan, and the selection is quite variable and worthy of additional collection. One such plant possessed fat, axillary, white flowers to 1¹/₂ in. (3.8 cm) in length! This would surely make a more ornamental addition to the garden than the clones currently under cultivation in the West.

Polygonatum humile is diminutive, but it is hardly the smallest of the *Polygonatum* species. *Polygonatum hookeri* grows to only 2 in. (5 cm) in height, spreading rapidly to form low mats of broad and blunt, oppositely carried leaves to 2 in. (5 cm) in length. Solitary and relatively large upturned flowers, purplish pink or white in color, are produced from the axils of the lower leaves in May and June, providing a most remarkable un-*Polygonatum*-like effect. *Polygonatum hookeri* is an adaptable and hardy species that thrives in the light shade of our woodland with adequate summer moisture, though it would do equally well in more exposed sites in cooler climates. It occurs naturally in high alpine meadows from Uttar Pradesh in northern India to southwestern China, on open slopes at elevations of 11,000–16,700 ft. (3300–5000 m), often growing at the base of shrubs.

Polygonatum hookeri (Photo by Lynne Harrison)

I observed *Polygonatum prattii* growing in very exposed sites in full sun or partial shade throughout much of northwestern Yunnan; it reminded me of stands of the red-berried *Gaultheria procumbens* that I grew up with in northern Michigan. In its native site, *P. prattii* rises to only 4 in. (10 cm) or less from spreading slender rhizomes, generally topped by a whorl of three rounded leaves that are green above and somewhat glaucous beneath. The reddish coral fruit can be hidden in the green foliage, but they shine in contrast to those plants that have yellowed in early dormancy. The flowers are reportedly purplish pink, though the seedlings that I germinated from seed collected in China have not blossomed to date.

Polygonatum graminifolium is a charming small species from southwestern China to the western Himalayas. Extremely narrow leaves are alternately arranged along 5- to 8-in. (12.5- to 20-cm) stems, and ascending, solitary, pink flowers are produced in April and May from the lower leaf axils. This species thrives in the woodland at Heronswood in well-drained soils with adequate summer moisture, though it could be expected to tolerate more open conditions with sharp drainage. My one clone of *P. graminifolium* was received from Elizabeth Strangman of Washfield Nursery in England.

It was exciting indeed to come across specimens of the striking *Polygonatum falcatum* in the wilds of Japan, on the Kii Peninsula southeast of Wakayama. Here astounding plants bore lanceolate leaves to nearly 1 ft. (0.3 m) in length and only 2 in. (5 cm) in width along stems that grew to 6 ft. (1.8 m). The drooping axillary flowers, produced in pairs from branched pedicels, result in large, succulent blue fruit. The excitement was not based so much on the intrinsic beauty held by this species, but more on the fact that *P. falcatum* was one of the very species that we were hoping to locate in the wild in this part of Japan. It is extremely rare in cultivation, though one would never guess as much from the number of catalogs in Europe and North America that list *P. falcatum*. For years, plants that made the horticultural rounds under this name were actually *P. odoratum*. Frustratingly, convincing horticulturists of both continents to consider giving the true *P. falcatum* a try will be an uphill battle; it is a supremely more striking garden plant.

During my travels in Japan and Korea in 1997, I encountered numerous specimens of *Polygonatum involucratum* as well as a closely allied species known as *P. inflatum*. The former grows to 15 in. (38 cm) high, with sparse ovate leaves to 4 in. (10 cm) and one or a few axillary clusters of two tubular, creamy white flowers to 1 in. (2.5 cm) in length attended by a shorter pair of green, leaflike, involucre bracts to ¹⁄₂ in. (1.25 cm) long. The pair of blue fruit subtended by these bracts provide an easy method of identifying *P. involucratum* in autumn. *Polygona-*

tum inflatum is similar in appearance, though it reaches 2 to 3 ft. (0.9 m) in height and bears narrow-lanceolate foliage to 4 in. (10 cm) and three to five clusters of two flowers each that are shorter than the subtending narrow whitish green bracts. It might be of interest to note that a third closely related species known as *P. cryptanthum* occurs in Japan. Similar to *P. involucratum*, *P. cryptanthum* rises to 15 in. (38 cm) and is few flowered, but its greenish flowers, held in pairs, extend to only ½ in. (1.25 cm) and are subtended by truncate whitish green bracts to ¼ in. (0.6 cm).

I found this good form of *Polygonatum falcatum*, with its stem nearly 6 ft. (1.8 m) long, growing on the Kii Peninsula in Japan in 1997 (Photo by Darrell Probst)

Common throughout the higher altitudes of the Korean Peninsula is the lovely but infrequently cultivated species *Polygonatum lasianthum*. It superficially resembles *P. odoratum*, with narrow foliage held somewhat upright on 18-in. (45-cm) stems. The flowers of this species are borne in axillary pairs from a branched pedicel that extends to the side of the stem. Due to the congested nature of the foliage and flowers, the flowers take on a false two-ranked appearance, seemingly borne in opposite pairs on the stem, while in fact they are arranged in an alternating fashion at each axil. These white, tubular flowers, to 1 in. (2.5 cm), result in blue fruit that are also held out from the stem, appearing at the same level or sometimes above the foliage, allowing for ease in identification in the field. The size of the flowers in relation to the overall size of the plant makes *P. lasianthum* a striking addition to the shaded garden.

The majority of *Polygonatum* species are terrestrial, but they do occasionally appear as epiphytes, and I observed two species growing in this format in eastern Nepal in the autumn of 1995. The 18-in. (45-cm) stems of *Polygonatum punctatum*, with whorled or alternately arranged glossy foliage, hung from large specimens of *Rhododendron arboreum* in relatively low elevations of the Milke Danda. Clusters of two to three purple-flecked flowers form in the leaf axils from pinkish buds, though I only observed the dull reddish fruit that are presented afterward. *Polygonatum punctatum* has thrived in my light woodland soil for some time, although the foliage, which wishes to remain evergreen, is often burnt during cold winters, and I suspect that this species will prove to have limited hardiness across much of the United States. A second epiphytic species grows on the same rhododendrons of the Milke Danda. The species is quite similar in appearance to *P. punctatum*, except that the glossy, ovate-lanceolate evergreen foliage of *P. oppositifolium* is borne in pairs (as the name implies) along arching 3-ft. (0.9-m) stems. Scarlet berries were present in great abundance on the plants that I observed, having followed the three- to eight-flowered axillary clusters of long, dull white flowers that are produced in April and May. While *P. punctatum* occurs

Polygonatum punctatum (Photo by Lynne Harrison)

throughout the eastern Himalayas and in southwestern China, *P. oppositifolium* is found only in central Nepal to Sikkim and at slightly lower elevations than the former. Both exist in a very narrow altitudinal band.

While in eastern Nepal, I also collected an epiphytic species known as *Polygonatum cathcartii* (HWJCM 500), which had hitherto been known only from collections east of the Kanchenjunga. Although for some time *P. cathcartii* was considered synonymous with *P. oppositifolium*, the glossy, ovate-lanceolate leaves, to 3 in. (7.5 cm) in length, are alternately arranged only at the first node and are borne in pairs along the rest of the blushed-purple stem. The creamy yellow, axillary flowers of *P. cathcartii* are borne singly or in pairs and result in crops of reddish brown fruit.

At elevations approaching 12,000 ft. (3600 m) in eastern Nepal, I collected seed from what was thought to be robust specimens of *Polygonatum verticillatum*. The rather erect stems possessed many whorls of four to eight narrow-lanceolate leaves, which bore in their axils branched clusters of lovely red fruit. The pendulous, green-tipped white flowers that preceded the fruit had blossomed in May to July. These specimens grew among hummocks of *Berberis* and other shrubs, which provided support for the stems to rise to 8 ft. (2.4 m) as well as protection from grazing animals.

Polygonatum verticillatum has a very broad distribution from southwestern Tibet, across Asia Minor, into Europe and north to Siberia, at elevations of 1600–12,000 ft. (500–3600 m) along forest margins and open slopes. The variants found within this vast range are not fully understood. A lovely garden form is occasionally available as *P. verticillatum* var. *rubrum*, with dark purple-suffused stems and foliage that are especially intense when emerging from the ground in spring. The young shoots are eaten by the hill tribes of the Himalayas.

In Nepal, Japan, and China I have collected numerous species of *Polygonatum* that possess accentuated coil-like, or cirrose, leaf tips, presumably an adaptation to facilitate clambering through the shrubby undergrowth of their natural environment. Several of the described species superficially resemble one another, and many years of study lie ahead before the nomenclatural confusion that surrounds them can be sorted out. Henry Noltie, of the Royal Botanic Garden in Edinburgh, has suggested treating all the taller growing, cirrose leaf-tipped species under the umbrella name of *Polygonatum sibiricum* in the broad sense, also referred to as the Sibiricum Group, though much of the literature still delimits separate taxa, including *P. cirrhifolium*, *P. curvistylum*, *P. fuscum*, and *P. stewartianum*.

Polygonatum sibiricum, as I have grown it, fits into this complex and makes a

Polygonatum sibiricum (Photo by Daniel J. Hinkley)

Polygonatum cirrhifolium, a species grouped within *Polygonatum sibiricum* in the broad sense, displaying its handsome, translucent red fruit (Photo by Daniel J. Hinkley)

very worthy garden plant. It rises to 5 ft. (1.5 m) or more when established and bears whorls of gray-green foliage with the aforementioned cirrose leaf tip. The elegant leaves are linear to narrow-lanceolate with inrolled margins and are produced in whorls of three to six, though I have often witnessed as many as ten leaves per whorl on some plants. In June, two to thirty short-stalked, white flowers, tinged with purple or green, emerge in paired pendulous clusters from the leaf axils. *Polygonatum sibiricum*, which is found throughout much of southwestern and north-central China in addition to Mongolia and southern Siberia, shows a great deal of ambiguous variation in its southern range. These may prove ultimately to be simple geographical variants, once this species is studied further.

In my observation, *Polygonatum curvistylum* is distinct from the other cirrose-foliaged members of the Sibiricum Group in that it rarely grows over 15 in. (38 cm) in height. I saw *P. curvistylum* commonly growing in the cracks of rocks in open and exposed areas throughout northwestern Yunnan Province. Clusters of two to eight bright coral-red fruit were ripening on the collapsed, yellowing stems quickly slipping into dormancy. It is a lovely species for fruit effects alone and will ultimately make a good addition to full-sun rock gardens across North America.

I observed a remarkable array of *Polygonatum sibiricum* types in Yunnan and Sichuan Provinces, ranging from plants with broad and glossy foliage and rising to 4 ft. (1.2 m) in full sun to an astounding narrow-foliaged, 13-ft. (3.9-m) plant growing in semishade and rising through the lower branches of the Chinese larch (*Larix potaninii*). This 13-ft. specimen was collected as *Polygonatum* sp. DJHC 600. Its leaves are borne in whorls of six to ten, each to 5 in. (12.5 cm) in length, and the axillary clusters of up to 20 flowers result in large blue fruit that have a distinctive greenish overtone. Seed from this collection germinated in the spring of 1998, and ultimately these seedlings will help broaden our knowledge of this and related species.

Polygonatum geminiflorum has few references in the literature, but it is common in Sikkim at high elevations and likely in China as well. It has proven to be both a handsome and robust species in cultivation, forming stiffly upright stems to 1½ ft. (0.5 m) and whorls of three broad leaves. Pairs of creamy white, pendant flowers are produced from the leaf axils in late spring and are followed by red berries. Interestingly, the plant displays two distinct forms of rhizomes, and I assume they change with age.

Polygonatum geminiflorum (Photo by Lynne Harrison)

Hardiness: As a whole, the genus *Polygonatum* seems to be quite forgiving of low temperatures, and many species thrive in the heat and humidity of the Southeast. The majority of the species discussed have limited use in cultivation, and so it is nearly impossible to assign USDA zones. It can safely be assumed that if you succeed with *Polygonatum* ×*hybridum*, *P. odoratum*, or *P. biflorum*, then the remainder of the genus will offer their ornament to your garden.

Cultivation: The true solomon's seals desire a somewhat sheltered and cool location with rich, humusy soil that is well drained. The epiphytic species are best planted in soil, rather than trying to duplicate their mode of survival in the wild, though mild maritime climates could accommodate an attempt at aerial cultivation. Most are vigorously rhizomatous and will form large, spreading colonies over time. Siting should allow for this tendency by keeping more diminutive treasures away from the taller members of this genus, as they will assuredly be overtaken. Additional summer moisture will aid the vigor of these plants, as will a yearly application of a well-balanced fertilizer.

Propagation: Easy by division of the rhizome in early spring. Seed is readily produced in cultivation and should be cleaned of all flesh and sown fresh. *Polygonatum* experiences double dormancy, and germination will generally not occur until the second year, though I have had first-year germination of *Polygonatum cirrhifolium*.

Disporum

At least 40 species of *Disporum* are known to exist worldwide, the majority being Asiatic in origin. Compared to *Polygonatum*, however, this genus is more generous to North America in its distribution, with a total of five species native to the East and West Coast. Morphologically, *Disporum* differs from *Polygonatum* in that it sometimes possesses branched stems, while lacking the thickened rhizome found in *Polygonatum*. The flowers of *Disporum*, terminal as well as axillary, are formed toward the apex of the stem, and the fruit is always a fleshy berry with few to many seeds held inside; depending on the species, the fruit is blue, yellow, or orange-red in color. The genus name is based on the presence of two ovules per carpel.

The three western North American species of *Disporum*, which are closely related to the genus *Uvularia*, make exceptional garden plants, even if Reginald Farrer denigrated *Disporum hookeri* var. *hookeri* as a "dingy . . . species of small merit." I take issue with Farrer on this matter; *D. hookeri* var. *hookeri* is a lovely and undeservedly scarce perennial in woodland gardens of zones 6–9 (and perhaps colder regions as well). The branched stems rise to 2½ ft. (0.8 m) in dense shade—they will be more compact under brighter conditions—carrying prominently veined, 3- to 4-in. (7.5- to 10-cm) leaves with long and elegant drip tips. Terminal umbels of three to four long-stalked flowers are produced in midspring to early summer, each bearing six pristine white tepals to ¾ in. (1.9 cm). The tepals are somewhat reflexed, and the stamens with creamy white anthers are tucked within. Orange-red fruit take the place of the flowers later in the season. *Disporum hookeri* var. *hookeri* is native from southern California to southern Oregon, where it grows in moist, shaded localities along the western slopes of the Cascade Mountain range as well as in the Siskiyous. The variety *D. hookeri* var. *oreganum* extends farther northward and eastward into Montana, and it differs from the type by its pubescent rather than glabrous styles and ovaries and its anthers that extend beyond the tepal. *Disporum hookeri* is readily distinguished from the similar *D. smithii* by its shorter petals, which allow a full view of the stamens.

When not in fruit, *Disporum trachycarpum* is difficult to distinguish from *D. hookeri*, as they share common territory, at least in the Pacific Northwest. Though the rough-fruited fairy bell, as *D. trachycarpum* is commonly known, lacks the elegant acuminate foliage tip that is found on *D. hookeri*, a more reliable identifying characteristic reveals itself once the red, albeit scabrous fruit is produced from the clusters of white flowers.

Much rarer in cultivation, and holding a tenuous standing in some areas of

Disporum hookeri var. *hookeri* (Photo by Lynne Harrison)

its natural range as well, *Disporum smithii* produces longer, 1-in. (2.5-cm), creamy white tepals that do not fully open and beyond which the stamens do not venture. The flowers result in striking orange-red, fleshy fruit that provides further interest to the garden in late summer through autumn. *Disporum smithii* is found growing naturally in moist, shaded woods along the West Coast, from British Columbia to central California, where its populations have suffered from the cutting of the much-needed overstory. In a garden setting in zones 6–9, this species will thrive in moist soils and makes an excellent choice for streamside plantings in shade. A striking white-margined variant of *D. smithii* exists but is currently quite rare in cultivation.

Disporum lanuginosum and *D. maculatum* are restricted to the East Coast of North America, and my experience with both species in cultivation is quite limited. They are decidedly different in appearance from their western counterparts, holding greater affiliation to the Asiatic species of the genus. *Disporum lanuginosum*, with erect, branched stems to 2 ft. (0.6 m) or taller, brandishes terminal clusters of nodding, yellow flowers. It is native along the eastern seaboard from Maine to Georgia. *Disporum maculatum* forms clumps of low, branched stems to 15 in. (38 cm), with nodding, purple-spotted white flowers produced in

Disporum smithii (Photo by Lynne Harrison)

May and June. Ranging from Newfoundland southwestward to Michigan, it is common along the shaded coastal dunes of northern Lake Michigan near the village of Arcadia, where I spent countless hours roaming as a child.

I collected seed of *Disporum cantoniense* in eastern Nepal, but this species exhibits a broad distribution, throughout the Himalayas and into southwestern China, and is represented by many different varieties. The form that I collected, from a shaded, moist situation nearly 8000 ft. (2400 m) above sea level, produces dramatic branched stems rising to 4 ft. (1.2 m) and carrying lovely and large crops of blackish blue fruit among the glossy evergreen foliage. The fruit follow pendulous, purple-red or white flowers that are produced in late April and early May. Since *D. cantoniense* is found at relatively low elevations of its native range, growing in near subtropical conditions, it may prove to have limited adaptability for most of the United States, although it seems quite content in my zone 8 woodland. *Disporum nantauense* was collected by Bleddyn and Sue Wynn-Jones in Taiwan under the name *D. cantoniense* var. *kawakamii*, and it too has been an exceptional performer in our garden. Its low, widely spreading and branched stems to 10 in. (25 cm) carry extremely narrow, 4-in. (10-cm) leaves, creating glossy green and highly textural colonies in the woodland. In midspring, terminal clusters of large, pendulous, creamy white flowers are produced, later resulting in handsome blue fruit.

Disporum nantauense (Photo by Lynne Harrison)

Disporum bodinieri and *D. megalanthum* are very similar in effect to *D. cantoniense*, and they also grow at relatively low elevations in their native territory in Sichuan and Yunnan Provinces of China. *Disporum bodinieri* produces tall stands of branched stems rising to 6 ft. (1.8 m), which are sheathed at the lower nodes with a light brown, papery bract. Terminal clusters of nodding, creamy white bells emerge in late spring and result in large crops of dark blue fruit. This species was common along road cuts and shaded ravines in both Chinese provinces, where it grew with *Disporopsis perneyi* and *Asarum chinense*. I observed *Disporum megalanthum* on the upper reaches of Emei Shan in Sichuan Province. This robust evergreen species grew up to 6 ft. (1.8 m) tall in some localities, always in fairly moist, shaded sites. It too produces large crops of blackish blue fruit, which create a remarkable scene in late autumn. The pure white flowers, with yellow stamens, appear in terminal clusters soon after the stems emerge in spring, later expanding to the plant's full height. I suspect that these species, which are similar to *Polygonatum sibiricum* in terms of nomenclatural flaws, will ultimately be lumped under an umbrella species with several recognized varieties.

Disporum sessile is common throughout eastern Asia, though it is infrequently found in cultivation in its typical form. On the other hand, *D. sessile* 'Variegatum' is remarkably abundant throughout the shade gardens of North America and Europe, and for good reason. Brightly striped and margined in white, the handsome sessile leaves are carried along 1-ft. (0.3-m) branched stems, which

Disporum sessile 'Variegatum' (Photo by Lynne Harrison)

emerge from vigorously spreading rhizomes that form sizable colonies. The large, creamy white, nodding flowers, produced from the upper leaf axils in early summer, are also variegated, and though the effect can be lost among the foliage, it is really quite splendid. The Japanese have been selecting variegated forms of *D. sessile* for countless generations, and so the cultivar name 'Variegatum', even in the United States, must be taken with a grain of salt. I have seen 40 or more forms of this species offered for sale in nurseries in Japan, but I could not in good conscience use the adjective "distinctive" to describe them. The most spectacular forms—that is, the forms with the most variegation—have proven to be the weakest in growth and should be avoided, except by those who covet the rare wares this sport has to offer. As *D. sessile* comes from summer-warm and humid areas of East Asia, it colonizes more vigorously in similar climates under cultivation. It does perform quite well in the cool maritime climate of the Pacific Northwest, but here I consider it more of a weaver than an actual groundcover.

Disporum uniflorum, previously and still widely known as *D. flavens*, is a superb plant from Korea and northeastern China. It creates columns of bright green, clasping foliage on erect, clumping stems to 3 ft. (0.9 m). Striking long and narrow, soft yellow flowers, similar in effect to those of *Uvularia grandiflora*, are formed in terminal umbels in midspring to early summer. Later, very pretty, oblong, bluish black fruit are produced in abundance. I have seen masses of this species growing on the west coast of South Korea as well as on Ullung-do in the Sea of Japan, where it produced magnificent stands of stoloniferous branched stems and enormous crops of blue fruit.

Elegance incarnate, *Disporum uniflorum* (Photo by Lynne Harrison)

In growth habit, and somewhat in fruit, *Disporum uniflorum* is similar to *D. viridescens*, which occurs in both Korea and Japan. (*Disporum uniflorum* is absent from Japan.) The terminal flowers of this vigorous species are more greenish white compared to the saturated yellows of the previous species, while the black fruit is perfectly rounded rather than oblong. *Disporum viridescens* forms expansive colonies of stoloniferous stems to 2½ ft. (0.8 m) in shaded, well-drained sites. I have observed the species growing commonly in moist sites on northern Honshu as well as in more well-drained locations on Mount Chiri in South Korea. One particularly fine stand grew as a herbaceous groundcover, with *Calanthe bicolor* and *Smilacina japonica*, beneath enormous virgin specimens of the rare conifer *Torreya nucifera* on Cheju Island. Witnessing this pristine, undisturbed, but greatly reduced ecosystem was an extraordinary experience, and I am thankful that this area is highly valued by the Korean government and has been preserved as a national monument.

Disporum lutescens is much of the same ilk—and in fact has been called *D. viridescens* var. *lutescens*, an invalid name—only it possesses lovely yellow, nodding flowers that arise from the upper leaf axils. I have found this species to be resentful of too much moisture during the winter season and prone to rot. It is native only to Japan, occurring on Honshu and Kyushu.

More demure in habit, *Disporum smilacinum* grows abundantly throughout South Korea as well as Japan, and it is also known to occur throughout much of eastern China. Low stoloniferous colonies of stems rise to between 4 and 18 in. (10 to 45 cm). The handsome creamy white, starry flowers are borne singly or in terminal pairs and are followed by rounded blue fruit, which look quite out of proportion on such a diminutive plant. It is frequently found growing in open deciduous woods within its natural habitat under rather dry summer conditions, and its performance has translated well to my garden, where it is thriving under a high overstory of Douglas firs in well-drained soil. Numerous exceedingly good

A lovely, golden-margined selection of *Disporum smilacinum* (Photo by Lynne Harrison)

Japanese selections of *D. smilacinum* are available with foliage broadly margined in bright yellow as well as pure white. Depending on their rarity, these forms can command princely sums, but they will quickly create expansive and extraordinarily handsome colonies.

Hardiness: The deciduous species of *Disporum* are sufficiently hardy in zones 4–9; the evergreen species are not fully tested in colder climates. These evergreen species, *Disporum bodinieri* and *D. cantoniense*, lose their stems in colder winters, but they are replaced readily in spring, with increased vigor on a yearly basis.

Cultivation: As noted for *Polygonatum*.

Propagation: By division in early spring as well as by seed. The seed of *Disporum* does not exhibit the double dormancy of most *Polygonatum* species and, if sown fresh, will germinate the following spring. Remove the seed from the flesh of the fruit before sowing.

Smilacina

The genus *Smilacina*, false solomon's seal, is among the showiest in flower of this lot of woodland herbs, and many of the 30-odd species possess an opulence in foliage that is beyond compare in the early spring garden. The unbranched stems rising from a thickened rhizome and the terminal clusters of small flowers superficially set this genus apart from other closely related genera in the Liliaceae. Four species are native to North America, though only two, *Smilacina racemosa* and *S. stellata*, are commonly cultivated. *Smilacina sessilifolia* and *S. trifolia* complete the quartet.

Smilacina racemosa is found throughout the continent, exhibiting substantial phenotypic differences between the plants on the two coasts. The East Coast version of *S. racemosa* is substantially smaller in all regards, rising to only 18 in. (45 cm) in height. As is the case in the two forms of *Polygonatum biflorum*, the more robust western form of *Smilacina racemosa* is a polyploid of the eastern diploid, and it manifests the exuberance that only a double dose of chromosomes can, with plants rising often to over 4 ft. (1.2 m) in content individuals. *Smilacina racemosa* var. *amplexicaulis* is found only in the western states and differs in its leaves, which are clasping and sessile rather than short petioled.

I am partial to the western form of *Smilacina racemosa*, which rises in early spring with bright green, parallel-veined leaves along stems that are topped by large, frothy panicles of creamy white flowers in June. The flowers are followed by extraordinary clusters of marbled pink and mauve fruit that ripen to rich orange-red or, infrequently, yellow. It is common on the western slopes of the Cascades from British Columbia to California, as well as south to Arizona, in moist and partially shaded sites. It is stunning in combination with the evergreen fronds of the western sword fern (*Polystichum munitum*). Among the numerous exotic *Smilacina* species under evaluation at Heronswood, our native species holds its own.

More prim in habit, *Smilacina stellata* rises to 12 to 15 in. (30 to 38 cm) in height, with small but charming terminal clusters of white stars produced late in the season, often not appearing until mid-August. These result in green fruit striped with black that later turns to red, though the fruit does not compete in effect with that of its more robust cousin, *S. racemosa*. The floral display is somewhat of a disappointment after the dramatic foliage unfurls, with leaves often expanding to 5 in. (12.5 cm) or more, alternately arranged along the squat stems. *Smilacina stellata* may be too rampant in growth for the small woodland garden, though I find it to be a lovely running and knitting species in our rather expansive woodland site.

The western North American form of *Smilacina racemosa* is decidedly more robust than the eastern counterpart and may represent a tetraploid of the species (Photo by Lynne Harrison)

In appearance, *Smilacina japonica* is closely allied to *S. stellata*, but this species carries more appeal to the garden. *Smilacina japonica* has somewhat larger leaves that are sessile to the decidedly pubescent 2-ft. (0.6-m) stems. Panicles of small, white flowers cap the stems in June and July. I have encountered this species throughout South Korea as well as in Japan, where the heads of ripened red fruit add color and a bit of excitement to the autumn mountain flora. For some time I have cultivated in my garden the golden-berried form of the species, *S. japonica* var. *luteocarpa*, which makes a distinctive and handsome addition to the woodland. *Smilacina japonica* var. *robusta* is encountered in northern Honshu and Hokkaido, and this variety is indeed more robust in all aspects, with stems rising dramatically to 5 ft. (1.5 m). The foliage of *S. japonica* var. *robusta* also possesses a short petiole and is not fully sessile. Of the two varieties, var. *robusta* is probably the one that should be sought out for inclusion in the moist, shaded garden. I saw a striking variegated form of this variety offered for a princely sum at a nursery in Japan, but my wallet would have suffered more than my garden would have benefited.

Larger and more dazzling in all regards is *Smilacina hondoensis*, a dioecious species from central and northern Honshu. Erect stems bear handsome lance-shaped leaves to 8 in. (20 cm) in length, deep green in color and prominently veined. The flowers of white are produced on pink pedicels in large terminal panicles, followed by handsome red fruit on female plants. Though *S. hondoensis* and *S. japonica* var. *robusta* both have hairy stems, this species differs from *S. japonica* var. *robusta* by possessing, in addition to minor floral differences, foliage that is fully sessile to the stem.

Smilacina hondoensis shows great affinity to a collection of *S. formosana* made in Taiwan by Bleddyn and Sue Wynn-Jones. *Smilacina formosana* is a superb and much-under-cultivated species that offers dark, glossy, lance-shaped, deeply veined leaves along gracefully arching stems to 5 ft. (1.5 m), which are capped in late spring by panicles of pristine white flowers. It is a most handsome species in foliage alone.

Another dioecious species from northern Japan is *Smilacina yezoensis*. It possesses foliage that is as dramatic as that of its Taiwanese brethren, deeply veined and extending to 6 in.

Smilacina formosana (Photo by Daniel J. Hinkley)

(15 cm) in length. The male inflorescence is a multiple raceme of greenish flowers, whereas the female inflorescence is a simple raceme, also green flowered, that results in brownish red fruit. The species occupies the same area of north-central Honshu as *S. hondoensis*, in moist, shaded sites at moderate altitudes.

Growing at fairly high elevations on Mount Odae in South Korea, with carpets of the rare *Iris odaesenensis* in a rich deciduous oak wood, the rare and demure *Smilacina davurica* forms low, arching stems to 6 in. (15 cm) that terminate in a simple raceme of green flowers in June, followed by lovely red fruit. The species was so plentiful at this location, along with *S. japonica* and *Disporum smilacinum*, that the ground was a dazzling display of colorful fruit from these species. *Smilacina bicolor* grows farther to the north, across the North Korean border, though it is quite rare in cultivation. Similar to *S. davurica* in appearance, it is somewhat larger, with stems to 18 in. (45 cm). A slightly branched raceme of green flowers is produced on the male plants; on the females, ruddy brown flowers result in orange-red fruit.

Perhaps most exciting for me are the numerous species of *Smilacina* that are native to southwestern China and the Himalayas but are virtually unknown in cultivation. I have growing in my garden three species of *Smilacina* that I first observed in eastern Nepal in 1995: *Smilacina fusca*, *S. purpurea*, and *S. oleracea*. The forms of *S. fusca* and *S. purpurea* that I grow are similar to one another in flower and foliage. They possess small, airy inflorescences of minute, purple flowers and elegant lanceolate leaves that grow to 6 in. (15 cm) in length and have leaf margins fringed with fine hairs (ciliate). *Smilacina purpurea* produces nar-

Smilacina fusca (Photo by Lynne Harrison)

Smilacina purpurea (Photo by Daniel J. Hinkley)

row, upright stems to 3 ft. (0.9 m) in height, and the narrow, terminal raceme, to 10 in. (25 cm) in length, is held stiffly erect or occasionally pendulous and is infrequently branched. Though my solitary garden specimen of this species fits perfectly its specific epithet by offering purple flowers, a white-flowered form is frequently encountered in the wild. In contrast, *S. fusca* is a rather demure, arching species, reaching only 15 in. (38 cm) in height. Terminal, pendulous panicles bear purplish brown flowers, and the leaves and stems of this species are coated in fine pubescence. Both species have made handsome additions to my woodland garden, thriving in a shaded position adjacent to *Disporum hookeri* and *Streptopus amplexifolius*.

I consider *Smilacina oleracea* the queen of the genus. I first encountered this spectacular, robust species in the rich wooded areas below Topke Gola in eastern Nepal, and I observed it again in Yunnan Province in 1996. Large, terminal heads of pastel-pink flowers are held atop 8-ft. (2.4-m) stems in early summer, followed by succulent orange fruit. The elegant lanceolate leaves, to 8 in. (20 cm), and stems are totally glabrous, lacking the pubescence found on the other Himalayan species. As with *S. purpurea*, a white-flowered form is known to occur throughout its range.

A new encounter for me personally was *Smilacina wilsonii*, which I saw for the first time during my 1996 trip to Yunnan. It offers enormous 10-in. (25-cm) long, ovate, felted leaves on stems to 4 ft. (1.2 m), the last 18 in. (45 cm) of

Smilacina oleracea (Photo by Lynne Harrison)

which forms a many-branched panicle. This grows in rich, moist locations in fairly dense shade along streams throughout the high mountains flanking the Tibetan Plateau. I was disappointed in the paucity of fruit found on this species, until, near the end of the trip, I ventured up a small rocky stream at the crest of Emei Shan in Sichuan. Here full heads of translucent orange-red fruit covered every boulder along the shaded stream; I strongly suspect that this was the identical species that I observed earlier in Yunnan. I now have the resultant seedlings growing in my nursery. When I returned to the same area of China in the autumn of 1998, not a single seed was left on any of the plants I encountered, making more apparent to me the vagaries of seed collection in the wild and the importance of taking the time to collect seed, in a discriminate fashion, when and if they are made available to you in the field.

The assemblage of plants that I collected during my trips to China in 1996 offered a challenge in assigning species names, and because of this I was most excited to return in 1998 to observe their distribution and growth habits. I was ultimately able to properly identify two species that grew in great abundance in the same localities of the Zhongdian Plateau. The one that I had collected in 1996 under the name *Smilacina* sp. DJHC 321 turned out to be precisely the same species I had collected earlier in eastern Nepal in 1995: *Smilacina purpurea*. Here, in its more easterly distribution, the species grows as a handsome, few-stemmed perennial with arching stems to 24 in. (60 cm) and simple racemes to 8 in. (20 cm) carrying exquisite, translucent red berries. It grew side by side with a vigorously clumping, more upright species that proved to be *S. forrestii*, which I had collected as *Smilacina* sp. DJHC 541 during my first trip to China. It shows great affinity to a plant that I received from Elizabeth Strangman of Washfield Nursery in England under the collection number of *Smilacina* sp. CLD 0383. Collected in the same area by James Compton in 1987, *S. forrestii* has performed beautifully in my garden, forming robust colonies in a rather short period of time and offering dark purple stems rising to 18 in. (45 cm) and lanceolate leaves to 3 in. (7.5 cm). In early spring, pristine white flowers are carried on stiffly upright branched racemes to 5 in. (12.5 cm) in length, resulting in striking crops of orange fruit.

Of all the puzzles yet to solve, I am most excited to put a name to *Smilacina* sp. DJHC 381. In the spring of 1997, I entered my greenhouse to find a most remarkable fragrance filling the enclosed space. With more than a little surprise, I discovered the source to be a single stem of this plant, which I had collected the previous autumn in Yunnan Province near Zhongdian. The deeply impressed, ovate leaves, to 3 in. (7.5 cm), are carried along notably hairy, 10-in. (25-cm) stems, while the green flowers are produced on 5-in. (12.5-cm) terminal racemes.

Hardiness: As this is primarily a genus from northerly latitudes and high elevations, most, if not all, *Smilacina* species will be hardy in zones 4–9. Obviously, little data exists for many of the species discussed.

Cultivation: As noted for *Polygonatum*.

Propagation: The seed exhibits a double dormancy and will not germinate for two seasons in most instances. Division in early spring is easily accomplished.

Streptopus

A genus of superb woodland, circumboreal plants, *Streptopus* is found in moist, shaded soils of the Northern Hemisphere, and it deserves greater use in our gardens for its charming floral display and striking sets of fruit. The generic name translates literally to "twisted foot," and the genus is known in the vernacular as twisted stalk, describing the kinked pedicel that is common to members of the genus. We may never understand the reason behind this odd bend in the stem, but it represents one of the billions of marvelous mysteries that surround us in the natural world. Nonetheless, this signature pedicel makes for an easily identified characteristic of the genus. To correctly identify the individual species, however, is a totally different story, and I can offer no simple solutions.

Three species of *Streptopus* exist in the mountains of western North America, and one of these is found, in a varietal form, in Asia as well. The most commonly encountered species is *Streptopus amplexifolius*, which makes a lovely component of the woodland garden. The thin leaves clasp the stems (that is, the leaves are amplexicaul, as suggested by the specific name), and the stems are branched and rise to 3 ft. (0.9 m) or even more. Solitary, axillary, whitish green, bell-shaped flowers are produced in abundance in spring at the ends of ¾-in. (1.9-cm), sharply bent pedicels. While hiking the Chilkoot Trail in southeastern Alaska with Robert L. Jones in 1992, I came upon immense stands of this species bearing spectacular crops of large, red fruit; *S. amplexifolius* is a highly ornamental woodland plant in this regard. I have also seen this species growing in the Cascade and Olympic Mountain ranges of the Pacific Northwest, always in dense shade and often along running water in somewhat mucky soils.

Streptopus roseus is a striking species in flower that is represented in the west by the variety *curvipes*, which differs little from the eastern counterparts, var. *roseus* and var. *pectinatus*. *Streptopus roseus* var. *curvipes* grows in damp, shaded sites at lower elevations of the Olympic Mountains along with *Disporum hookeri* and *Smilacina stellata*. In fact, I had been looking long and hard for this species for many years, not realizing until recently that I was practically walking on it; I had

Streptopus amplexifolius (Photo by Lynne Harrison)

The succulent fruit of *Streptopus amplexifolius*—note the kinked pedicels that give the genus its common name, twisted stalk (Photo by Daniel J. Hinkley)

Streptopus amplexifolius flower (Photo by Lynne Harrison)

assumed the plants were the superficial look-alike, *Disporum hookeri*. *Streptopus roseus* produces axillary flowers of pink along unbranched stems to 15 in. (38 cm). Great variability exists with regard to the richness of flower color, and selection work should be done to introduce into general cultivation some of the better colored forms.

With a name like *Streptopus streptopoides* (a streptopus that resembles a streptopus), one must presume this to be the mother of all twisted stalks. Though the native stands of this species, found at relatively high elevations in the Olympics and Cascades, are far from imposing, producing rather short unbranched stems, a varietal form, *S. streptopoides* var. *japonica*, which I observed on northern Honshu in Japan, forms quite remarkable plants to 4 ft. (1.2 m) and taller. Both types produce axillary, starlike flowers of light pink or white followed by large, red berries possessing many seeds.

Assuredly, numerous species of *Streptopus* native to the vast, underexplored regions of China deserve more attention. Near Zhongdian in northwestern Yunnan Province, beside Tianchi Lake at 12,000 ft. (3600 m) in altitude, I collected fruit of a low-growing species with clasping foliage and stems to 10 in. (25 cm) that grew with *Beesia calthaefolia* and *Arisaema elephas* in a damp, shaded situation near the lake margin. I have been unable to provide a species name.

Hardiness: Collectively, *Streptopus* represents very cold-tolerant plants that may not be useful in areas with excessive summer warmth and extreme dryness. Zones 4–9.

Cultivation: As noted for *Polygonatum*, but these are certainly more tolerant of poorly drained sites.

Propagation: Easy by seed or by division in early spring. Seed may exhibit double dormancy and will not emerge until the second year. Remove all pulp and dry slightly before sowing.

Disporopsis

The genus *Disporopsis* is relatively new on the scene, but in the short period of time since its introduction, it has already created quite a stir among plant aficionados. As with all newly introduced genera, especially with a paucity of different clones available for study, the taxonomy of *Disporopsis* is still rather lacking, and many taxonomic errors can be identified in commerce. Some taxonomists estimate that as many as 20 species can be found in China, and the natural distribution of the genus extends to Taiwan and the Philippines.

All species of *Disporopsis* possess evergreen stems, thick spreading rhizomes, and axillary flowers. *Disporopsis perneyi* is the best-known to date and makes a handsome addition to the bright, shaded garden. Slightly nodding stems to 15 in. (38 cm) are produced on a yearly basis, with very pretty clusters of tubular, axillary flowers forming along the stems in late spring and resulting in striking sets of blue fruit. The leathery, dark green, glossy leaves are retained throughout the winter, though they become quite weather-beaten by spring, and I prefer to remove the old stems before growth resumes. I observed this species in Sichuan Province growing on a steep, moist bank in a narrow canyon just above Ya'an. Here it grew in a rich association with *Disporum bodinieri*, *Asarum chinense*, and *Epimedium acuminatum*. *Disporopsis perneyi* has proven hardy across much of North America, creating sizable stoloniferous colonies in humus-rich soils.

I currently cultivate two clones of *Disporopsis arisanensis*, though I have not observed this species in the wild; it is found only in Taiwan and not on mainland China. Both clones that I cultivate bear stems that are shorter and more arching than those of *D. perneyi*, growing to 8 in. (20 cm) in height, and the foliage is somewhat larger, to 3 in. (7.5 cm) in length, and dark, shiny green in color. The few axillary flowers are tubular bells produced in early to late spring. The creamy white flower color is variable, as some display a whitish green hue, while others are pale to deep yellow and heavily marked with purple on the inside. *Disporopsis arisanensis* is rhizomatous and will form rather expansive colonies in the garden when fully established. It may prove useful to areas of North America with mild winters.

Disporopsis arisanensis is often and incorrectly sold as *D. fusca-picta* in the trade, but the true *D. fusca-picta* is a much more robust species and is easily recognizable by its very distinct rhizome, which is knobby with short, contracted internodes. I witnessed *D. fusca-picta* at lower elevations of Emei Shan, where it formed dark green, glossy foliage on stems to 3 ft. (0.9 m) in height. I currently have a handful of clones of this species under cultivation, and I await their inaugural flowering.

Hardiness: Though there has been very little testing of this genus around the country, initial reports seem encouraging from colder climates. *Disporopsis perneyi* has been reported to survive unprotected in Missouri (zones 5–6). The other species may be more tender and should be protected with a heavy mulch, until further data proves to the contrary. *Disporopsis fusca-picta* is probably too tender for much of the country where extreme cold temperatures exist; if provided plenty of summer moisture, however, it will certainly thrive in areas with excess warmth and humidity.

Cultivation: All species of *Disporopsis* should be planted in a sheltered location with humus-rich, well-drained soils. The newly produced shoots should be protected from slugs as they emerge in spring. Because of the evergreen nature of *Disporopsis* foliage, one might consider steps to prevent damage by strawberry root weevils (several nonchemical means are available). As stated earlier, we cut the stems back in late winter to remove the old stems and rather unsightly foliage; this should be done long before growth resumes, to prevent damage to the emerging stems.

Propagation: *Disporopsis* can be propagated by division in early spring and by seed. The seed has shown a tendency toward double dormancy, so seed pots must be retained for at least two years. The presence of more than one clone will result in better seed set.

Disporopsis perneyi (Photo by Lynne Harrison)

Disporopsis arisanensis (Photo by Lynne Harrison)

Uvularia

The genus *Uvularia* claims only eastern North America as its native haunts, though it is quite common in deciduous woods from Newfoundland to Florida and west to Kansas. I have cultivated the four species of *Uvularia* in my garden for many years, and they are exceptionally carefree and lovely additions to the spring woodland. Superficially resembling the disporums, they differ most in possessing dry, three-lobed capsules rather than berries as fruit. The smallest of the lot is *Uvularia sessilifolia*, which has a wide distribution in deciduous woods from eastern Canada to Alabama and west to South Dakota. The finely textured leaf stems rise to 16 in. (40 cm) in height, and the 3-in. (7.5-cm) leaves are sessile to the stem. Pendulous, greenish yellow, tubular flowers are produced in the apex in late spring and early summer. I currently grow two variegated cultivars of this species: *Uvularia sessilifolia* 'Variegata', which has a clear white margin to the foliage, is a rather stubborn performer for me; and *U. sessilifolia* 'Cobblewood Gold' offers a lovely rich yellow variegation throughout the foliage. The latter was introduced by Darrell Probst of Massachusetts, in 1997, and it has proven to be an exceptionally beautiful and vigorous clone.

Uvularia caroliniana is slightly taller than *U. sessilifolia*, reaching up to 20 in. (50 cm) in height, and its natural range is somewhat more restricted, from New Jersey south to Georgia and west to Alabama. Like that of *U. sessilifolia*, the foliage is sessile to the stem and grows to 3 in. (7.5 cm) long, but it differs from that of the previous species by being minutely serrate along the margin. The flowers are a similar greenish yellow and are borne in terminal clusters. The styles of both are divided, with those of *U. caroliniana* parted to at least half of its length, while the styles of *U. sessilifolia* are divided to only one-third. *Uvularia caroliniana* can be found in the trade under several names, including *U. pudica* and *U. puberula*.

The $3\frac{1}{2}$-in. (9-cm) leaves of *Uvularia perfoliata*, which are glabrous on both sides, totally clasp the stems and provide the best method of identification of this species. The stems rise to 2 ft. (0.6 m), and soft yellow flowers to $1\frac{1}{4}$ in. (3 cm) in length are held in terminal clusters. The pendulous, deeply colored lemon-yellow flowers of *U. grandiflora* are much larger, to 2 in. (5 cm) long, emerging on $2\frac{1}{2}$-ft. (0.8-m) stems and blossoming in late spring. The floral display makes *U. grandiflora* the boldest and most beautiful member of the genus, and the colonies of leafy, spreading stems are also striking. The foliage clasps the stems on this species as well, but it can be differentiated from *U. perfoliata* by the fact that its leaves are longer, to 5 in. (12.5 cm), and are pubescent beneath.

Uvularia sessilifolia (Photo by Lynne Harrison)

Uvularia grandiflora (Photo by Lynne Harrison)

Uvularia grandiflora occurs in the deciduous woods of mid-central Michigan, which I explored as a youth, hunting in early spring for the elusive morel mushroom, amidst *Trillium grandiflorum, Dicentra cucullaria, Sanguinaria canadensis,* and *Hepatica nobilis* subsp. *americana. Uvularia grandiflora* 'Pallida' offers a paler butter-yellow flower that is quite good, but it is not significantly different from the type species to justify expending a great deal of energy to obtain it. Predictably, 'Pallida' is more widely available in Europe than in the United States—another example of a native American selection being embraced more passionately by European gardeners and nurserypeople than by those of the plant's homeland.

Hardiness: All species are considered quite hardy to zone 4.

Cultivation: All *Uvularia* species are easily cultivated in moist but well-drained, humus-rich soils in partial to full shade. They combine beautifully with the later trilliums, such as *Trillium erectum,* or various species of *Meconopsis.*

Propagation: *Uvularia* has proven so easy to propagate by division that I have not bothered to collect seed.

Uvularia grandiflora 'Pallida' (Photo by Lynne Harrison)

Croomia

The genus *Croomia* is infrequently encountered, and I include it only because I was so intrigued by its presence in the woodlands of Shikoku Island, Japan, where I saw it in 1997. The similarity to *Polygonatum* in stem and foliage is uncanny, though the flowers and fruit are significantly different. *Croomia japonica*, which I observed in wooded situations in association with *Arisaema sikokianum*, possesses succulent stems that rise in zigzag fashion to 10 in. (25 cm) and bear ovate, deeply ribbed leaves to 5 in. (12.5 cm). Wiry, 3-in. (2.5-cm) pedicels carry small, solitary, axillary flowers with four strongly reflexed tepals. The species is native to Japan in the moist woodlands of Honshu and Kyushu. *Croomia heterosepala* has somewhat broader foliage, while its flowers are held on equally long pedicels but are composed of two broad and two smaller rounded white tepals, appearing more like a *Cardamine* flower than a woodland lily. The fruit is composed of a two-carpelled, green capsule subtended by a persistent corona. All in all, nothing about these plants will set the gardening world afire, but I consider them among the most precious plants in my collection.

Hardiness: Uncertain at present; my specimens have not yet been trialed in the garden, though they assuredly are hardy in zones 7–10.

Cultivation: As noted for *Polygonatum* and other woodland lilies: moist, humus-rich soils in shaded sites.

Propagation: Division of the rhizome in early spring is a distinct possibility, as is propagation by seed, though I have not had experience with either.

Croomia japonica (Photo by Lynne Harrison)

CHAPTER 26

Gargantuan Lilies:
The Genus *Cardiocrinum*

What must the mid-nineteenth-century Scottish plant explorer Robert Fortune have felt when he first saw the erect, towering stems of *Cardiocrinum giganteum* thrusting through the rich vegetation of Yunnan Province? No Westerner before him had witnessed its remarkable presence or had even contemplated a scene that to this day demands a second look by jaded plantspeople and beginning gardeners alike.

Indeed, few scenes are as provocative as a stand of *Cardiocrinum giganteum* in full blossom at the end of June. The glossy green basal foliage is heart-shaped (as suggested by the generic name) and up to 18 in. (45 cm) long by 10 in. (25 cm) wide on blossoming-sized plants. After seven years of building strength, the enormous bulbs of this species are fully primed to send their treelike flowering stems skyward to 15 ft. (4.5 m) or higher. The stems are capped by a dozen fragrant, pendulous white trumpets to 10 in. (25 cm) in length; at Heronswood, the shaded garden is awash with fragrance from the flowers in late June. After fertilization takes place, the swollen, globular ovaries take an upward stance, offering a much longer, somewhat more subtle, but equally dramatic effect to the summer and autumn garden. Even in autumn, when the fruit capsules have turned to tawny brown and opened to spill their seed about the garden, like a thousand silken coins, the gigantic stems can be cut and stored for an incredibly long-lasting ornamental effect.

Cardiocrinum giganteum covers a rather broad natural range, from Kashmir in the west, across the Himalayas, to southwestern China. In nature, the species is delineated into two varieties. The type, *C. giganteum* var. *giganteum*, possesses green stems and petioles, whereas these features in the western counterpart, *C. giganteum* var. *yunnanense*, are a startling deep burgundy-purple. The latter,

After a seven-year voyage to maturity, the flowering stems of *Cardiocrinum giganteum* var. *giganteum* tower to nearly 15 ft. (4.5 m) (Photo by Lynne Harrison)

which I have observed both along the eastern flank of the Cang Shan in Yunnan Province as well as on Emei Shan in Sichuan Province, should be sought over the green form, though both will certainly add distinction and wonder to the well-appointed woodland.

While in Chiba Prefecture on Honshu in 1995, I encountered the more diminutive but equally desirable *Cardiocrinum cordatum* var. *cordatum* growing in the low, wooded hills of this area with *Arisaema limbatum*, *Hydrangea involucrata*, and *Stachyurus praecox*. *Cardiocrinum cordatum* var. *cordatum* takes a similarly long time to flower from seed, at which time it will rise to 4 ft. (1.2 m) high while producing numerous fragrant, ivory-colored flowers in late summer. The five to nine irregular-shaped blossoms are composed of three bottom petals that form a lip and two upper petals that construct a flattened lid. Like those of *C. giganteum*, the seed capsules of *C. cordatum* align themselves vertically after fertilization and spilt open into three equal parts to disperse the seed.

A more northerly and robust counterpart, *Cardiocrinum cordatum* var. *glehnii*, extends through Hokkaido and into Sakhalin and the southern Kuril Islands. In

1997, I encountered vast stands of this variety near Lake Towada on northern Honshu, where dried stems rising to 6 ft. (1.8 m) in height were chock full of seed. So plentiful was this variety here that one could not take a step without disturbing the stems and filling the air with its sparkling, translucent seed. It is a scene that I will not soon forget. This variety differs from the southern form by its greater height and more flowers, up to 20 per stem.

In flower, *Cardiocrinum cathayanum* appears quite similar to the closely related *C. cordatum*. In late summer, atop 3- to 4-ft. (0.9- to 1.2-m) stems, the upper two petals incurve to form a curious, flat-topped flower. The foliage of *C. cathayanum* emerges in spring with a startling coppery tone, later fading to deep, glossy green. I received bulbs of this species from the curator of the Asian Collection at the U.S. National Arboretum in Washington, D.C., but I have been unable to procure collection data or references to this species in the literature. It flowered for me for the first time

The flowers of *Cardiocrinum giganteum* var. *giganteum* (Photo by Lynne Harrison)

in the late summer of 1995, and since then I have had specimens in flower every year from one bulb or another.

Hardiness: *Cardiocrinum* is much hardier than most people realize, surviving to flowering size in zone 5 on a consistent basis, though it is risk-free in zones 6–9. It will not tolerate the summer-humid areas of the deep South and Southeast. The bulbs migrate to the surface as they mature, in fact the apex of the bulbs ultimately appears slightly above the soil line, and so mulching in late fall will be beneficial in colder areas.

Cultivation: Cardiocrinums respond best to a rich diet and plenty of moisture. Given this, they do not necessarily need a shaded site, though that is their preference in nature. Provide with an additional application of slow-release fertilizer during the first five or six years after planting and before blossoming. Do not fertilize the bulbs in their blossoming year; I have had stems collapse to the ground from their own mass due to spring fertilization of mature bulbs. The best flowering effects come from seedling-grown plants that have been in place for several years before flowering. Younger bulbs slip into early dormancy in midsummer, and so their position should be noted, lest one disturbs their territory. Although the mother bulb dies after flowering (anything would die after giving birth to such enormity), offsets are produced in abundance, and these should be dug and replanted throughout the garden in autumn or early spring, not left in place to compete with one another. Protect the foliage of young plants from slug damage.

Propagation: Seed is certainly the best method of propagation, and once you have successfully blossomed one plant, a sufficient supply of fresh seed will not be a concern. Seed takes two years to germinate and another six to seven years before flowering. Self-sown seedlings in the garden should be protected from slug damage. As stated above, offset bulbs do provide an easy method of propagation while producing a garden population of diverse maturity that will offer up at least a few flowering stems on a yearly basis. Large offset bulbs often will blossom the following year and are generally a disappointment, producing stems that belie their full potential.

Cardiocrinum cathayanum (Photo by Daniel J. Hinkley)

CHAPTER 27

Boggy Beauties:
Helonias and *Heloniopsis*

In the bog outside the window of my office grows a small colony of *Heloniopsis*, which I received originally from the knowledgeable Seattle gardener Elisabeth C. Miller. Every year, in late winter, I delight in hearing the exclamation of visitors to the garden when seeing this quiet, beguiling, and refined plant in blossom. It represents to me the startling beauty that exists unknown throughout the natural world, and comforts me in the realization that no matter how exuberantly, how passionately I confront the kingdom of plants, endless peaks remain to climb, explore, and marvel.

Heloniopsis orientalis creates glossy green rosettes of broad, spear-shaped foliage to 8 in. (20 cm) in length. In early spring, the nodding and spidery, rich pink flowers are formed atop stout, 10-in. (25-cm), sheathed flowering stems. I observed *H. orientalis* in South Korea growing in dense shade on moss-covered islands in a small river. Later, I found it in a decidedly different habitat, creating exasperatingly expansive colonies in much drier situations, growing beneath large specimens of *Clethra barbinervis*. How I would have loved to see this remarkable colony in full blossom.

The taxonomy of *Heloniopsis orientalis* is rather complicated, with its broad geographical range offering several distinctive varieties. I currently grow *Heloniopsis orientalis* var. *kawanoi*, which is a Lilliputian variant of the species. Miniature rosettes of foliage, to 3 in. (7.5 cm) across, send forth towering 4-in. (10-cm) stems carrying demure, light pink flowers in midspring. *Heloniopsis orientalis* var. *breviscapa* represents the southerly range of the species, and it differs mainly in its paler pink or pure white flowers. *Heloniopsis orientalis* var. *flavida* is somewhat taller than the type, with quite intriguing greenish white flowers atop 18-in. (45-cm) stems.

Native to acidic, boggy sites along the Atlantic seaboard, *Helonias bullata* is a monotypic species that is profoundly deserving of greater use throughout the country. In foliage it possesses an affinity to *Heloniopsis orientalis*, a close relative in the lily family. In midspring, dense heads of fleshy pink flowers are held above the rosettes of broad, green foliage on stout stems to 18 in. (45 cm) or more, though I profess to not having brought this to flower in my own garden. As the Asiatic counterparts of *Helonias*—that is, the genus *Heloniopsis*—thrive so well, and as my garden plants are apparently quite healthy, I suspect that simple patience is the key.

Hardiness: Both genera are adaptable to zones 5–10, perhaps colder with some winter protection. *Heloniopsis orientalis* var. *breviscapa* exhibits greater tenderness than the northerly forms.

Cultivation: I successfully cultivate *Helonias* and *Heloniopsis* in an artificially created, perpetually moist bog, though these plants surely will also survive in well-amended soils that receive adequate moisture throughout the seasons.

Propagation: Seed is infrequently set on these plants in cultivation, but several methods of asexual propagation readily lend themselves to the task of increasing these species for further garden use. Tubercles are produced in abundance by helonias, and they can be removed and sown, as for seed; these will quickly develop as clonal offspring. *Heloniopsis orientalis* often produces new plants from the flowering scape after it has faltered and comes into contact with moist soils. Both genera can be easily divided in early spring.

Helonias bullata (Photo by Daniel J. Hinkley)

CHAPTER 28

Paris in the Springtime:
The Genera *Paris, Trillidium,* and *Scoliopus*

Paris

I have come to grow and collect certain genera of plants that I simply know to be good but can offer few reasons as to why I think that. They often do not possess showy flowers or ethereal fragrance. They may not be difficult to grow but are certainly not carefree. Yet when I look into their blossoms, witness their foliage or fruit, I sense deeply that they are undeservedly scarce in our gardens. Surely, I think, they would be more popular if only more people knew of them.

To be sure, for a genus with a name like "Paris," I might be tempted to think that it is the simple association with pleasurable passages of time in my youth— vagabond days along the Champs-Élysées, a superb meal at a bistro, my first encounter with Winged Victory—that has endeared the plants to me. Yet I must admit that the attraction here is purely botanical. I have traveled and labored to witness this genus in the wild, for I thought intuitively that it was worthy. After a decade of cultivation, exploration, and introspection, I remain unscathed by self-doubt. The genus *Paris* and its close allies comprise an assemblage of simply good garden plants that shout for attention from a greater gardening audience.

As with many genera of plants that have subjected themselves to closer inspection by taxonomists, *Paris* isn't what it used to be. It has been sliced up into three different genera, *Paris, Kinugasa,* and *Daiswa,* only to be pasted back together under the single grouping of *Paris.* A profoundly limited study in the West means that still much is to be learned about this group of plants, and it is certain that further major modifications will be made. For the purposes of this book, I have adopted the most recent trend of treating all as species of *Paris.* It is an exciting time in horticulture and botany, and any frustration toward these changes should be tempered by the realization that we are slowly but surely becoming more confident in our translation of the natural world.

Herb paris, as *Paris quadrifolia* is known commonly, is a pleasing species to cultivate in the moist woodland and will set about to form rather large colonies of low stems to 6 in. (15 cm) or slightly more, capped by four ovate leaves. Rising above on 3- to 5-in. (7.5- to 12.5-cm) pedicels, an intriguing solitary flower is composed of four rather large, leafy sepals and eight threadlike, golden petals. A knobby, purple pistil sits nestled inside surrounded by eight or more stamens. *Paris quadrifolia* thrives in a perpetually moist area in our woodland garden, adjacent to *Dactylorhiza foliosa*, a terrestrial orchid. A European native, *P. quadrifolia* is the only representative of the genus to occur outside of Asia.

The genus name *Paris* has its roots in the Latin word *par*, meaning equal, due to the corresponding number of leaves and flower parts, although it is now apparent that when Linnaeus first applied this name to *Paris quadrifolia*, he had not seen the several species that disregard such regularity. Nevertheless, once you have made the acquaintance of a single *Paris* species, you most likely will recognize other species as close relatives, as the common format, though variable, is discernible. My first encounter with a wild species of *Paris* was in South Korea, where *P. verticillata* is relatively common in moist, heavily shaded deciduous woods, often in valley bottoms. The broad, 5-in. by 2-in. (12.5-cm by 5-cm),

Paris quadrifolia (Photo by Lynne Harrison)

heavily veined leaves of this species are found in false subterminal whorls of five to eight (though I have only encountered plants with seven leaves) atop 8- to 16-in. (20- to 40-cm) stems. In spring, the stems are capped with four-merous (parts in fours or multiples thereof) flowers that are similar in appearance to those of *P. quadrifolia*, though the threadlike petals (or inner tepals) become strongly reflexed after opening. The fruit is a purplish berry containing several seeds. *Paris verticillata* has proven to be an easy garden plant in our woodland, planted in moist, humus-rich soils. This species has a large distribution across Eurasia, and I have observed it in both Korea and Japan. It is only in Japan, however, that *P. verticillata* can be found growing with a more rarely encountered species known as *P. tetraphylla*. I observed this Japanese endemic in 1995 growing side by side with *Trillium tschonoskii* in the moist soils along a stream in northern Honshu. *Paris tetraphylla* has responded well to cultivation in my garden, where it has produced a rather large stoloniferous colony of stems rising to 8 in. (20 cm). The plants display four broad, acuminate leaves and diminutive but charming flowers of reflexed green sepals and bright golden stamens surrounding the plump purplish ovary; petals are absent. This species is quite common in the area surrounding Lake Towada, where I witnessed it with its plump, shiny black berries intact above the dying, straw-colored foliage. Thus far it has also delighted the few who have encountered it in blossom in my garden.

A rather mystical plant that has long drawn admiration by plant collectors worldwide, *Paris japonica* (previously known as *Kinugasa japonica*) is found only in the mountains of central and northern Honshu; it is especially common in moist meadows on mid-elevations of Mount Fuji. Thought by taxonomists to represent a natural intergeneric hybrid of *P. verticillata* and *Trillium tschonoskii*, this species is as easy to recognize as it is challenging to cultivate. The brilliant flowers, which contain eight or more white sepals (or outer tepals) and narrow white petals (or inner tepals), are produced in early spring above magnificent 15- to 30-in. (38- to 75-cm) stems. The dramatic whorls of foliage consist of 8 to 10 leaves, each to 1 ft. (0.3 m) in length. The fruit is a dark purple berry, which is eaten in Japan. (The fruit of *Paris quadrifolia* is considered poisonous!)

Reticent to sacrifice plants to the garden until I garner more experience growing this species, I have successfully brought *Paris japonica* to flower under cultivation in containers. As the species is found naturally in moist, volcanic soils at high altitudes, I have tried to replicate these conditions by providing an extremely well-drained, peat-based medium in a cool location and with plenty of moisture throughout the growing season. A dry, cool dormant period is required.

The members of the genus that were previously lumped together as *Daiswa* represent the most dramatic species within *Paris*. From the charming and diminutive *Paris violacea*, with striking variegated foliage, to the imposing 7-ft. (2.1-m) tall *P. hainanensis* (which my friends Bleddyn and Sue Wynn-Jones collected in Taiwan and have in cultivation at their nursery, Crûg Farm Plants, in northern Wales), there is nothing understated about these species in foliage, flower, and overall stature.

During the 1980s and '90s, countless plants experienced a remarkable increase in their understanding by botanists, their demand by a growing legion of sophisticated gardeners, and their general availability on a commercial scale. The plant now known as *Paris polyphylla* (and at other times known as *Daiswa polyphylla*) represented to me the Holy Grail, the ultimate prize for searching hard enough and long enough. Though still far from common, this species is at long last readily available to gardeners who desire it for their woodland plantings.

I received my first division of *Paris polyphylla* from a lusty clump growing in the rock garden of the University of British Columbia Botanical Garden, shared with me by curator of collections, and a close friend, Gerald Straley. To my knowledge, at that time only a few other plants of the species were in cultivation in North America. This plant has thrived in my garden, where it produces up to 30 stems rising to 3 ft. (0.9 m), topped by a false whorl of 10 to 12 leaves, each 7 in. (18 cm) long, on purple-suffused petioles. Carried 6 in. (15 cm) above the foliage in early summer, the large flowers have broad, green sepals to 3 in. (7.5 cm) in length and golden, threadlike petals.

Paris polyphylla is the most widespread of the species and likewise is the most variable. Among the plants that I cultivate under this name, those that originated from higher elevations of northern India are amazingly distinct, but they possess the required diagnostic features to place it in this taxon. These produce blossoms

Paris japonica (Photo by Daniel J. Hinkley)

Paris polyphylla (Photo by Lynne Harrison)

on 6-in. (15-cm) stems in early spring, long before the plants of my taller growing clone have even begun to emerge from the ground.

Due to the separation in flowering time of the two clones of *Paris polyphylla* that I grow, and because at least two clones must be present for fruit production, I have never witnessed their fruitful ornament in my garden. This failure to set seed has been somewhat bittersweet. The lack of fertilization means that the extraordinary flowering effects are incredibly long-lived, in fact up to four months! It was not until I was in eastern Nepal in 1995, however, that I realized just how spectacular the heads of ripened red fruit can be. I had been told repeatedly by those who preceded me to this part of the world that I would indeed see "masses" of *Paris* in the wild, an experience that I looked forward to with great anticipation. Thus, as I faced the last days of the expedition without having seen a single specimen, I became enormously disappointed. On the last full day of hiking back to the village of Tumlingtar, whence we had begun our journey a month earlier, we approached the last mountain pass of the trek that brought us to moderate elevations and cooler temperatures. Here in a magical, climax wood-

Where more than one clone are grown together, *Paris polyphylla* forms a striking set of fruit, as shown on this specimen in an expansive colony in eastern Nepal (Photo by Daniel J. Hinkley)

land surprisingly untrammeled by the local population, we came upon drifts of *P. polyphylla* in perfectly ripened fruit; the broad stars of glossy scarlet berries lit the forest floor like a treasure chest of ruby brooches. I slept that last night on the trail, staring into the brilliant sweep of the Milky Way, counting my good fortune, and warmed by the overall experience.

I encountered countless members of the genus while in Yunnan and Sichuan Provinces of China in 1996 and again when I returned to Sichuan in the autumn of 1998. Because of the great variability that exists within its ranks, however, I could only positively identify a few from the rather enormous contingent. Three species possess foliage that is sessile or subsessile to the stem, which readily partitions them from the petiolate species. *Paris thibetica* is an elegant species and one of the easiest to identify due to its striking golden stamens, each of which bears a long, threadlike appendage (known as free connective) attached to the tip. The foliage of this species is equally distinctive and elegant, with whorls of 7 to 11 extremely narrow, sessile leaves, though it is quite variable in regard to leaf number, length, and width.

While botanizing the slopes of Emei Shan in the autumn of 1998, I observed a species of *Paris* that is quite distinct from those that I had observed further to the south in Yunnan Province and in eastern Nepal. *Paris lancifolia* is much like a more robust specimen of *P. thibetica.* The lanceolate foliage is composed of five to eight sessile leaflets to 6 in. (15 cm) atop stems rising to 2 ft. (0.6 m). Five to seven persistent green sepals remained on the plants when I came upon them. The fruit consists of a five-segmented capsule that opens to expose a flat, bright-orange fleshy seed coating, though the seed coat of *P. lancifolia* does not possess the translucence of that of either *P. polyphylla* or *P. yunnanensis.*

On the western slopes of the Cang Shan, an immense chain of moderately high peaks to the west of Dali in Yunnan, the Sino-British Expedition found the third sessile species, *P. violacea,* in 1981. It is described as a charming species to 8 in. (20 cm) in height, with four to six dark green leaves etched in silver along the veins. The flowers are composed of four to six variegated sepals and shorter, threadlike golden petals. Short, golden stamens surround a globose pistil; the purplish stigma, which lies flush with the receptacle, and the three purple styles, which rise from the stigmatic disk, give the plant its specific epithet.

Interestingly, in the same area of Yunnan where the aforementioned expedition observed *Paris violacea,* a variant of *P. polyphylla* also was first discovered

Paris thibetica (Photo by Lynne Harrison)

and described. Known as *P. polyphylla* var. *alba*, it is a startling plant in blossom, offering bright yellow sepals and petals, a whitish ovary, and bright yellow styles. It is currently available in specialty nurseries in Britain for a hefty sum, though I currently have seedlings of this plant germinating in my nursery, supplied to me by my friend Jim McClements from Maryland.

Throughout much of Yunnan, especially in the open and dry woods above Lichang, *Paris yunnanensis* grows among *Pinus yunnanensis*, *Dipelta yunnanensis*, and *Quercus monimotricha*. It is similar to *P. polyphylla* in appearance, though they differ on several counts. The leaves of *P. yunnanensis*, like those of *P. polyphylla*, are borne on rather long petioles; the petioles of *P. yunnanensis* can be as long as the leaf blade itself, whereas those of *P. polyphylla* are shorter. A quick check of the number of lateral veins on each leaf blade will also be useful for distinguishing the two. *Paris yunnanensis* has two laterals on each side of the main vein, while *P. polyphylla* generally possesses only one. I will always remember trying to identify this species in the field in Yunnan in 1996, as I was never fully comfortable with my diagnosis. I look forward to returning to this part of the world to observe these and other species again and to test whether my skills in identification have improved.

During my expedition to Emei Shan in 1998, I encountered another very distinct species of *Paris*. Not as frequently observed as *Paris lancifolia*, though certainly not uncommon at the higher elevations above 7500 ft. (2250 m), a low, four-leaved, petiolate species known as *P. fargesii* grows no taller than 6 in. (15 cm). Each leaflet is nearly as broad as it is long, 4 in. (10 cm) by 3½ in. (9 cm). A large, single, deep orange-red berry emerges slightly above and is surrounded by four persistent sepals. Like *P. tetraphylla*, *P. verticillata*, and *P. quadrifolia*, this species is distinctive in that its fruit does not split open upon ripening. Unfortunately, most of the fruit had long departed by the time I got there, and I left mostly empty handed, though armed with the greater self-confidence that I had actually come closer to understanding this genus.

Hardiness: The provenance of the original collection will have tremendous bearing on how hardy each individual clone is. Clones of *Paris polyphylla* from higher altitudes can be assumed to be hardy throughout zones 4–9. Most oth-

Paris yunnanensis, photographed in Yunnan Province above Lichang in 1996 (Photo by Daniel J. Hinkley)

ers have not been adequately tested in cultivation, though initial reports show successes for most if not all to the cooler reaches of zone 6. *Paris* is resentful of the humid conditions of the Southeast.

Cultivation: As for trilliums, cultivate in well-drained but humus-rich soils in partial shade, although I have seen *Paris polyphylla* cultivated in full sun and plenty of moisture. A yearly application of a well-balanced fertilizer in late winter will stimulate growth of dormant buds below the ground and provide a much larger colony in a shorter period of time.

Propagation: Propagation by seed is slow and results are inconsistent. The seed has been shown to exhibit a mycorrhizal symbiosis (a mutual association of the root cells with certain fungi), which is necessary for, or at least greatly augments, germination. A small vial of soil taken from near the parent plant and added to the seed compost will improve chances. In addition, *Paris* demonstrates a double dormancy, and most of the seed will not germinate until the second spring. An additional five to six years will be required to bring the seedlings to blossoming size. Division is certainly a more acceptable method of propagation and should be performed in late summer or early autumn before growth resumes. Care should be taken to prevent drying of the new root growth. If this occurs, the plants will emerge the following spring but will quickly slip into dormancy; the plants will reappear the following spring if left in place. *Paris* species are currently protected by the Chinese Government due to the medicinal properties they possess, and special permission must be granted to collect and/or export the seed of this genus.

Trillidium

With exceptional treatises on the genus *Trillium* recently published (including *Trilliums* by Frederick W. and Roberta B. Case, published in 1997), it is unnecessary for me to further illuminate their charms, though they remain a most cherished component of my woodland garden. Although I have long been keen on the American contingent of *Trillium* species, which represents a cache of exceptional garden plants, observing the Asiatic species in their native habitat is always an especially thrilling experience. On numerous occasions, I have encountered *Trillium camschatcense* in the densely shaded and moist forests of northern Japan and Korea, as well as *Trillium tschonoskii* growing on the peaks above Pulchoki on the outskirts of Kathmandu in Nepal. These are well established in my garden, thriving in rather boggy situations in partial shade adjacent to *Lysichiton americanus* and *L. camtschatcensis*.

I also observed a rare *Trillium* relative near Pulchoki in Nepal, at elevations above 7000 ft. (2100 m). Though the proper placement of *Trillidium govanianum* in the plant kingdom is still in deliberation (some refer to it as *Trillium govanianum*), most taxonomists agree that the floral features of this species are significantly distinct to warrant placing it outside the realm of the genus *Trillium*. *Trillidium govanianum* produces a diminutive plant, similar in effect to a minute *Paris*, with flowers consisting of whorls of three narrow, greenish purple sepals and identical petals (thus more correctly referred to as tepals) to less than 1 in. (2.5 cm) in length. The flowers are borne on short pedicels above the foliage. Ovate leaves to 1 in. (2.5 cm) in length are held in whorls of three and are sessile or subsessile to the stem. The entire plant rises no higher than 4 in. (10 cm).

Hardiness: Little data exists with regard to the hardiness of *Trillidium govanianum* in the United States, though one can use the accepted rating for *Trillium tschonoskii* as a reference point, since the two species share the same range in the wild. The latter is hardy in zones 6–9.

Cultivation: Plants under cultivation in my garden have thus far thrived in a moist, peaty location in partial shade. Because of its small proportions and darkness in flower, *Trillidium* might be considered for cultivating in a shaded trough or container to better protect the emerging plants from slugs as well as to allow easier observation of the charming Lilliputian floral display.

Propagation: I have not had experience growing *Trillidium* from seed, but as is the case with *Trillium*, I assume that it will exhibit a double dormancy. The seed of both genera has a high-protein appendage, known as an elaiosome, attached to the outside of the seed coat. This aids in the dispersal and planting of seed by ants, which consider it a tasty morsel worthy of taking home to the family. Seed should be gathered just as the ovary splits and sown immediately. I suspect that seed of this rarity will, for the time being, be a seldom-encountered commodity. Division in late summer as root growth resumes will certainly be an easier and more auspicious approach.

Scoliopus

Closer to home, in northern California and southern Oregon, a genus known as *Scoliopus* shares digs in the Liliaceae with the above-mentioned taxa. Of the genus's only two species, *Scoliopus bigelowii* is the one that I have had the most intimate associations with, having seen it colonizing densely shaded areas under immense specimens of *Sequoia sempervirens* in northern California. From seed that

I raised, I now have flowering-sized plants established in my woodland. *Scoliopus bigelowii* forms ever-increasing colonies of stems, each of which contains two 5-in. (12.5-cm) linear leaves that emerge in late winter with handsome liver-colored spots, reminiscent of a good clone of *Tricyrtis maculata*. As the foliage emerges, the plants produce an umbel of up to 12 flowers, each composed of three greenish purple sepals and very narrow, erect, purplish brown petals. The flowers possess a quiet to completely mute beauty; add to this its carrion-like fragrance, and one wonders how this species could possibly be considered essential for cultivation. Relax. *Scoliopus bigelowii* blossoms so early in the season that its meat-casserole-gone-over fragrance is nearly undetectable. It forms an exceedingly handsome clump of foliage over time, and the floral effects are curiously beautiful. Admittedly, it will certainly have a limited appeal to all but the best of gardeners with the most exceptional tastes.

The second species, *Scoliopus hallii*—known under the rather delicious vernacular as Oregon fetid adder's tongue—is found growing from Tillamook on the northern Oregon coast to the Siskiyou Mountains on the California border. Like its southern cousin, *S. hallii* is found in the cool maritime forests of the Coast Range and the western slope of the Cascades, where it prefers moist soils along mountain streams. In February and March, the linear, nonmottled leaves appear in pairs, from which arise one to several stems each carrying a single flower. The flowers are composed of three purplish-streaked, greenish white sepals, which grow to $1/3$ in. (0.8 cm) and reflex at the tips, and three erect, linear petals. It is a rarely encountered woodland plant that will certainly add distinction to the collector's woodland, though it will never set the horticultural world ablaze.

Hardiness: The two species of *Scoliopus* are well adapted to the maritime Northwest, where the summers are cool and the winters mild and moist.

Cultivation: Because of the plants' early emergence, siting must take into consideration the susceptibility to damage by slugs and late frosts. Provide as rich and moist an environment as possible.

Propagation: Seed capsules are produced after flowering on stems that bend to ground level. If the seed is sown fresh upon harvesting, most of it will germinate the following spring; if, however, it is allowed to dry out before sowing, it will not emerge for an additional year. Refrain from transplanting the delicate seedlings until the second or third year; it is more appropriate to allow the parent plant to handle the vagaries of raising their offspring. Transplant self-sown seedlings when they are large enough to handle the move. Divide plants in midsummer as they go dormant, or in early spring as growth resumes.

U.S.D.A. HARDINESS ZONE MAP

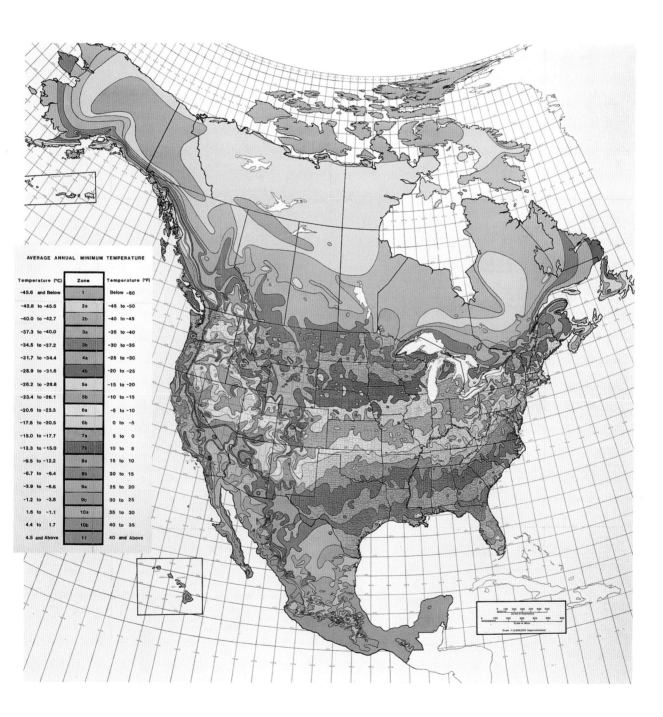

AVERAGE ANNUAL MINIMUM TEMPERATURE

Temperature (°C)	Zone	Temperature (°F)
-45.6 and Below	1	Below -50
-42.8 to -45.5	2a	-45 to -50
-40.0 to -42.7	2b	-40 to -45
-37.3 to -40.0	3a	-35 to -40
-34.5 to -37.2	3b	-30 to -35
-31.7 to -34.4	4a	-25 to -30
-28.9 to -31.6	4b	-20 to -25
-26.2 to -28.8	5a	-15 to -20
-23.4 to -26.1	5b	-10 to -15
-20.6 to -23.3	6a	-5 to -10
-17.8 to -20.5	6b	0 to -5
-15.0 to -17.7	7a	5 to 0
-12.3 to -15.0	7b	10 to 5
-9.5 to -12.2	8a	15 to 10
-6.7 to -9.4	8b	20 to 15
-3.9 to -6.6	9a	25 to 20
-1.2 to -3.8	9b	30 to 25
1.6 to -1.1	10a	35 to 30
4.4 to 1.7	10b	40 to 35
4.5 and Above	11	40 and Above

MAIL-ORDER SOURCES OF PLANT MATERIAL

Postage costs may be associated with the catalogs of the nurseries listed. North American gardeners should enclose international postage vouchers when requesting catalogs of European nurseries.

United States

Arrowhead Alpines
P.O. Box 857
Fowlerville, MI 48836

Asiatica (limited mail-order)
P.O. Box 270
Lewisburg, PA 17339

Camellia Forest Nursery
125 Carolina Forest Road
Chapel Hill, NC 27516

Collector's Nursery
16804 NE 102nd Avenue
Battle Ground, WA 98604

Forestfarm Nursery
990 Tetherow Road
Williams, OR 97544-9599

Garden Visions
63 Williamsville Road
Hubbardston, MA 01452-1315

Geraniaceae
122 Hilcrest Avenue
Kentfield, CA 94904

Gossler Farms Nursery
1200 Weaver Road
Springfield, OR 97478-9691

Heronswood Nursery, Ltd.
7530 NE 288th Street
Kingston, WA 98346

Klehm Nursery
4210 North Duncan Road
Champaign, IL 61821

Logee's Greenhouses
141 North Street
Danielson, CT 06239

Niche Gardens
1111 Dawson Road
Chapel Hill, NC 27516

Oregon Trail Gardens
1810 SE Troge Road
Boring, OR 97009-9646

Plant Delights Nursery
9241 Sauls Road
Raleigh, NC 27603

The Primrose Path
R.D. 2, Box 110
Scottdale, PA 15683

Roslyn Nursery
211 Burrs Lane
Dix Hills, NY 11746

Siskiyou Rare Plant Nursery
2825 Cummings Road
Medford, OR 97501

Wayside Gardens
P.O. Box 1
Hodges, SC 29695-0001

The White Flower Farm
P.O. Box 50
Route 63
Litchfield, CT 06759-0050

Yucca Do Nursery
P.O. Box 104
Hempstead, TX 77445

United Kingdom

Axletree Nursery
Starvecrow Lane
Peasmarsh, Rye
East Sussex TN31 6XL

The Beth Chatto Gardens, Ltd.
Elmstead Market
Colchester
Essex CO7 7DB

The Botanic Nursery
Atworth Plant Centre
Bath Road
Atworth, nr Melksham
Wiltshire SN12 8NU

Cally Gardens
Gatehouse of Fleet
Castle Douglas
Scotland DG7 2DJ

Crûg Farm Plants
Griffith's Crossing
nr Caernarfon
Gwynedd LL55 1TU

Fillan's Plants
Pound House Nursery
Buckland Monachorum, Yelverton
Devon PL20 7LJ

Great Dixter Nurseries
Northiam, Rye
East Sussex TN31 6PH

Green Farm Plants
Bury Court
Bentley, Farnham
Surrey GU10 5JX

Greenway Gardens Nursery
Churston Ferrers
Brixham
Devon TQ5 0ES

Hadspen Garden & Nursery
Castle Cary
Somerset BA7 7NG

Hopleys Plants, Ltd.
High Street
Much Hadham
Hertfordshire SG10 6BU

Perry's Plants
The River Garden
Sleights, Whitby
North Yorkshire YO21 1RR

Stillingfleet Lodge Nurseries
Stillingfleet
Yorkshire YO4 6HW

Washfield Nursery
Horn's Road
Hawkhurst
Kent TN18 4QU

The Netherlands

Coen Jansen
Ankummer Es 13 a
7722 RD Dalfsen

De Hessenhof
Kwekerij 'De Hessenhof'
Hessenweg 41
6718 TC Ede

Piet Oudolf
Kwekerij Oudolf
Broekstraat 17
6999 De Hummelo

Pieter Zwijnenburg Jr.
Halve Raak 18
2771 AD Boskoop

GLOSSARY

acuminate: tapering to a point

alternate: foliage arrangement in which leaves grow singly along a stem; the converse of an opposite arrangement

amplexicaul: clasping the stem

anther: the pollen-bearing part of the stamen

apetalous: lacking petals

auricle: an earlike growth or appendage

axil: the upper angle between a stem and any outgrowth from the stem, such as a leaf

axillary: located in or growing from an axil

bifid: divided into two parts or lobes by a cleft

bipinnate: pinnate foliage in which the leaflets are themselves pinnate

biternate: ternate foliage in which the leaflets are further divided into three parts; also referred to as twice ternate

bract: a modified, reduced leaf

bracteole: a secondary bract

bulbil: a small bulb that grows from a leaf axil or in an inflorescence

calyx (*pl.* calyces): collective term for the sepals of a flower

carpel: a simple pistil or a segment of a compound pistil bearing an ovule

caudate: tapering into tail-like appendage

caulescent: producing a developed stem aboveground

cirrose: coil-like

clone: an asexually produced plant, which is genetically identical to its parent

cordate: heart-shaped

coriaceous: having a leathery texture

corona: a crownlike or cuplike appendage in a flower

363

cyme: an inflorescence in which the central or terminal flower opens first

dentate: having a toothed margin; compare with serrate

digitate: having leaflets or lobes that radiate from a center, as in fingers on a hand

dioecious: having the male and female reproductive organs on separate plants

double flower: a flower that contains more than the normal number of petals, usually concealing or replacing the stamens and pistils

edaphic: the chemical and physical characteristics of the soil

endemic: confined to a particular region

epiphyte: a plant that grows on another plant but is not parasitic and produces its own food

glabrous: smooth, without hair

glaucous: coated with a waxy bloom that can be rubbed off

hastate: arrow-shaped, triangular

inflorescence: the arrangement of flowers on a stem or axis

intergeneric: between genera, as in a hybrid cross involving more than one genus

interspecific: between species, as in a hybrid cross involving more than one species in the same genus

involucre: a pair or group of bracts at the base of a flower or inflorescence

laciniate: deeply and unevenly cut

lanceolate: narrow and tapering, or lance-shaped

-merous: having a specified number of parts, given with a number; for example, *three-merous* means parts arranged in threes

monocarpic: flowering and bearing fruit only once, and then dying

monoecious: having the male and female reproductive organs on a single plant but in separate flowers

monospecific: having only one species, said of a genus

monotypic: having only one component, as in a genus with one species

nutlet: a small nut or nutlike fruit

obovate: egg-shaped, with the narrower end nearest the base

offset: a side shoot, as from a bulb or tuber, that roots and forms a new plant

opposite: foliage arrangement in which leaves grow in pairs on opposite sides of a stem; the converse of an alternate arrangement (see also whorl)

orbicular: round and flat

ovate: egg-shaped, with the broader end nearest the base

palmate: having three or more leaflets or lobes radiating from a center, in a palmlike manner

panicle: a branched inflorescence in which the lower flowers of the branches open first

pedate: palmately lobed, with the two outer lobes further divided

pedicel: the stalk of an individual flower or fruit

peduncle: the stalk of an inflorescence

peltate: shield-shaped, with the leaf stalk attached to the lower surface of the leaf margin rather than at the edge

perfoliate: surrounding the stem, as in a leaf whose basal lobes unite around the stem

petal: a usually showy leaflike segment of the flower, distinguishable from a sepal

petaloid: resembling a petal

petiolate: having a petiole

petiole: a leaf stalk

pinnate: a featherlike arrangement, with the leaflets arranged in rows on each side of the axis or rachis

pistil: the female, seed-bearing reproductive organ of a flower, usually consisting of the ovary, style, and stigma

plantlet: a secondary plant that develops on a larger plant

polyploid: having more than the normal two sets of chromosomes

propagule: a small piece of a plant that can be propagated to form a new plant

pubescent: covered with soft, fine hairs

raceme: an unbranched inflorescence in which the individual pediceled flowers are arranged along the stem, the lower flowers opening first

rachis: the main axis of a compound leaf or inflorescence

receptacle: the enlarged end of the flowering stalk where the flower parts grow

recurved: curved backward or downward

reflexed: curved backward or downward, more sharply than recurved

reniform: kidney-shaped

rhizomatous: bearing rhizomes

rhizome: a creeping stem lying at or below the ground surface that produces roots as well as stems, leaves, and flowers

rootstock: a synonym for rhizome

rosette: a circular cluster of leaves or flowers radiating from a common center

rugose: wrinkled or corrugated

scandent: climbing or scrambling, as in a vine or lax shrub

scape: a leafless flower stalk that rises directly from the base of the plant

semidouble flower: a flower that contains more than the normal number of petals, but not enough to completely conceal the stamens and pistils

sepal: the leaflike, outermost segment of the flower; unit of the calyx

serrate: having a toothed or sawlike margin; a serrate margin is distinct from a dentate margin by having the notches pointing toward the apex of the leaf

sessile: lacking a petiole, as in a leaf attached directly to the stem

spadix (*pl.* spadices): a fleshy spike of the inflorescence, usually enclosed within the spathe

spathe: a large, leaflike appendage that encloses a spadix or other inflorescence

spike: an unbranched inflorescence bearing stalkless flowers

stamen: the male, pollen-bearing reproductive organ of a flower, usually consisting of a slender stalk (filament) and an anther

stigma: the upper surface of the pistil that receives the pollen

stolon: a creeping stem lying at or above the ground surface that will root and produce plantlets

stoloniferous: bearing stolons

style: the slender part of the pistil located between the ovary and the stigma

subsessile: having a partial or minute petiole

taxon (*pl.* taxa): a group of plants (or animals) at any level in the taxonomic hierarchy; for example, the species *Anemone nemorosa* is a taxon, the family Ranunculaceae is a taxon

tepal: a leaflike segment of the flower when sepals and petals cannot be differentiated

terminal: growing at the tip or apex of a stem

ternate: growing in threes, as in a compound leaf composed of three leaflets

tetraploid: having four sets of chromosomes, as opposed to the typical two sets

tomentose: covered with a dense layer of short, woolly hairs

trifoliate: three-leaved

tripinnate: bipinnate foliage in which the second divisions are themselves pinnate

triternate: biternate foliage in which the leaflets are further divided into three parts; also referred to as thrice ternate

tuber: a swollen, usually subterranean root or stem, from which new plants develop from buds or "eyes"

tubercle: small tubers that form on a plant bearing a tuberous root system

type: the standard or definitive form or specimen

umbel: an inflorescence with multiple flower stalks emanating from a single point at the apex of the main flower stalk

vegetative: the nonreproductive parts of a plant, such as the stems and leaves; in vegetative propagation, such as cuttings, plants are multiplied from vegetative parts

whorl: arrangement in which the parts grow in a circle around a single point or node

BIBLIOGRAPHY

Alpine Garden Society China Expedition. *Quarterly Bulletin of the Alpine Garden Society* vol. 64 (June 1996), no. 2.

Armitage, Allan M. *Herbaceous Perennial Plants.* 2nd ed. Champaign, Ill.: Stipes Publishing, 1997.

Barker, David G. *Epimediums and Other Herbaceous Berberidaceae.* The Hardy Plant Society, December 1996.

Bath, Trevor, and Joy Jones. *Hardy Geraniums.* Portland, Ore.: Timber Press, 1994.

Beckett, Kenneth A. "Gunnera in Cultivation." *The Plantsman* vol. 10 (December 1988), pt. 3.

Case, Frederick W., and Roberta B. Case. *Trilliums.* Portland, Ore.: Timber Press, 1997.

Clark, Lewis J. *Wildflowers of the Pacific Northwest, from Alaska to Northern California.* Sidney, B.C.: Gray's Publishing Ltd., 1976.

Clausen, Ruth R., and Nicolas H. Ekstrom. *Perennials for American Gardens.* New York: Random House, 1989.

Cobb, James L. S. *Meconopsis.* Portland, Ore.: Timber Press, 1989.

Compton, James. "Reclassification of *Actaea* to include *Cimicifuga* and *Souliea*: Phylogeny inferred from morphology, nrDNA ITS and cpDNA sequence variation." *Taxon* vol. 47 (August 1998).

Coombes, Allen J. *Dictionary of Plant Names.* Portland, Ore.: Timber Press, 1994.

Eastman, Donald C. *Rare and Endangered Plants of Oregon.* Wilsonville, Ore.: Beautiful America Publishing Company, 1990.

Elliott, Jack. *The Smaller Perennials.* Portland, Ore.: Timber Press, 1997.

Farrer, Reginald. *The English Rock Garden.* 2 vols. Edinburgh: T. C. and E. C. Jack, Ltd., 1922. Reprint, Little Compton, R.I.: Theophrastus, 1976.

Gusman, Guy. "What is *Arisaema erubescens* (Wall.) Schott?" *Sino-Himalayan Plant Association Newsletter*, no. 16 (1998).

Jeffrey, C. "*Polygonatum* in Eastern Asia." *Kew Bulletin* vol. 34, no. 3.

Jelitto, Leo, and Wilhelm Schacht. *Hardy Herbaceous Perennials*. 2 vols. Portland, Ore.: Timber Press, 1985.

Lancaster, Roy. "*Deinanthe bifida* and *D. caerulea*." *The Garden* vol. 121 (June 1996), pt. 6.

————. *Plant Hunting in Nepal*. Portland, Ore.: Timber Press, 1982.

————. "*Saruma henryi*." *The Garden* vol. 123 (April 1998), pt. 4.

————. *Travels in China*. Woodbridge, Suffolk: Antique Collectors' Club, 1989.

Lee, Yong No. *Flora of Korea*. Seoul, Korea: Kyo-Hak Publishing Co. Ltd., 1996.

Lord, Tony (ed.). *The RHS Plant Finder, 1998–99*. London: Dorling Kindersley, 1998.

Mayo, S. J., J. Bogner, P. C. Boyce. *The Genera of Araceae*. Kew, England: Royal Botanic Gardens, 1997.

Mitchell, Bob. "Paris—Part I." *The Plantsman* vol. 9 (September 1987), pt. 2.

Nakai, T. "Japanese Hepatica." *Japanese Journal of Botany* vol. 13 (1937), pt. 5.

The New Royal Horticultural Society Dictionary of Gardening. 4 vols. London and Basingstoke: Macmillan Press Ltd., 1992.

Ohwi, Jisaburo. *Flora of Japan*. Washington, D.C.: Smithsonian Institution, 1984.

Phillips, Roger, and Martyn Rix. *The Random House Book of Perennials*. 2 vols. New York: Random House, 1991.

Polunin, Oleg, and Adam Stainton. *Flowers of the Himalaya*. Delhi: Oxford University Press, 1984.

Pradhan, Udai C. *Himalayan Cobra-Lilies (Arisaema): Their Botany and Culture*. Kalimpong, West Bengal, India: Primulaceae Books, 1990.

Probst, Darrell. *The Epimedium Newsletter* vol. 1 (Spring 1998), no. 1.

Rice, Graham. *Hardy Perennials*. Portland, Ore.: Timber Press, 1995.

Staff of the Liberty Hyde Bailey Hortorium. *Hortus Third*. New York: Macmillan Publishing Co., Inc., 1976.

Thomas, Graham Stuart. *Perennial Garden Plants*. 3rd ed. Portland, Ore.: Sagapress/Timber Press, 1990.

White, Robin, and Sue White. "Information Sheet on Epimediums in Cultivation." Blackthorn Nursery, 1994.

Yinger, Barry. "Asarums." *Bulletin of the American Rock Garden Society* vol. 51 (1993), no. 2.

INDEX OF PLANT NAMES